PRINTERS AND
PRESS FREEDOM

8—

PRINTERS AND PRESS FREEDOM

The Ideology of
Early American Journalism

Jeffery A. Smith

Oxford University Press
New York   Oxford

Oxford University Press

Oxford   New York   Toronto
Delhi   Bombay   Calcutta   Madras   Karachi
Petaling Jaya   Singapore   Hong Kong   Tokyo
Nairobi   Dar es Salaam   Cape Town
Melbourne   Auckland

and associated companies in
Berlin   Ibadan

Library of Congress Cataloging-in-Publication Data

Smith, Jeffery Alan.
   Printers and press freedom.

   Bibliography: p.
   Includes index.
   1. Freedom of the press—United States—History.
   2. Journalists—Legal status, laws, etc.—United States—
History.   I. Title.
KF4774.S64   1988   323.44'5'0973   87-7206
ISBN 0-19-505144-0
ISBN 0-19-506473-9 (Pbk.)

10 9 8 7 6 5 4 3 2 1
Printed in the United States of America

To Robert and Dorothy Smith

Preface

Few nations have ever actually embraced the idea that a right to criticize government is healthy for the political system. Many countries now have constitutional protections for freedom of expression, but only a minority interpret that liberty to mean acceptance of a free and independent press. In the United States, the press has sometimes been described as an unofficial fourth branch of government, a branch which serves as a check on the other three and provides the information necessary for a democracy to function.[1] The basis of this structural rationale for press freedom lies in the political and intellectual experiences of eighteenth-century America, experiences which shaped what is today the world's oldest written constitution still in use. Part of this frame of government is the First Amendment, which guarantees but does not define "freedom . . . of the press." Courts and scholars have usually assumed the First Amendment was not written and ratified to provide an absolute protection for expression, but they typically have undertaken only fitful struggles with the issue of what legal limitations were originally intended or assumed.

If rights exist as the result of an interaction of principles, practices, and institutions, then eighteenth-century concepts of press freedom should be studied within the contexts of Enlightenment thought, party politics, and the political tensions created by oligarchical patterns of government. In particular, our interpretations of journalistic rights ought to be examined in the light of recent historiographical efforts to comprehend the influence of the English "radical Whig" or "country" ideology on political thought in early America. This set of perceptions and prescriptions portrayed freedom and power as constantly at odds and maintained that liberty would be preserved only where independent, public-spirited individuals were practicing the classical republican virtues of honesty, frugality, industry, and vigilance. It was reflected in the sublime rhetoric of Jefferson and in the satires and simple adages of Franklin. An ambition to serve friends and the public was welcome, *Poor Richard's Almanack* said, "But the Ambition that has *itself* only in View, is restless, turbulent, regardless of publick Peace, or general Interest, and the secret Maker of most Mischiefs, between Nations, Parties, Friends and Neighbours."[2]

English libertarian doctrine—with its distrust of corrupting power and its promotion of popular sovereignty—was routinely used by eighteenth-century journalists to justify writings critical of official conduct. Political theorists also perceived the implications of radical Whig ideology for the press. In condemning the Sedition Act of 1798, James Madison pointed out that old legal notions of seditious libel, which denied a fundamental right to criticize official actions and policies, were inappropriate in a nation which had erected a limited government responsible to the people. Moreover, he observed, the First Amendment was ratified by a country where the press had habitually censured public men and where independence and the federal constitution might not have existed without free journalistic debate. The right of freely discussing public issues and public persons, Madison maintained, was "the only effectual guardian of every other right."[3]

Madison and his contemporaries came to see liberty of the press as a natural part of a democratic system. The objectives of this study will be to explore how they reached this conclusion and to determine what limitations libertarian thought and editorial policies placed on this newly conceived freedom. I agree with Professor Leonard W. Levy that "libertarian" is a relative term, but I would maintain—contrary to Professor David A. Anderson—that libertarian press ideology was remarkably lucid and dynamic in the eighteenth century.[4] My purpose, then, will be to identify and analyze the elements of early American press theory and to investigate how this journalistic ideology was carried into practice.

The research for this undertaking has included reading more than eight thousand issues of eighteenth-century newspapers and visiting sixteen libraries and archives in six states. Many people have been helpful, but I particularly appreciate the forbearance and expertise of the staff of the State Historical Society of Wisconsin where most of my research was completed. I also wish to acknowledge a travel grant from the Graduate School of the University of Wisconsin–Madison, a Ludwig von Mises Fellowship from the Center for Libertarian Studies, and the support services of University House, University of Iowa.

My greatest debts, however, are to a number of individuals. For sharing with me their knowledge of history, I thank Professors James L. Baughman, Paul S. Boyer, David S. Lovejoy, Harold L. Nelson, Norman K. Risjord, MaryAnn Yodelis Smith, and Stephen Vaughn. I thank also my wife, Geneviève, and my children, Vincent and Claire, for their patience and encouragement.

Iowa City J.A.S.
April 1987

Contents

PRINTERS AND PRESS FREEDOM

Introduction

Courts offer various rationales for their decisions on constitutional issues. They sometimes formulate or follow general doctrines and they often employ particular structural, prudential, or ethical arguments in the course of balancing competing interests. Such approaches may be used in an effort to achieve justice or to secure the public welfare, but they may lack a clear connection to the original intent of the Constitution. Indeed, legal scholars have questioned the extent to which the initial meaning can be known or should be followed. "The Founding Fathers—and their intentions—are clothed in mystery," Arthur S. Miller has written, adding that the history of the period is incomplete, that courts abuse it at will, and that it settles little that is worth arguing about. "Questions of constitutional law involve matters of public policy which should not be decided merely because of the original meanings of words in the Constitution," Leonard W. Levy has maintained. "They must be read as revelations of the general purposes which were to be achieved, or as expressions of imperishable principles that are expansive and comprehensive in character."[1]

With remarkable uniformity but only a little use of history, some scholars have identified certain "underlying principles" or "values" embedded in the press clause of the First Amendment. These have been discussed in terms of functions served by freedom of expression and include the discovery of truth, the maintenance of democratic processes, and the facilitation of necessary change and personal fulfillment. While some suggest that modern court decisions have been

3

generally consistent with these broad purposes of the press clause, others maintain that the original conception is irrelevant because it was so constricted.[2]

Following an often-cited thesis advanced by Leonard Levy, Philip B. Kurland has stated that "the most widespread definition" of press freedom at the time of the First Amendment was Sir William Blackstone's position that it meant the absence of prior restraints upon publication and did not prevent subsequent punishment for expression deemed dangerous to the government or offensive to religion. Kurland remarked that in its early press freedom cases decided in the years following World War I, the Supreme Court "began to create and recreate its own versions of the first amendment" invoking "magic phrases" and "more or less meaningless epigrams" such as " 'chilling effects' " and " 'market place of ideas'." Levy has argued that freedom of expression was understood narrowly in early America and that libertarian conceptions of the First Amendment have been concocted on fictitious pretenses. "The Constitution," he wrote, "designed by an eighteenth-century rural society, serves as well today as ever because an antiquarian historicism that would freeze its original meaning has not guided its interpretation and was not intended to."[3]

The position that the original intentions are unknowable or irrelevant in fact runs counter to the firm admonitions of the Framers and their contemporaries. Those who would interpret the document, Thomas Jefferson wrote, had to take themselves "back to the time when the constitution was adopted, recollect the spirit manifested in the debates, and instead of trying what meaning may be squeezed out of the text, or invented against it, conform to the probable one in which it was passed." James Madison insisted that there was a duty to support the Constitution's "true meaning as understood *by the nation* at the time of its ratification." He repeatedly stated that the intentions were to be found in "contemporaneous expositions" or the "comments prevailing at the time it was adopted."[4] Prompted by the scholarship of Leonard Levy, legal historians have begun reexamining contemporary sources on the press clause and have opened a debate that should last for many years.

I

Levy maintained in his book *Legacy of Suppression,* first published in 1960, that the generation that framed the First Amendment "did not intend to give free rein to criticism of the government that might be deemed seditious libel." The Framers were Blackstonians who thought press freedom meant freedom from licensing and censorship, Levy wrote, and "the American experience with freedom of political expression was as slight as the theoretical inheritance was narrow." Scholars responded by challenging Levy's belief that the press was not free and aggressive in practice prior to the First Amendment. "Despite the law, there was freedom of expression in fact," Merrill Jensen wrote in a review of *Legacy of Suppression.* "No governmental institution, political faction, or individual was free from attacks such as few newspapers today would dare to print."[5]

In a revision of his book, published in 1985 as *Emergence of a Free Press,* Levy recanted his claim about press practice and admitted that he had "ignored the nearly epidemic degree of seditious libel that infected American newspapers after Independence." He continued to contend, however, that "the revolutionary generation did not seek to wipe out the core idea of seditious libel, that the government may be criminally assaulted by mere words." Levy reiterated his assertion that he had disproven notions about the demise of seditious libel before the First Amendment, views held by some U.S. Supreme Court justices and by scholars such as Henry Schofield and Zechariah Chafee, Jr. What had been his revisionist heresy in 1960, Levy said, has become "a new orthodoxy" to generate dissent.[6]

Early dissenters countered the Levy thesis by locating evidence of uninhibited conduct by the press and by citing statements on journalistic freedom which appeared to go beyond Blackstone. Still, no study has matched the scope of Levy's book or has offered a comprehensive alternative interpretation of the ideas and events that led to the press clause. The most thorough critique of Levy's work to date is a 1983 law journal article by Professor David A. Anderson. Anderson closely examined the sparse history of the drafting of the First Amendment during the First Congress and discussed the changes in language which occurred as the various versions were written. He concluded that there could be "little doubt that press freedom was viewed as being closely related to the experiment of representative self-government." Anderson directed several perceptive questions to adherents of the Levy thesis. He asked, for instance, why the press clause, which the public demanded and the states ratified, would have been aimed merely at prior restraint which had not been an issue for almost seventy years in America.[7]

Still, many aspects of the Levy thesis remain unscrutinized. Significant portions of his evidence require further consideration and additional sources should be examined. Too many issues remain unclear for Levy's interpretation to be a "new orthodoxy" or, as Anderson put it, "the conventional wisdom of our generation."[8] Levy's books have complicated First Amendment history. It is now apparent that the meaning of press freedom in the eighteenth century consisted of many strands and many colors. Much remains to be unraveled for analysis.

One of the central problems has been why so much press freedom existed in practice if the law on the books was so suppressive and the theory in people's minds so narrow. Levy admitted that he was "puzzled by the paradox." Since the British Constitution protected an oligarchy and Parliament had virtually unlimited power, English precedents were often inappropriate to a democratic republic in America where popular sovereignty had been achieved. Yet, it was difficult to emerge from a legal system dedicated to social control at the expense of the public will. When the Federalists tried to muzzle their Republican opponents with the Sedition Act of 1798, the majority party adopted the Blackstonian definition of press freedom as a justification for the statute. To some extent, Blackstone may have been "the oracle of the common law in the minds of the American Framers" as Levy claims, but Sir William was an apologist for the status quo in England and promoted legal theories clearly at odds with the fundamental principles of the United States Constitution.[9] Anachronistic precedents can be dredged up to suit political ends long past the time they can logically be accepted.

In addition, sociologists of the law point out that the influence of law is not as direct and powerful as might be expected and that people, individually and in groups, find subtle and not so subtle ways of evading the restrictions it imposes. They explain that social fields and networks are private governments that act as alternative institutions to regulate much of the behavior in society.[10] Accordingly, it becomes necessary to study such specific factors as connections within the printing trade and such general influences as republican political theory to understand the context of the writing of the press clause.

Understanding of republican theory in early America has advanced significantly since the publication of *Legacy of Suppression,* but this awareness is entirely absent in *Emergence of a Free Press.* Levy ignores the insights into the political culture provided in the work of such historians as Bernard Bailyn, Gordon Wood, and Lance

Banning. They and other scholars have begun to trace the powerful influences of England's "radical Whigs" on America and to describe the distrust of government and attachment to the principles of liberty that their doctrines entailed. Although the relationship seems apparent, historians have not yet carefully investigated the connections between republican thought as explicated in recent historiography and the ideology of eighteenth-century journalism. Following the radical Whig tradition, colonial journalists proclaimed their independence of factions and declared the importance of their serving as checks on government. In practice, of course, political pressures took their toll on journalistic ideals. The editorial policies of printers were periodically overturned in times of war and party strife, but the occupational ideology itself was deeply entrenched and was, in repeated instances, supported by the public as represented in mobs and in juries.[11]

With the endorsement of libertarian political doctrine and an underpinning of public support, aggressive journalism developed rapidly in America. Contrary to the assumptions of Levy and a number of other historians including Daniel Boorstin and Arthur M. Schlesinger, Sr., religious beliefs and political authority were being actively challenged in newspapers and pamphlets for decades before the Stamp Act Crisis. The colonies had a relatively small urban population and a limited number of presses, but the amount of contentious, antiauthoritarian writings was sufficient to contribute substantially to radical political theory and practice before the Revolution. Freedom of the press, said an essay published in the *Boston Gazette* in 1755, meant a right to expose abuses of power and was considered "essential to and coeval with all free Governments."[12]

II

Any study of the meaning of liberty of the press in the eighteenth century should take into account the actions of legislatures against the journalists and the statements made by politicians, printers and others who discussed freedom of expression. Statements on press freedom are important because interpretations of the right were frequently offered in official proceedings and in the press. The shades of opinion on the issue are revealed by examining such contemporary sources. The efforts made by legislatures to confront writers for their "contempt" or "breach of privilege" should be understood because court trials for seditious libel were no longer a threat to colonial printers after the much heralded acquittal of John Peter Zenger in 1735. The legislatures, as Levy correctly noted, were the principal menace to press freedom because they could use their contempt powers to punish political expression.[13] Still, Levy's work has misconstrued both the breach of legislative privilege cases and the positions taken on journalistic rights in early America.

In at least twenty instances, colonial legislatures summoned and interrogated journalists who published writings critical of the provincial government. In some cases, individuals were jailed for breach of privilege until the end of a legislative session if they were defiant or if they sufficiently angered a majority of the members. Levy suggests that such episodes effectively kept the crime of seditious libel alive in America after the failure of the Zenger prosecution. The matter is of course confused by the fact that legislatures—particularly the lower houses—perceived themselves as guardians of the people's rights and that parliamentary privilege had developed historically out of an actual need to protect members from the displeasure of the monarch and government officials.[14] Although it was no doubt an abuse of authority when used against journalists, the use of legislative power in such instances manifested a conflict between institutions—representative bodies and the press—both of which were understood as serving the interests of the public. The action itself was thus not without its libertarian dimension when it was employed to protect assemblies that were resisting royal authority. That it was used vindictively or with little regard for freedom of expression is merely one more example of the human propensity to ignore principles when lashing out at real or imagined enemies.

Levy's treatment of the subject is not convincing. His determination that the actions "effectively subdued the printers" neither fits his revised conclusion about the actual freedom of the press nor even matches his own evidence in most cases. Printers fought back with a variety of weapons, including publicity, lawsuits, and appeals to other bodies. Levy's *Legacy of Suppression,* for instance, overlooked the fact that Daniel Fowle fought the Massachusetts legislature for twelve years after being jailed for five days in 1754. The printer was accused of publishing a pamphlet opposing a provincial excise tax. The General Court voted to pay his expenses in 1764 and damages in 1766.[15]

Levy's assertion that only three journalists—William Smith, Thomas Powell, and Isaiah Thomas—ever invoked freedom of the press in defending themselves against legislative actions assumes that everything publishers said has been preserved for historians. When the Massachusetts legislature jailed James Franklin for a month in 1722 after he published a satirical news story about provincial authorities, his brother Benjamin took over the paper and reprinted a large portion of a spirited essay on freedom of thought and liberty of speech in free governments. Such statements are not considered in Levy's interpretation because the term "freedom of the press" was not used. Statements made at other times are also apparently dismissed. James Parker and Wiliam Weyman, for instance, spent ten days in jail in March 1756 after a letter in their *New-York Post-Boy* argued that the New York legislature was failing to provide an adequate defense in the French and Indian War. There is no evidence to suggest they brought up press freedom at the time, but a month later a paper Parker published in New Haven, the *Connecticut Gazette,* discussed the natural right of the British subject "to complain when he thinks himself agrieved" and the role reason would play when both sides of a controversy were published. In November the printers of the *Post-Boy* introduced an essay on press freedom noting that they had "seen and felt many oblique Strokes at the LIBERTY OF THE PRESS."[16]

Printers showed few signs of being intimidated. James Franklin and James Parker spent more time in jail for contempt than any other printer yet neither altered his behavior. Moreover, the use of breach of legislative privilege—sporadic as it was—seems to have died out after the Revolution. Levy says that "parliamentary privilege did not disappear after Independence," but he is unable to cite any instances of it being used between 1776 and 1791 when the First Amendment was ratified. On the other hand, Levy noted that the wording of Pennsylvania's 1776 constitution clearly allowed a freedom to criticize governmental proceedings and that in 1779 only one member of Congress voted in favor of a motion to summon John Dunlap for publishing a trenchant attack on its management of the country's finances. Instead of jailing Dunlap, members of Congress used the occasion for orations on liberty of the press.[17]

Support for the right to criticize even the patriots was demonstrated in Congress and in the state legislatures. In 1776 a Congressional resolution noted that there were loyalists who had been "deceived and drawn into erroneous opinions respecting the American cause" and it suggested that state and local governments protect the country against its enemies. Levy found the resolution ominous, but what Congress then proposed was "to treat all such persons with kindness and attention" and "to view their errors as proceeding

rather from want of information than want of virtue or public spirit."
The resolution recommended that the governments distribute copies
of publications which tended "to elucidate the merits of the American cause." The only other specific suggestion was to disarm loyalists and to take dangerous ones into safe custody. The states passed
loyalty laws, but could demonstrate remarkable concern for the press.
In 1777 and again in 1779 William Goddard was accosted by patriot
mobs for printing letters in the *Maryland Journal* that angered Baltimore's Whig Club. Legislative hearings were held at Annapolis after
both incidents. In 1777, when Goddard complained that the patriots
were "violently invading the Liberty of the Press," the Assembly
rounded up the members of the mob that could be found and made
them admit their mistakes.[18]

Levy's principal thesis, that the revolutionary generation did not
intend to eliminate the idea that government could be criminally assaulted by words, rests primarily on his reading of statements made
by politicians and journalists. Levy finds seeming contradictions in
libertarian arguments which extol the press as a means of exposing
wrongdoing in government and yet acknowledge that journalists can
be tried under some circumstances for publishing such writings. The
problem was that thinking on libel law had created a morass. Libertarians then, as now, believed the press should scrutinize government
and express opinions freely, but thought that the press had to accept
some degree of responsibility in its treatment of the personal reputations of public officials. Although they rejected the notion of government itself being defamed, libertarians usually said that journalists
could be successfully sued or prosecuted for libelling public officials
if they did not have an appropriate defense. Ideas on what constituted an appropriate defense varied, but a generally accepted one
was truth. Truth was the standard used by John Peter Zenger's lawyer, Andrew Hamilton, but Hamilton was among those who realized
that defendants who could not prove everything they wrote could be
found guilty.[19] Thus, he understood a need to rely on the sympathies
of jurors.

Levy often presents libertarians as oppressive and ignores the distinctions made in their arguments. He accuses Andrew Hamilton of
twice participating in legislative actions taken against a Philadelphia
printer, Andrew Bradford, for printing insulting articles in his *American Weekly Mercury*. On the first occasion, in 1722, Hamilton did
no more than attend a Council meeting and listen to Governor Wil-

liam Keith direct the printer to submit to censorship, an order which he seems to have ignored. In the second episode, in 1729, Hamilton may have taken testimony from Bradford in his capacity as the city's recorder, but if he did so it was in compliance with a Council order and there is no actual evidence to show that he did anything on his own. Hamilton's defense of Zenger in 1735 is dismissed in *Emergence of a Free Press* as having never made "a frontal assault on the concept of seditious libel." In fact, Hamilton's courtroom speech celebrated the role of the press in criticizing government. He said, however, that writers could be punished for making false accusations against a "private person" or a "public magistrate."[20] Levy fails to see that libertarians were recognizing a liberty to discuss government freely, but thought that there could be limits on what was said about individuals who had some right to their reputations.

Libertarians routinely distinguished between the freedom to discuss public issues and the limited right to discuss public persons. Benjamin Franklin wrote in a newspaper essay published in 1789, the year the First Amendment was written, that legislation should be passed to protect personal reputations, but that liberty of the press could be unlimited for "discussing the propriety of public measures and political opinions." Nine of the eleven revolutionary-era state constitutions had, in fact, declared that liberty of the press ought to be inviolable or ought never to be restrained. Still, a desire to protect personal reputation existed. In his proposal for Virginia's 1776 constitution, Thomas Jefferson wrote that "presses shall be free, except so far as by commission of private injury they may give cause of private action." Levy nevertheless concludes that neither Franklin nor Jefferson ever went on record opposing "seditious libel."[21]

III

Since Levy's thesis stumbles on crucial points, there is a need for a more accurate understanding of what was meant by the term "freedom of the press" in the century that produced the First Amendment. Legal historians, however, will undoubtedly find it difficult to draw general conclusions. Individuals' actions and stated opinions varied with changing circumstances, so Levy's attempts to portray inconsistencies are not all groundless. Libertarians did not always exercise perfect self-control or flawless adherence to their principles. Scholars have, for instance, been particularly drawn to the case of Thomas

Jefferson who ardently championed freedom of the press, but seemed unable to endure it while serving as president.[22] Yet, libertarian principles were expressed and were followed to a remarkable extent.

The most accomplished journalist early America produced was indisputably Benjamin Franklin. As a printer, politician, and propagandist, he was in an unsurpassed position for observing and participating in the growth of the eighteenth-century press. When he was born in 1706, the colonies had only one newspaper, the tame, plodding *Boston News-Letter* which was "Published by Authority." As late as 1721, he recalled in his autobiography, his older brother James was considered foolish for starting to print the *New-England Courant* in Boston. "I remember his being dissuaded by some of his Friends from the Undertaking, as not likely to succeed," he wrote, "one Newspaper being in their Judgment enough for America."[23]

After helping his brother battle attempts by Massachusetts authorities to silence the *Courant,* the younger Franklin took over a dying newspaper in Philadelphia and began establishing other publications elsewhere. Sufficiently successful after twenty years to retire from active participation in his business, he devoted more time to science, philanthropy, and statesmanship, but also continued to use his pen to promote his causes and to participate in the affairs of his first profession, as it outgrew government supervision and public indifference. In the year of his death, 1790, one hundred newspapers were engaged in a spirited pursuit of readership, and the states were voting to ratify a Bill of Rights specifically guaranteeing "freedom . . . of the press."

Franklin's career illuminates the issues of what "freedom of the press" meant in the eighteenth century and of how journalism became in his lifetime a powerful force in public affairs. Franklin has, however, been an extraordinarily elusive historical figure. Historians have accordingly drawn differing conclusions about his press theory and practice. Leonard W. Levy has, for instance, found Franklin's thought on the subject to be superficial if not sinister, while Clinton Rossiter has stated that he had "the most intense personal reasons for championing freedom of expression" and never "shrank from active conflict with those who would suppress it." James A. Sappenfield has discerned a "spirit of recklessness" in his approach to journalistic controversy. Yet Stephen Botein has portrayed Franklin as the prime example of what he has seen as a pattern among colonial printers— the cultivation of an image of blandness and impartiality to avoid making enemies and losing business.[24]

The problem of interpreting how Franklin and other journalists used and supported the press is one of reconciling their pragmatism and idealism and their combativeness and moderation. As one of the transcendent geniuses of the eighteenth century, Franklin, in particular, possessed all of these qualities.[25] He endorsed liberty of the press as resolutely as any other freedom, but was not always prepared to say that the rights he expected for himself should be extended to a business competitor or a political adversary. (See chapters VI through IX.) As a writer, Franklin displayed a talent for virtually any approach from light, disarming humor to searing personal attack. Capable of waiting for the best opportunities, he was silent in some controversies and prepared to give detailed, reasoned opinions in others. Such finesse led one exasperated opponent, addressing Franklin from a rival's paper in 1740, to point to "the Caution with which you usually act in Matters where your Interest is concerned," but to observe that "you can, upon some Occasions, strike a bold Stroke, and then depend upon your Wit to bring you off."[26]

The following study, then, is in part intended to consider how one preeminent Enlightenment writer and statesman conducted himself as a patriarch of American journalism and an advocate of liberty of the press. Moreover, it is an effort to explore—through other printers, philosophers, and politicians—the development and justification of assertive religious and political communication in the formative period of a nation's history. Part One surveys the European events, ideas, and ideals which tended to shape early American debate on freedom of the press. Part Two is devoted to the political and legal questions faced by eighteenth-century writers and publishers. Together, Parts One and Two form the basis for Part Three, which focuses on the press theory and practices of the most prominent network of journalists in America—Benjamin Franklin and his immediate associates in the printing business.

The study as a whole offers evidence that colonists were publishing and justifying aggressive journalism for decades before the Revolution. The study further suggests that by the time of the First Amendment, Americans had forged a general libertarian press ideology that was incompatible with the idea of seditious libel. The components of this theoretical perspective came from practical experience as well as from radical Whig and Enlightenment thought.

PART ONE

Philosophies and Practices

I

The English Experience

In 1754 Benjamin Franklin was performing his duties as a member of the Pennsylvania Assembly, as one of two deputy postmasters general for North America, and as a delegate to the Albany Congress which adopted his proposals for uniting the colonies against the French. He was also preoccupied with the task of starting a printing business in New Haven, Connecticut. After receiving an honorary master's degree from Yale the previous autumn, Franklin had determined, as he wrote to William Strahan, his London business associate, that the location offered "a considerable Town in which there is an University, and a Prospect that a Bookseller's Shop with a Printing House may do pretty well." Franklin asked Strahan to ship books, stationery, type, and a press modified to meet his specifications.[1]

Delays developed in the shipment from England, but Franklin also had difficulties finding a printer. In prior ventures, he had selected a journeyman from his shop in Philadelphia and had made him a partner. Using this system, he had dispatched Thomas Whitmarsh to Charleston in 1731, Lewis Timothy—after Whitmarsh died—to Charleston in 1733, James Parker to New York in 1742, and Thomas Smith to Antigua in 1748. He also set up a partnership in 1748 with his foreman, David Hall, to free himself from most of the daily responsibilities of his Philadelphia office. Franklin offered the new position in Connecticut to each of the two nephews he had helped to establish in the trade—James Franklin, Jr., who was at Newport,

Rhode Island, and Benjamin Mecom, who had gone to Antigua when Smith died in 1752. After both relatives declined, Franklin turned to Parker, who already had presses in New York and New Jersey, and persuaded him to undertake the firm on a trial basis.[2]

When James Parker arrived in New Haven at the end of December 1754, he brought an appointment from Franklin to serve as local postmaster. He also had plans to "beat the Way" for a nephew of his own or, otherwise, to employ John Holt, a bankrupt merchant he was training as a favor to Franklin. Holt's brother-in-law was Franklin's fellow deputy postmaster general, Virginia printer William Hunter. Parker soon had orders from Yale College and its contentious New Light president, Franklin's friend Thomas Clap. Parker was also in a position to receive government printing as he, Franklin, and the Timothy family already had in other colonies. On April 12, 1755, Parker published the first issue of the *Connecticut Gazette*.[3]

Starting a newspaper was one of the priorities in each of the businesses Franklin founded. A publication promoted printing shop merchandise and services and brought in income from advertising and subscriptions. Printers were anxious to point out, however, that the newspaper was not merely a means of making money, but was also part of a vital intellectual process. "The PRESS is not so much considered, as the Property of the Men who carry on the Trade of Printing, as of the Publick," the *Connecticut Gazette* editorialized. A free press was "highly esteem'd by Britons" as a method for "asserting all their just Rights, redressing Grievances, detecting Error, advancing useful Knowledge, and making an Appeal to the Reason and Justice of the whole Race of Mankind."[4]

Parker, who had spent more than a decade in the cross fire of New York politics as the publisher of the *New-York Weekly Post-Boy,* used the first page of the first issue of the *Gazette* for a rousing rendition of reasons to uphold press freedom. The editor declared that liberty of the press would surely "be always zealously preserved inviolate" in "a Land possess'd by the Offspring of a People, who bravely fought the howling Wilderness with all its savage Terrors, rather than become the servile Slaves of bigotted Tyrants." He contrasted the spirit of England's Glorious Revolution with the suppressive measures endured by "the unenlightened People of Rome or Spain" where the "bigotted Priesthood and Inquisition prevails" and by those in France where "the volatile Humour of the People keeps them from sinking under their great Load of Chains, whilst he who dares to murmur, soon finds Reward in the Bastile." Parker observed that the utility of newspapers was "universally acknowledged" in an English country and he invited readers to submit pieces that would advance virtue, commerce, and liberty. He cautioned against personal defamation, but remarked that only the guilty feared free expression and that few, if any, could judge when that right was being truly abused since the opinions of mankind differed. "The press has always been an Enemy to Tyrants," he insisted, "and just so far as Tyranny prevails in any Part of the World, so far the Liberty of the Press is suppressed."[5]

Far from being unique, Parker's inaugural essay in the *Connecticut Gazette* represented the conventional libertarian wisdom that press freedom fostered progress and provided a measure of a nation's political liberty. The only recognizable change in the standard recital of benefits of a free press came at the time of the Revolution when unfettered expression was identified as an American rather than a British birthright. Writing in Boston's *Herald of Freedom*, "Philalethes" declared in 1788 that the liberty of a country could "generally be calculated by the liberality and free state of the press" and that his fellow citizens had to preserve this "sublime" and "darling" freedom. "They are nurtured in the ennobling idea," Philalethes said, "that to *think* what they please, and to *speak, write* and *publish* their sentiments with decency and independency on every subject, constitutes the dignified character of Americans."[6]

When Francis Bailey began his *Freeman's Journal* in Philadelphia in 1781, he remarked that the New World had begun "to emerge from the fangs and tyranny of the Old" and that "wanton and unhallowed restraints" had been placed on printing where countries were in decline. "This is not a place for tracing facts; every novice in history must know them," he told his readers. "The Freedom, then, of these states, now exalted into empire, must rise or fall with the freedom of the press." Bailey then reprinted a poem on liberty of the press from Benjamin Franklin's *Poor Richard's Almanac* for 1757 which said:[7]

> This *Nurse of arts*, and *Freedom's fence*,
> To chain, is treason against sense;
> And liberty, thy thousand tongues
> None silence who design no wrongs.

While printers invariably had personal, financial, and political positions to consider in the conduct of their businesses, many were prepared to proclaim that the owner of a press had a particular obligation to the principles of knowledge and liberty. As a potential target of public resentment or partisan reprisal, the printer naturally had a vested interest in supporting the ideals of free expression if only as a matter of self-defense. In any case, however, arguments for press freedom were made and were presented as the essence of practical wisdom and common justice. The main sources of this press ideology were the ideas and rationales that profoundly influenced the American Revolution, the Constitution, and what Jefferson called the "revolution of 1800"—the philosophies of the Enlightenment and of England's libertarian tradition.[8]

I

Like orthodox religion, press control was never completely successful in England. Just as church authorities battled sects, superstition, and skepticism, secular leaders struggled to manage or suppress political expression.[9] The ingenuity of the government in imposing press restraints was matched only by the resourcefulness of those who sought to evade them. As this conflict continued for centuries, writers and politicians who sought expanded freedom fashioned cogent arguments for liberty of the press.

After the first presses were established in Britain at the end of the fifteenth century, the Tudors brought the new technology within the royal grasp with decrees, proclamations, monopolies, and licensing. The restrictions were extensive and were backed by punishments extending from fines and warnings to torture, maiming, and execution. The elaborate system, however, left some printers discontented enough to risk all for profit or principle. The result was that individuals—such as the Puritans who moved a secret press around England to produce the Martin Marprelate tracts in 1588 and 1589—could achieve publication if they were sufficiently determined.[10]

The governments of the turbulent seventeenth century were repeatedly stung by a lack of compliance with press restrictions. During the reigns of James I and Charles I, the first English newspapers were censored or closed down, but only with difficulty. In the years Charles attempted to rule without Parliament, the arbitrary proceedings of his Court of the Star Chamber against Puritan writers like William Prynne—who was twice maimed for seditious libel—merely added to public resentment. As Parliament moved toward a military solution to its problems with the king, press controls disintegrated, the Star Chamber was abolished, and printers began turning out unprecedented numbers of religious and political publications. Prynne was released from prison and was greeted by a crowd of ten thousand as he returned to London. An essay which appeared in the *Boston Gazette* more than one hundred years later went as far as to assert that "the original, true and real Cause" of the English civil war was suppression of the press and that "had not *Prynn* lost his *Ears,* K. *Charles* would have never lost his Head."[11]

With the Commonwealth, the Protectorate, and finally the Restoration came the revival of earlier methods of restraint, but enforcement proved inadequate. Although presses were confiscated and printers imprisoned, unlicensed pamphlets were published and sold with virtual impunity. Almanac writers competed with each other in the production of partisan diatribes, crude humor, and scurrilous personal attacks. William Lilly, the foremost astrological propagandist of the seventeenth century, was arrested nine times in his career but knew how to use perjury and prominent friends to avoid the consequences of his boldness. Censorship removed Lilly's more blatant reflections on government and warnings to the king, but this left intriguing blank spaces in his almanac for his tens of thousands of devoted readers to ponder.[12]

In the aftermath of the Glorious Revolution of 1688–89, prior restraints appeared to be not only ineffective, but also clearly unpopular. Licensing ended permanently in 1694 when the House of Commons refused to renew the printing act then in effect. In a document drafted by John Locke and approved by the Commons in 1695, the controls developed under the Tudors and Stuarts were depicted as impractical and as detrimental to the trade of printing. The Commons maintained that the system hindered scholars and subjected printers to improper searches and excessive penalties. Moreover, licensing was said to lack set standards and to allow "great Oppression."[13]

A more subtle method of press control—the combination of taxation and subsidization—was used in the eighteenth century, but without impressive results. Printers found loopholes in the stamp laws and practiced fraud and evasion. The effort to extend stamp duties to America in 1765 was an outright failure. Still, the taxes were a form of prior restraint and made it difficult for English newspapers to survive without the financial support of a party or the ministry. At the height of its efforts to buy journalistic favor, the Walpole administration may have spent as much as £10,000 a year. Bolingbroke's *Craftsman,* the leading opposition publication, calculated a figure twice as high in 1731 for printing and postage without including the costs of "Prosecutions, Evidence, and some other Articles of secret Service" and of what it called Walpole's "standing Army of Writers." Being an antiadministration penman could also be profitable, as William Guthrie demonstrated in 1746 when he began receiving a pension of £200 a year simply for agreeing to stop writing against the government.[14]

By the accession of George III, the press had become too much a part of England's political culture to be easily repressed or manipulated by government. For more than a century, newspapers and pamphlets had been strewn across the tables of clubs, inns, taverns, and coffeehouses and had fueled animated exchanges which filled the air along with the tobacco smoke. London had nearly ninety newspapers in 1760 and improvements in roads and the post office made the publications of the metropolis readily available elsewhere. Provincial centers were also acquiring newspapers of their own as Samuel Johnson observed in the *Idler,* saying that "almost every large town has its weekly historian, who regularly circulates his periodical intelligence, and fills the villages of his district with conjectures on the events of war, and with debates on the true interest of Europe."[15]

As they increased awareness of public affairs, periodicals helped to lift the veils of awe and mystery surrounding politics. Although Parliament prohibited the reporting of its debates, handwritten newsletter accounts of the proceedings had begun to appear regularly in the late seventeenth century. Unauthorized publication continued in the eighteenth century in Abel Boyer's *Political State of Great Britain* and in *Gentleman's Magazine* and *London Magazine.* Occasionally reprimanded for their activities, publishers of the debates took the precaution of disguising the names of the speakers or attributing the proceedings to mythical clubs or assemblies. Thus *Gentleman's* employed Samuel Johnson to report on "Walelop" (Walpole) and the "Senate of Magna Lilliputia." An essay on liberty of the press in *Gentleman's* in 1738 stated that it was the "undoubted Right" of the people to be informed of the opinions, actions, and interests of governors and that to claim otherwise was the assertion "only of *Priestcraft* and *Tyranny,* for they alone would have the People ignorant who desire to deceive them."[16]

Freedom of the press and individual liberties were salient political issues early in the reign of George III—largely because of John Wilkes. He and his supporters countered the government's irregular and maladroit moves to punish him for seditiously libelling the king in the forty-fifth issue of his *North Briton* and to disqualify him from taking a seat in Parliament. As the reading public of England and America was provided with fresh and conclusive evidence that the ruling oligarchy was oppressive and corrupt, the cause of Wilkes was celebrated in toasts and popular demonstrations throughout the nation. When Wilkes won reelection to Parliament in 1768, Benjamin Franklin witnessed mobs illuminating London for two nights and "requiring gentlemen and ladies of all ranks as they passed in their carriages to shout for Wilkes and liberty, marking the same words on all their coaches with chalk, and No. 45 on every door." Franklin considered it "really an extraordinary event" to find such support for "an outlaw and exile, of bad personal character, not worth a farthing."[17]

The irreverent triumphs of Wilkes appealed to a literate, self-confident people denied meaningful political participation. Wilkes and others were awarded substantial damages in cases arising from mass arrests the government made in response to the *North Briton* Number 45. Juries also frustrated prosecutions of the various newspaper publishers who printed the insulting "Letter to the King" written by the brilliant but unidentified journalist "Junius" in 1769. Members of the opposition and London radicals led by Wilkes could hardly believe their good fortune in 1771 when the Commons majority made the blunder of attempting to stop newspaper publication of the House debates. Wilkes and his compatriots took steps to obstruct and embarrass the government, and three of the eight printers summoned to the Commons received the protection of the city of London which claimed the exclusive authority of arrest within its boundaries. In the ensuing struggle, no one—including the king—wanted to press the matter when Wilkes refused to appear before the House, but Lord Mayor Brass Crosby and Alderman Richard Oliver were committed to the Tower until the end of the session. Reacting to the spectacle, a mob menaced Parliament and attacked Lord North, the head of the ministry, demolishing his coach. Newspapers, meanwhile, continued to publish the debates and the Commons gave up trying to stop them.[18]

George III and his ministers did, of course, have their defenders in the years preceding the American Revolution. William Strahan, who was appointed King's Printer in 1770, wrote a stream of letters to David Hall in Philadelphia warning him not to believe what he read in the English press. Hall, a former journeyman of Strahan's who had taken over the *Pennsylvania Gazette* from Franklin, was told in 1771

that Wilkes was "perhaps the best Manufacturer of paragraphs that
ever lived" but that he and Junius were sinking in popularity. "The
Discontents and Scurrility with which our Newspapers are constantly
filled," Strahan wrote to Hall a year later, "exist only in *them,* and
are the Productions of a few profligate Individuals." Tobias Smollett,
a literary figure who—like Defoe, Addison, and a number of other
prominent writers—was not above receiving political patronage, put
out the weekly *Briton* on the side of the government when Wilkes
was publishing the *North Briton.* In his novel *Humphry Clinker*
(1771), Smollett complained that party spirit encouraged dishonesty
and defamation and that "every rancorous knave—every desperate
incendiary" could "skulk behind the press of a newsmonger, and
have a stab at the first character in the kingdom, without running the
least hazard of detection or punishment." Describing the popularity
which could be gained as "a martyr to the cause of defamation," one
of Smollett's characters remarked that prosecuting a publisher "is so
far from being considered a punishment, *in terrorem,* that it will
probably make his fortune."[19]

II

As partisanship stretched the practical limits of journalism in eighteenth-century England, general ideas about the meaning of press
freedom also took shape. Like parties themselves, combative publications were questioned as to their legitimacy at first, but came to be
regarded as inevitable and even as necessary for the preservation of
liberty. Positions on press freedom were not associated so much with
the increasingly hollow "Whig" and "Tory" designations as with the
fact of being in or out of power. While administration supporters
were anxious to maintain their dignity in the eyes of the public, members of the opposition were ready to proclaim the importance of free
political expression in checking the misuse of authority. The crude
propaganda tactic of pushing the adversary's position to its extreme
was used with the predictability and embellishment of solemn ritual.
One side was accused of fomenting sedition and the other of fostering slavery. "A Tory under Oppression, or out of a Place, is a Whig;
and a Whig with Power to oppress, is a Tory," "Cato" explained in
the *British Journal* in 1722. "The Tory damns the Whig for maintaining a Resistance, which he himself never fails to practise; and the
Whig reproaches the Tory with Slavish Principles, and yet calls him
a Rebel if he does not practise them."[20]

"Cato," the pen name of John Trenchard and Thomas Gordon, was the leading luminary of eighteenth-century libertarian press theory. Drawing on the "radical Whig" or "commonwealth" ideology of seventeenth-century writers like James Harrington, Robert Molesworth, and Algernon Sidney, Cato stressed the dangers of arbitrary rulers, money interests, and public corruption. He also dismissed the doctrines of the divine right of Kings and passive obedience and reasoned that governments were established by men for the good of mankind. Trenchard and Gordon's essays appeared in the *London Journal* from 1720 until 1722 when their criticism of government policies led Walpole to buy off the owner of the paper. Their collaboration continued in the less important *British Journal,* but ended in 1723 with Trenchard's death. Editions of *Cato's Letters* were published and republished for decades in Britain and were immensely popular in America, where journalists and political theorists praised and imitated the authors.[21]

Cato's sharply antiauthoritarian temperament was particularly evident in his four essays on the right of expression. "Freedom of Speech is the great Bulwark of Liberty; they prosper and die together," he wrote, "And it is the Terror of Traytors and Oppressors, and a Barrier against them." He regretted that the liberty to criticize government had "been approved or condemned by all Men, and all Parties, in proportion as they were advantaged, or annoy'd by it." Cato argued that the freedom should rather be understood as a means of making the public vigilant and keeping the powerful honest. He told his readers that press controls were ineffective and that officials were more of a threat to a nation than the public. Saying that "almost all over the Earth, the People, for One Injury they do their Governors, receive Ten Thousand from them," Cato suggested that the burden of patience be on the rulers more than the ruled. He ridiculed the pretensions of leaders who "called every Opposition to their wild and ravenous Schemes, and every Attempt to preserve the People's Right, by the odious Names of Sedition and Faction" and advised those in authority that the best way to prevent libels was not to deserve them. "Guilt only dreads Liberty of Speech, which drags it out of its lurking Holes," Cato said, "and exposes its Deformity and Horror to Day-light."[22]

Among Cato's professed admirers was the rakish, freethinking Henry St. John, Viscount Bolingbroke. An ambitious Tory secretary of state in the last years of Queen Anne's reign, Bolingbroke was immediately discarded by George I and driven from England by vindictive Whigs in 1715. He joined the Pretender in France, but soon disavowed the Jacobite cause and was eventually allowed to return to England. Attempting to unite Tories and opposition Whigs, Bolingbroke, his political ally William Pulteney, and their editor, Nicholas Amhurst, used the pages of the *Craftsman* for a ten-year campaign against the Walpole ministry's taxes, treaties, economic policies, and systematic corruption of Parliament. Although not ultimately successful with his brand of democratic Toryism, Bolingbroke proved to be a brilliant journalist and inspiration to Americans—especially in the South where newspaper essayists seem to have preferred him to Cato. Thomas Jefferson, among others, appreciated his rational approach to religion and his "country" ideology which condemned the wickedness of the city and court.[23]

Liberty of the press was a constant topic in the *Craftsman* for twelve months beginning early in 1731 when its printer, Richard Francklin, was charged with seditious libel for publishing an embarrassing letter on European treaty negotiations. One periodical reported that a "vast Crowd" gathered around Westminster Hall for preliminary proceedings and that when Pulteney emerged from the building he was loudly cheered. "Which," the journal noted, "shews the Fondness of the People of *England* for the Liberty of the Press." Francklin, who had been pronounced not guilty by the jury in a 1729 prosecution, was convicted by a "special jury" packed with crown officers, but Bolingbroke's publication used the occasion to blast the precedents and procedures used against the printer. The *Craftsman* emphasized its editorial affinity to "Cato's immortal letters" and quoted Trenchard and Gordon at length on corruption and the right of expression. The paper stated that freedom of the press meant the examination of "all Matters of Religion and Government" and "the Liberty of censuring the Conduct of Men in Power, whenever We think their Measures deserve it."[24]

Ministerial writers heaped scorn on Bolingbroke and accused him of running a "School of Sedition." One of Walpole's journalists, William Arnall, produced a pamphlet saying that the *Craftsman* wanted "an unbounded License to abuse all Persons, and all Things" and that Bolingbroke, contrary to his assertions of his leniency, had taken vigorous action against the press two decades earlier when he was in office. The pamphlet listed printers, publishers, and booksellers who had been taken into custody on his warrants and pointed out his participation in unsuccessful attempts to pass legislation forbidding anonymous publications and requiring the registration of presses. Ridiculing the pamphlet and admitting only that some prosecutions had been forgotten, the *Craftsman* ended its year-long promotion of press freedom, but not before denying a government newspaper's charge that Bolingbroke had tried to influence a member of Francklin's jury. "It would be endless to pursue these Writers through all their Dirt and Scandal," the paper said.[25]

After his failure to engineer a repeal of the Septennial Act in 1734, Bolingbroke retired from politics, but the *Craftsman* held its course. Henry Haines, the *Craftsman*'s printer after Francklin's conviction, was arrested twice in 1737—the first time for publishing observations comparing George II to Shakespeare's King John. The prosecutions prompted newspaper debate in which the *Craftsman* defined press freedom as being limited only by a "proper Regard to Decency and good Manners"—a concern which could give way "in Case of Extremity, to the publick Good." The paper said liberty "was always understood to imply a Right of enquiring into the Expediency of *publick Measures*" and quoted John Peter Zenger's attorney, Andrew Hamilton, defending the right to criticize those "who injure and oppress the People under their Administration." *Common Sense,* another opposition journal, offered the view that "all Restraints upon Freedom of Writing and the Press, have never been, nor can be made of any other Use, than to promote the Designs of Oppression and arbitrary Power." Meanwhile, the Walpole ministry's *Daily Gazetteer* accused the *Craftsman* and *Common Sense* of "openly Abusing all Government" and of appealing to "many giddy, and not a few evil-minded Persons, ready to lay hold of such Suggestions, and, in consequence thereof, to disturb the publick Peace." The *Gazetteer* pointed with horror—the *Craftsman* with pride—at the events of 1733 when Bolingbroke's paper had spurred the frenzied propaganda and public outcry that defeated Walpole's cherished exise scheme. On that occasion, the prime minister told the House of Commons that excise opponents were "stirring up the people to mutiny and sedition." Walpole was, in fact, forced at one point to flee an angry crowd outside Parliament.[26]

The founding of *The Champion* in 1739 brought Henry Fielding and James Ralph to the forefront of opposition journalism. Ralph, a Philadelphian who had formed a friendship with Benjamin Franklin and sailed with him to England in 1724, had initially intended to establish himself as a poet. Franklin tried to discourage him, but he wrote verse long enough to become one of the objects of ridicule in Alexander Pope's satirical *Dunciad*. Ralph also had a brief career assisting Fielding in antiministerial stage productions before Walpole imposed theater censorship in 1737. The two writers then collaborated on *The Champion,* which used the formulas of Cato and the *Craftsman* to scorch the administration. Writing as "Lilbourne" in *The Champion,* Ralph justified the paper's editorial stance with an essay recalling the Prynne prosecution and the Glorious Revolution and expounding on liberty of the press as "the Right of a Freeman to utter his thoughts on State-Affairs freely." Not finding the paper profitable, Fielding withdrew in 1741 and, after the fall of Walpole, became a government journalist. Ralph continued *The Champion* for a time and then wrote for other opposition papers while attempting to auction off his mediocre talents. In 1753 he finally obtained an annual pension of £300 to abstain from political topics.[27]

Despite the rhetoric of press freedom, the English political journalist was sometimes considered no more than a talented clerk or the producer of a commodity. As long as government in effect rewarded both praise and criticism of itself, whatever convictions journalists had tended to be secondary to opportunity or necessity. In 1758, Ralph published *The Case of Authors by Profession or Trade* in which he deplored the insecurities and inhumanities of Grub Street. Asserting that there had come to be no difference between "the Writer in his Garret, and the Slave in the Mines," he complained of a decline in worthwhile patronage. In a list of authors he felt had been properly compensated in the past, he included the name of Thomas Gordon, who, he noted, had been appointed a commissioner of wine licenses by Walpole after he finished attacking his administration in *Cato's Letters.* Ralph added that the people, if they were sincere about the importance of free expression, would take liberty of the press "out of the Hands of Faction" and make use of it "to bring their Grievances, if any, to a fair, full, and effectual Audit."[28]

In Ralph's native country, meanwhile, the idea of the free press being the vox populi could be taken more seriously. With little or nothing to offer the mercenary writer, colonial journalism was generally left to the believers in causes and to the printers themselves. British Americans were, moreover, in a position to employ opposition ideology in all its intensity as an explanation for their own distinct anxieties and to adopt its approach in a place where the authority and inducements of government were relatively weak. From this perspective, support in England for civil liberties could appear cynical. A poem on liberty of the press published in the *South-Carolina Gazette* in 1765 said:[29]

> In good Queen Anna's days, when Tories reign'd,
> And the just Liberty of the Press restrain'd.
> Sad Whigs complain'd, in doleful notes and sundry,
> O Liberty! O Virtue! O my Country!
> But when themselves had reach'd the day of grace,
> They chang'd their principles, as well as place,
> From Messengers secure no printer lies,
> They take Compos[i]ters, Press men, Devils, Flies,
> What means this change? The sum of all the story's,
> Tories deprest are Whigs, and Whigs in pow'r are Tories.

While writings as admired as *Cato's Letters* or the *Craftsman* were often copied verbatim in America, lesser works or political acts might be simply imitated—although not always with notable success. In 1754 enough votes were found in the Massachusetts General Court to pass a liquor excise measure in spite of a spirited press campaign plainly modelled on the uncouth and frightening essays, broadsides, and ballads that demolished Walpole's excise plan in 1733. In 1770, colonial newspapers proclaimed Alexander McDougall "America's Wilkes" after the Son of Liberty was accused of publishing a seditious libel of the New York Assembly. Although supported with patriot toasts, gifts, and demonstrations patterned on those afforded the author of the *North Briton* Number 45, McDougall spent 162 days in confinement.[30]

The familiar themes of the people's right to know and the mob's threat to authority were given extended discussion in England in the wake of the Wilkes phenomenon and the Junius trials. In 1770, Parliamentary debates of the legal aspects of the cases turned inevitably to the broad issue of journalistic freedom. Both opponents and followers of Lord North's ministry expressed the by then commonplace sentiment that freedom of the press was the "palladium" or "bulwark" of English liberties, but differences emerged on what the freedom meant and on what had caused the public's fury. Since the publication of the *North Briton,* the prime minister said, a factious press had "overflowed the land with its black gall, and poisoned the minds of the people." Edmund Burke, who had earlier in the year published his *Thoughts on the Cause of the Present Discontents,* placed the blame squarely on the "grand criminals" of the ministry. He told the members that he could "see no reason for supposing that the people

have sunk to the very dregs of corruption, that they naturally delight
in slanders and detraction." Burke remarked that Junius, despite the
"rancour and venom" of his letter to the king, had written "many
bold truths by which a wise prince might profit."[31]

With the perennial impasse over freedom of the press again appearing, an additional concept was brought forward in the debates—
the idea that, after all, truth would emerge in journalistic argument.
"Truth will at last prevail," North said of the writings of Junius.
"The public will see and feel that he has either advanced false facts,
or reasoned falsely from true principles; and that he has owed his
escape to the spirit of the times, not to the justice of his cause." Not
everyone in the House of Commons was convinced by this proposition, however. One member complained that many people took anything they saw in print as gospel and that "not a stage, nor a fly, nor
a waggon goes down to the country without loads of magazines, pamphlets, and news-papers, and other literary manufactures, full of
nothing but misrepresentation and abuse." Alexander Wedderburn,
whose caustic opposition voice was about to be quieted with an appointment to the position of solicitor general, responded that if liberty of the press poisoned the minds of the people, it also provided
an antidote. "The same waggons, the same flys and stages that carry
down into the country the lies and abuse of faction, carry down also
the lies and abuse of the ministry," he said. "If any one is bit by the
tarantula of opposition, he is cured by the music of the court."[32]

II

The Marketplace of Ideas Concept

As long as the sport of British government was played by the rules of patronage, personality, and power, freedom of the press had an unsteady foundation. Printers practiced evasion, politicians changed principles, and journalists appeared opportunistic. Still, the cause of free expression had a vitality which ran deeper than the "court" and "country" distinction or the expedients of political controversy. The notion of democracy may have had little relevance in a system that rewarded greed, partisan loyalty, and electoral manipulations, but liberty had a talismanic quality which pervaded the political culture. The English civil war began ostensibly as an attempt to recover ancient freedoms, and the cry of the mobs in the 1760s was "Wilkes and Liberty." Ministry polemicists even justified corruption on the ground that it stabilized government and therefore sustained liberty.[1] The very word "freedom" in freedom of the press, then, was telling. Any attempt to restrict the right could be depicted as popish and oppressive. From a libertarian perspective, unfettered expression could be defended as a simple matter of intellectual fair play, as a kind of free trade in ideas.

I

The marketplace of ideas concept—the proposition that truth naturally overcomes falsehood when they are allowed to compete—was used continually during the eighteenth century as a justification for

freedom of expression. The belief that competing voices produce superior conclusions was, to some extent, already established, since it
was implicit in scientific reasoning, the practice of trial by jury, and
the process of legislative debate. Two philosophical positions provided support. One, as expressed by a Philadelphia newspaper essayist, was that truth acted "like a Spark upon Tinder" in the mind
and simply put falsehood to flight. On the other hand, Montaigne
had observed two hundred years earlier that human beings were born
to seek truth, but that truth and falsehood often looked alike and
that the mind was prepared to accept and even court deception. People, he concluded, should therefore be tolerant, suspicious of those
claiming knowledge, and ready to welcome contradiction as an opportunity for discussion and improved understanding. "I hate every
kind of tyranny," he wrote, "whether of words or acts."[2]

At the time Montaigne was writing his essays, similar sentiments
were being expressed in England to demand freedom of speech in the
House of Commons. Peter Wentworth, who was a Puritan agitator
during Elizabeth's reign, told his fellow members in 1576 that he
wished rumors of the queen's displeasure and her "Commanding or
Inhibiting" messages about matters under discussion were "Buried
in Hell." He argued that the queen was not without fault and that
unless there was freedom of speech, Parliament would be "but a
very School of Flattery and Dissimulation." Any harmful ideas, he
said, would do less damage if known and exposed. How, Wentworth
asked, "can truth appear and conquer until falsehood and all subtilties that should shadow and darken it be found out?"[3]

Individuals representing a broad spectrum of Protestant thought
were, in fact, prepared to recognize that truth was elusive and to
criticize ignorance, passivity, and suppression as holdovers from the
Roman Catholic Church. In his farewell address to the Pilgrims in
1620, pastor John Robinson stated that it was necessary to "examine
and compare" what was received as "further light" since Christianity
had come "so lately out of such thick Antichristian darknesse."
With the breakdown of press controls at the beginning of the civil
war came swarms of propaganda tracts for radical sects and political
groups and eventually published pleas for mutual forbearance. "That
since we know in part, and prophesy in part, and that we now see
through a glasse darkly," wrote Jeremy Taylor, chaplain to Charles
I, in 1647, "wee should not despise or contemn persons not so knowing as ourselves."[4]

In 1644, a momentous year in the military and religious developments of the civil war between the king and Parliament, a number of pamphlet writers who urged toleration on the basis of imperfect human knowledge took up the theme of the innate power of truth. Early in the year, Henry Robinson's *Liberty of Conscience: Or the Sole Means to Obtain Peace and Truth* was published. Robinson argued that persecution did not reform error, that it was enough that "by the incongruities and absurdities which accompany erroneous and unsound doctrines, the truth appears still more glorious, and wins others to the love thereof." By summer, readers had William Walwyn's *The Compassionate Samaritane,* which was careful to agree with laws restricting printing but suggested that those who were sure of their doctrines "should desire that all mens mouthes should be open, that so error may discover its foulnes and trueth become more glorious by a victorious conquest after a fight in open field." Walwyn, an admirer of Montaigne, thought that mankind's knowledge would always be uncertain, but that any future consensus would probably "proceed from the power and efficacie of Truth, not from constraint." Available by October was John Goodwin's *Œomaxia, Or the Grand Impudence of Men Running the Hazard of Fighting Against God, In Suppressing Any Way, Doctrine, Or Practice, Concerning Which They Know Not Certainly Whether It Be From God or No.* Error, Goodwin wrote, "cannot be healed or suppressed but by the manifestation of the truth, as darknesse cannot be destroyed but by the shining of the light."[5]

Out of this ferment came the classic *Areopagitica: A Speech of Mr. John Milton For the Liberty of Unlicenc'd Printing, To the Parliament of England* published in November of 1644. Having been threatened with punishment by the Commons several months earlier for heretical opinions in a tract on divorce, Milton concerned himself specifically with Parliament's strict Licensing Order of June 14, 1643, which had substantially reduced the number of uncensored publications. In *Areopagitica,* which was unlicensed as his divorce pamphlet had been, Milton did not break new ground so much as bring majestic prose and concentrated scholarship to the question of press freedom. He appealed to his beleaguered fellow revolutionaries to participate in "one generall and brotherly search after Truth" and to be "of a quick, ingenious, and piercing spirit, acute to invent, suttle and sinewy to discours, not beneath the reach of any point the highest that human capacity can soar to." Milton traced censorship back to Roman despots and popes and represented the licensing procedure as "apishly Romanizing," ineffective, arbitrary, and insulting.

Truth does not need protection, he declared. "Let her and Falsehood grapple; who ever knew Truth put to the wors, in a free and open encounter."[6]

The marketplace of ideas was thus depicted as reasonable and just, but few were prepared to comply with all its logical implications. Traces of the concept were soon to be found in Leveller demands for press freedom, but a more common reaction may have been that of the conservative Puritan Richard Baxter who had witnessed the expression of extremist religious opinions in the New Model Army. "Some think the truth will not thrive among us, till every man have leave to speak both in presse and pulpit that please; God forbid that we should ever see that day!" Baxter said in a pamphlet published in 1649. "If ten mens voyces be louder then one, then would the noyse of Errour drown the voyce of Truth."[7]

Milton himself, conforming to the existing Protestant notion that Catholicism represented idolatry and oppression rather than religion, explained in *Areopagitica* that he did not want his views to be understood as meaning "tolerated Popery, and open superstition." Apparently referring to blasphemy and defamation, he added that no law could possibly permit that which is "impious or evil absolutely either against faith or manners." Milton did technically become a licenser in 1651 while serving as a secretary to the Commonwealth's Council of State. His role, however, primarily consisted of the formalities of registering and overseeing the government's *Mercurius Politicus* edited by Marchamont Nedham. Milton did refer to the arguments of *Areopagitica* in 1652 when he faced official questioning for approving a catechism Parliament afterward condemned.[8]

Milton's pamphlet seems to have had little contemporary influence, but later polemicists used its reasoning and made its laissez-faire challenge the catchphrase of libertarian press theory. Adaptations of *Areopagitica*—with its marketplace principle intact—were made in Charles Blount's *A Just Vindication for Learning* in 1679 and William Denton's *An Apology for the Liberty of the Press* in 1681. Both authors opposed licensing by following Milton's arguments, but neither could match his original style and vision. Licensing ended in 1694, but the prospect of its revival kept the controversy alive. In 1698, Matthew Tindal, the famed deist, used *Areopagitica*'s image of victorious truth and relied heavily on other portions of Milton's essay to produce *A Letter To a Member of Parliament, Shewing That a Restraint On the Press Is Inconsistent With the Protestant Religion, and Dangerous to the Liberties of the Nation.* Francis Gregory, a former chaplain to Charles II, responded in the same year with *A Modest Plea for the Due Regulation of the Press,* which contended that Tindal placed too much faith in human reason. In 1699, a pamphlet attributed to Daniel Defoe, *A Letter to a Member of Parliament, Shewing the Necessity of Regulating the Press,* reacted to Tindal by saying that religious questions should be settled within the national church rather than in the press. In 1704 Tindal repeated his assertions in *Reasons Against Restraining the Press,* and Defoe, who could write on either side of an issue, attacked licensing in *An Essay on the Regulation of the Press.*[9]

In the eighteenth century, the marketplace of ideas concept was applied specifically and vigorously to secular matters. Anthony Ashley Cooper, the third earl of Shaftesbury, maintained in his "Sensus Communis: An Essay on the Freedom of Wit and Humour," that any opinions which would not bear ridicule should be suspect since truth " 'tis suppos'd, may bear *all* Lights." He spoke of "a Liberty in decent Language to question every thing" in friendly conversation since "amicable Collision" prevents "rust upon Mens Understandings." The belief that public political discourse should operate on the marketplace principle was promoted by Trenchard and Gordon, the authors of *Cato's Letters.* "Whilst all Opinions are equally indulged, and all Parties equally allow'd to speak their Minds, the Truth will come out," they wrote. "She has so many Advantages above Error, that she wants only to be shewn to gain Admiration and Esteem," they concluded, "and we see every Day that she breaks the Bonds of Tyranny and Fraud, and shines through the Mists of Superstition and Ignorance."[10]

II

In America, where both *Cato's Letters* and Milton's works were highly regarded, colonial journalists used the proposition to justify publishing controversial material. Benjamin Franklin used it in his *Pennsylvania Gazette* in 1731 and again in 1740 when Philadelphians objected to his handling of religious topics. An essayist in John Peter Zenger's *New York Weekly Journal* wrote in 1733 that people "recollect, enquire and search, before they condemn" and that when "Nonsense, Inconsistencies, or personal Reflections are writ, if despised, they die of Course." The writer said that "he is an Enemy to his King and Country who pleads for any Restraint upon the Press." The press must be "a Curb, a Bridle, a Terror, a Shame, and Restraint to evil

Ministers," the essay maintained, and even if good officials' "Characters have been clouded for a Time, yet they have generally shin'd forth in greater Lustre: Truth will always prevail over Falsehood."[11]

The promulgation of errors, journalists insisted, only made truth appear more radiant. In 1752 James Parker responded to a complaint about a deistic essay he printed in the *New-York Weekly Post-Boy* by saying that he was "willing to give the Advarsaries of Christianity a fair Hearing" since it could only make Christianity "shine brighter." Four years later, during the French and Indian War, Parker's partner, John Holt, defended the *Connecticut Gazette*'s publication of an essay criticizing New England troops by saying that editors should not let their mere prejudices determine newspaper content. Where there was liberty of the press, he said, "Truth, Innocence and Justice, can never be injured; for they will shine the brighter from the Attempts made to destroy or eclipse their Lustre."[12]

Doubts about the efficacy of truth were expressed, however, in the tumultuous years between the Stamp Act crisis and the Revolutionary War. William Bollan, a Massachusetts lawyer and colonial agent, remarked in his 1766 book *The Freedom of Speech and Writing Upon Public Affairs, Considered* that prejudice and passion often prevailed over reason even if truth was eventually victorious. "By her appearance in season she might have saved a person or a kingdom," Bollan said, "but by her delay she becomes a sharp accuser, and a helpless friend." John Holt, who had earlier strongly endorsed the marketplace of ideas concept in Connecticut, started his own *New-York Journal* with financial support from the Sons of Liberty in 1766 and made it a one-sided advocate of the patriot cause. He told his readers in 1775 that he wanted to publish both sides and that truth would "run no hazard in a fair contest with its adversaries." He did not wish to decline this combat, he went on to explain, but since "a weekly paper will contain but a small part of the pieces that are necessary to be published on the right side, I have been obliged, in great measure, to confine myself to such." A correspondent in Hugh Gaine's more conservative *New-York Mercury* pointed to the contradiction in Holt's logic and suggested that he seemed "anxious to wipe off the Imputation of Insanity, with which sensible people have charged him."[13]

While Bollan's thinking about free expression may have been colored by the frustrations inherent in promoting colonial viewpoints in England, Holt's position reflected the degrees of polarization and competitiveness that existed in American journalism by 1775. Taking a stance which was consistent with radical Whig disdain for parties, colonial printers had often proclaimed their impartiality, but Revolutionary America presented new political and economic realities. Holt's *Connecticut Gazette* was one of only twelve English-language papers in America at the beginning of 1756; by 1775 his *New-York Journal* was one of forty-four newspapers—seven of which were being published in Philadelphia, five in Boston, four in New York, and three in both Williamsburg and Charleston. The *Journal's* local rivals were Gaine's profitable, mercurial *Mercury,* James Rivington's fiercely loyalist *Gazetteer,* and after August, John Anderson's cutrate, outlandishly radical *Constitutional Gazette.* Deeply in debt to James Parker and finding it difficult to compete in New York, Holt announced in 1770 that he was receiving too many long, argumentative essays and that he had decided "to prefer those Pieces that come attended with Money." Answering charges made in Rivington's paper in 1774 that he was a "poor devil" perverting liberty of the press by selling himself to the highest bidder and sowing anarchy, confusion, and sedition, Holt said he served the public in general and propagated principles he would die to defend. Rivington, he said, would allow freedom of the press to "any Thing in Favour of the late Ministerial Measures and Claims upon the Colonies" while suppressing as licentious "All Pieces in Favour of the Rights and Liberties of the Subject."[14]

Neutrality became all but impossible during the Revolutionary War and with the peace came increasingly intense competition that further undercut the intellectual rationale for having each newspaper be impartial. As editors found it practical and even necessary to devote themselves to special political, economic, and ethnic interests, truth could presumably emerge from the clash of opinions between rather than within publications. The number of American newspapers grew from forty in 1782 to sixty-three in 1784 when Philadelphia had eleven, Boston had eight, and New York had six.[15]

One of the printers seeking public and party favor in Philadelphia was John Holt's son-in-law, Eleazer Oswald, whose *Independent Gazetteer* backed the "Republican" faction that was seeking to rewrite the state's radically democratic constitution of 1776. The paper professed to have been established "independent of Party, upon Principles of Public Utility," but more revealing was the masthead's statement that liberty of the press was the palladium of all rights, which was signed by "Junius," a writer known for his intense animosity toward England's public officials. When it was founded in 1782, the

Independent Gazetteer sought to show how brutal partisanship and editorial bias might be reconciled with the idea of fair play. Oswald's first issue laid the philosophical foundation for its subsequent accusations and personal abuse by presenting an anonymous statement that press licentiousness was no excuse for press restraints and that religion and liberty were always safe where the press was free. "He that has Truth, Reason and Justice on his Side," the essay said, "will always be an Overmatch for his Adversaries of equal Abilities." Oswald himself, writing in the same issue, said he believed truth prevailed when given the opportunity, but that not every matter could receive a full discussion, that much could be done to disguise truth, and that the printer therefore had a responsibility to make decisions about "the Propriety, Nature and Tendency" of material offered for publication. "Without a Capacity to judge in these Essentials," he concluded, "he is not qualified for his Business."[16]

Impartiality had been a byword of the colonial press, but open partisanship became typical by the end of the century. State and national parties grew potent and rancorous, and their animosities were quickly reflected in newspapers. As the number of American newspapers increased to well over two hundred by the year 1800, economic and political competitiveness reached new levels and editors were prepared to abandon all pretense of balanced journalism. "The American people have long enough been imposed upon by the pretended impartiality of printers," said Baltimore's *American and Daily Advertiser* in 1799, "it is all delusion; every party will have its *printer*, as well as every sect its *preacher.* . . ."[17]

The partisan journalism of the late 1790s was, in fact, perhaps the most vicious and vituperative in the nation's history. Editors nevertheless still insisted they served the cause of truth. William Cobbett advertised his invective-laden *Porcupine's Gazette* in 1797 as an antidote to the poisonous lies vomited by the Republican press. "A falsehood that remains uncontradicted for a month, begins to be looked upon as a truth," he wrote, "and when the detection at last makes its appearance, it is often as useless as that of the doctor who finds his patient expired." The answer, Cobbett said, was to fight for every inch of ground and "return them two blows for one."[18]

Benjamin Franklin Bache, Cobbett's chief adversary in Philadelphia journalism, began publishing his newspaper in 1790 with claims of impartiality and the motto "TRUTH, DECENCY, UTILITY." By 1794, however, his *Aurora* had become a champion of Jefferson's Republicans and he adopted a new motto: "SURGO UT PROSIM,"

I rise to be useful. Infuriated by Bache's attacks on Washington and Adams, Cobbett and other defenders of the Federalists depicted Bache as a paid agent of the French in 1798 as the United States and France appeared ready to go to war. Bache answered the accusations in his newspaper but also decided to distribute a pamphlet which he titled *Truth Will Out! The Foul Charges of the Tories Against the Editor of the Aurora Repelled by Positive Proof and Plain Truth and his Base Calumniators Put to Shame.* "The Editor has found it out of his power to make truth, in this transaction, pierce thro' the misrepresentation of bitter enmity and the prejudices of party malice," he explained in the preface. "Many presses published with avidity the charges against the Editor and have been dilatory or have altogether refused, to publish the vindication."[19]

III

Among those advocating the marketplace of ideas concept in the late eighteenth century were two prominent and perennial revolutionaries—Thomas Paine and Thomas Jefferson. Paine wrote in the first part of *The Rights of Man,* published in 1791, that the American and French revolutions had "thrown a beam of light over the world, which reaches into man" and that ignorance, once dispelled, could not be reestablished. "The mind, in discovering truth, acts in the same manner as it acts through the eye in discovering objects," he said, "when once any object has been seen, it is impossible to put the mind back to the same condition it was in before he saw it." In the second part of *The Rights of Man,* published a year later, Paine remarked that he did not expect monarchy and aristocracy to last more than seven years in any of the "enlightened countries" of Europe. "If better reasons can be shown for them than against them, they will stand; if the contrary, they will not," he contended. "Mankind are not now to be told they shall not think, or they shall not read; and publications that go no farther than to investigate principles of government, to invite men to reason and to reflect and to show the errors and excellencies of different systems, have a right to appear."[20]

Paine's sentiments were not shared by the English authorities, and he was quickly charged with sedition. The author, who had gone to France and taken a seat at the Convention, was not present at the trial, but Thomas Erskine, who defended him, quoted liberally from his works, often emphasizing the marketplace of ideas concept.

" 'Reason and discussion will soon bring things to right, however wrong they may begin,' " he told the jury, quoting Paine and arguing that "writings against a free and well-proportioned government need not be guarded against by laws" since the criticism would never have any effect. "I am not insisting upon the infallibility of Mr. Paine's doctrines," he explained, "if they are erroneous, let them be answered, and truth will spring from the collision." Erskine added Montesquieu's endorsement of the marketplace principle and quoted several passages from *Areopagitica*. "Let reason be opposed to reason, and argument to argument," Erskine said, "and every good government will be safe."[21]

The jury in *The Rights of Man* case was packed against Paine and he was convicted. The defense argument was nevertheless considered important enough to be reprinted in New York, New London, and Philadelphia in 1793. Erskine, a popular Whig orator who became Lord Chancellor of Great Britain in 1806, acted as counsel for the prosecution when a publisher of Paine's *Age of Reason* was convicted in 1797 for disseminating blasphemy. Erskine discussed the marketplace of ideas concept and said that Christianity could be decently investigated, but he maintained that the religion of the Scriptures should not be insultingly denied.[22]

Thomas Jefferson used the marketplace of ideas concept routinely but eloquently, beginning with his Bill for Establishing Religious Freedom in Virginia in 1779. "No government ought to be without censors: & where the press is free, no one ever will," he wrote to President Washington in 1792 to defend an antiadministration editor, Philip Freneau. "If virtuous, it need not fear the fair operation of attack & defence. Nature has given to man no other means of sifting out the truth, either in religion, law, or politics." The ideological contest of the 1790s and the jailing of Republican editors under the Sedition Act of 1798 did not extinguish his faith in tolerance and in the human intellect. "We are all republicans: we are all federalists," he said in his first inaugural address in 1801. "If there be any among us who would wish to dissolve this union or to change its republican form, let them stand undisturbed, as monuments of the safety with which error of opinion may be tolerated, where reason is left free to combat it."[23]

Jefferson's tone changed considerably during his presidency as he faced the batterings of the Federalist press. "Nothing can now be believed which is seen in a newspaper," he wrote to an aspiring journalist at the end of his second term. "Truth itself becomes suspicious by being put into that polluted vehicle." He told seventeen-year-old John Norvell, who had written to ask his advice, that those who did not read newspapers were better informed than those who did, "inasmuch as he who knows nothing is nearer to truth than he whose mind is filled with falsehood & errors." The letter, which was only one of a number he composed at the time denouncing the press, created a minor sensation when it was made public after his death. Attempting to explain the tirade, James Madison suggested in 1828 that Jefferson's objection was to "one-sided publications" which created delusions in the minds of their readers. "Could it be so arranged that every newspaper," Madison said, "when printed on one side, should be handed over to the press of an adversary, to be printed on the other, thus presenting to every reader both sides of every question, truth would always have a fair chance." Madison acknowledged, however, that "such a remedy is ideal."[24]

Jefferson's attitude did mellow during his retirement. As late as 1814, he still complained about "the putrid state" of newspapers and attributed the problem to party spirit. "As vehicles of information, and a curb on our functionaries," he said, "they have rendered themselves useless, by forfeiting all title to belief." By 1823, however, he could tell John Adams that the libels that had been written about himself had rarely been worth reading or remembering. Later in the year, Jefferson wrote to a French correspondent that a free press was a powerful means of obtaining peaceful political reform and was "the best instrument for enlightening the mind of man, and improving him as a rational, moral, and social being."[25]

III

The Ideals of the Enlightenment

Whatever its advantages may have been for libertarian press ideology, the proposition that truth would prevail in free and open debate did not by itself say that truth *should* conquer falsehood. Some eighteenth-century apologists for the status quo not only questioned whether illusion and error could be eradicated, but also feared the impact new truths would have on the stability and well-being of societies. Seeing themselves as realists, thinkers from Pierre Bayle to Frederick the Great to Antoine de Rivarol excused prejudices and official lies as useful and necessary. The faith of the Enlightenment, on the other hand, was that the public could use and should have both freedom and knowledge. Individual theorists differed on how quickly the old myths could be demolished without inviting moral and governmental chaos, but agreed that religious and political tyranny relied on widespread ignorance and acquiescence.[1] They consequently regarded a free press as their natural ally.

I

As glimmerings of the Enlightenment began to appear in the seventeenth century, the technology of printing was portrayed by some as a virtual panacea. To John Milton's friend, Samuel Hartlib, who worked for reforms in husbandry, industry, and education, the press was a simple and dramatically effective means of change. In *A*

Description of the Famous Kingdom of Macaria, a brief utopian tract written as the Long Parliament was abolishing the Stuart monarchy's most obnoxious powers, Hartlib could say that all kingdoms would eventually be ideal states, since "the Art of Printing will so spread knowledge, that the common people, knowing their rights and liberties, will not be governed by way of oppression." Once established, however, his Macaria was to maintain its serenity by leaving religious and political disputes to a "Great Council." The more adventurous eighteenth-century libertarian's view was neatly summarized in Bishop Thomas Hayter's *An Essay on the Liberty, of the Press,* which ranked the development of printing along with the introduction of gunpowder in importance to civilization. "Learning soon flourished; Superstition and Dulness were disgraced; Liberty was the Offspring of Learning and Truth; and by the quick Circulation and Collision of the Products of different Minds, Men were animated and enlightened," Hayter wrote. "They studied their Rights, and in some few Countries asserted and enjoyed them."[2]

At the other extreme were those who expressed deep-seated anxieties about the impact of the press. "I thank God, there are no free-schools, nor printing; and I hope we shall not have, these hundred years," Virginia's governor, William Berkeley, reported to his London superiors in 1671. "For learning has brought disobedience and heresy, and sects into the world; and printing has divulged them and libels against the best government: God keep us from both!"[3]

The press, however, proved difficult to resist or control. After the 1720s, royal instructions to colonial governors, which had noted that "great inconveniencies may arise by the liberty of printing," no longer pretended to require licensing, a procedure which had been discarded decades earlier in England. As the population of the colonies grew and became more dispersed, provincial governments began to recruit printers who could turn out legal forms, proclamations, and legislative acts. In some cases, religious groups or political factions sought out and supported new presses. By the time of the American Revolution, colonial journalism was robust and competitive. Individuals still loyal to Britain perceived the patriot printers and their publications as an immediate danger and desperately sought to restrain them. After repeated failures to obtain indictments of radical journalists in Boston, Chief Justice Thomas Hutchinson of Massachusetts told a grand jury in 1770 that he was discouraged in his attempts to stop criminal libels and that his only hope came "from finding that they multiply so fast, are becoming so common, so scandalous, so entirely false and incredible, that no Body will mind them; and that all Ranks among us will treat them with Neglect."[4]

Berkeley and Hutchinson may have indulged in wishful thinking, but their fears were not irrational. In their careers both had to confront the wrath of aroused public opinion and actual rebellion in a land brimming with angry outcasts, outspoken zealots, and self-reliant entrepreneurs. Although it may have served simply to vent some frustrations, a free press also complicated matters considerably for authorities by periodically helping to raise political temperatures. For advocates of change, the right to use printed communication meant the opportunity to promote the prerequisites of a more just and enlightened world—liberty, prosperity, and intellectual and cultural refinement.[5]

II

The leaders of America's revolutionary Enlightenment considered the education of the public essential to their success. Concerned with instilling republican virtues and the lessons of Whig history, Franklin and Jefferson in particular devoted themselves to the task of cultivating the minds and reading habits of their fellow citizens.

Although he was in the business of selling books, Franklin made the establishment of a subscription library in Philadelphia his first public project. He and his partners Lewis Timothy and James Parker each had occasion to serve as local librarians and Franklin made contributions to the libraries of Harvard, Yale, and other institutions. In the part of his autobiography written in 1771, he credited libraries such as the one at Philadelphia with making "common Tradesmen & Farmers as intelligent as most Gentlemen from other Countries" and with contributing "in some degree to the Stand so generally made throughout the Colonies in Defence of their Privileges." Both Franklin and Jefferson built private collections of books that were among the largest in America. In order to reestablish the Library of Congress after the British burned the Capitol in 1814, Jefferson sold ten wagon loads of his books to the federal government for considerably less than their value. He also provided the Library of Congress with a classification system it adopted. Jefferson selected books for his friends and for the major project of his retirement, the University of Virginia.[6]

As founders of educational institutions, Franklin and Jefferson sought to ensure that succeeding generations would share their convictions. Franklin intended in 1749 to start a nonsectarian, practically oriented academy which would use "Tillotson, Addison, Pope, Algernon Sidney, Cato's Letters, & c." as classics. For a quarter of a century, however, the College and Academy of Philadelphia was dominated by Provost William Smith, an Anglican clergyman who aligned himself with the Penns and argued against independence from Britain. In 1756 Smith bitterly attacked Franklin's antiproprietary politics in the press, and the board of trustees removed Franklin as its president. When some of the trustees proposed investigating Smith's actions, the provost's senior philosophy students signed a report saying that he had acted impartially in the classroom and had only advanced principles "warranted by our standard Authors, Grotius, Puffendorf, Locke, and Hutcheson; writers whose sentiments are equally opposite to those wild notions of Liberty that are inconsistent with all government." Franklin resented being thus ousted by "a Cabal" and remained an enemy of Smith's for the rest of his life. Franklin nevertheless remarked in his autobiography that a number of the college's students became "serviceable in public Stations, and Ornaments to their country."[7]

Jefferson's writings were replete with statements on the importance of formal education and proper principles. His "Bill for the More General Diffusion of Knowledge," written for Virginia in 1779, declared that certain kinds of government protected natural rights better than others and that the role of learning was "to illuminate, as far as practicable, the minds of the people at large" so that "they may be enabled to know ambition under all its shapes, and prompt to exert their natural powers to defeat its purposes." Jefferson in later years expressed specific apprehensions about "the wily sophistries" of David Hume's histories of Britain and William Blackstone's *Commentaries on the Laws of England* which he thought had "made tories of all England" and of some young Americans. Angry that lawyers nurtured on Blackstone "no longer know what whigism or republicanism means," Jefferson warned James Madison in 1826 that they would have to be "rigorously attentive" to the politics of a law professor to be selected for the University of Virginia. "It is in our seminary that that vestal flame is to be kept alive;" Jefferson said, "it is thence it is to spread anew over our own and the sister States."[8]

As a revolutionary faith, the American Enlightenment of Franklin and Jefferson did not go unchallenged. Yet the problem of political education for the country was understood largely as a simple matter of conveying facts and ideas. "A popular Government, without popular information, or the means of acquiring it, is but a Prologue to a Farce or a Tragedy; or, perhaps both," Madison wrote in 1822. "Knowledge will forever govern ignorance: And a people who mean to be their own Governors, must arm themselves with the power which knowledge gives." Madison then defined a free people's learning as "that light over the public mind which is the best security against crafty & dangerous encroachments on the public liberty." In an essay on public opinion published in the *National Gazette* in 1791, Madison listed ways of facilitating "a general intercourse of sentiments": domestic commerce, good roads, contact with representatives, a free press, and "a circulation of newspapers through the entire body of the people." These, he suggested, favored liberty by effectively shrinking the size of the country and thereby making public opinion easier to know and more difficult to counterfeit. "Public opinion sets the bounds to every government," Madison observed, "and is the real sovereign in every free one."[9]

American scholar-statesmen thus fashioned a concept of government which was consonant with the Enlightenment's ideal of widespread knowledge and the radical Whig belief that the people had to be informed in order to exercise their legitimate authority. One instance of this mingling of intellectual strains came in the carefully articulated address of the Continental Congress to the inhabitants of Quebec in 1774. Enumerating the rights "without which a people cannot be free and happy" and which Americans were ready to die defending, Congress included freedom of the press. Its importance, the document said, was in "the advancement of truth, science, morality, and arts in general" as well as in "its diffusion of liberal sentiments on the administration of Government, its ready communication of thoughts between subjects, and its consequential promotion of union among them, whereby oppressive officers are shamed or intimidated, into more honourable and just modes of conducting affairs." To Cato, who schooled generations of Americans in radical Whig thought, freedom of expression was the only alternative to having a world "overrun with Barbarism, Superstition, Injustice, Tyranny, and the most stupid Ignorance."[10]

Yet, however much eighteenth-century rhetoric may have been calculated to inspire or to warn of danger, American political thought was conditioned to a significant extent by skepticism and by the sense of living in what Franklin called the "Age of Experiments." Such outlooks also tended to support open inquiry and free discussion and presumably modulated public discourse. While freedom of expression was defended by radical Whigs as a means of stemming slavery and corruption and by revolutionaries as a way of spreading liberating political doctrine, Enlightenment skeptics like Voltaire and Hume, who admitted their uncertainties and denounced fanaticism, had their own reasons to object to suppression.[11]

Voltaire and other French *philosophes* preached tolerance and looked for a press that could be a forum for criticism as well as a channel for transmitting humanitarian ideals. As the bureaucracy of the *ancien régime* forced unacceptable writers to resort to elaborate subterfuge and their publishers to engage in smuggling operations, men of letters found themselves in the incongruous position of lying and skulking as they labored for the causes of honesty and human dignity. Some who resented their fate earned Voltaire's enmity by forming an illicit literary subculture inclined toward nihilism and political pornography. Voltaire, who endured imprisonment, exile, and book burnings, ridiculed press controls and declared that ambitious people, not words, did harm.[12]

As an Englishman, Hume did not have to confront the perils of Voltaire and his cohorts, although he took the advice of friends and delayed publishing some of his more unsparing views on religion. Hume, like Voltaire, praised the high degree of intellectual freedom in England and associated it with the nation's wealth. In his essay "Of Refinement in the Arts," he declared that "*industry, knowledge,* and *humanity* are linked together by an indissoluble chain" and that they all flourish in the more polished and luxurious times. "The spirit of the age affects all the arts, and the minds of men being once roused from their lethargy and put into a fermentation turn themselves on all sides, and carry improvements into every art and science," he wrote. "Profound ignorance is totally banished, and men enjoy the privilege of rational creatures to think as well as act, to cultivate the pleasures of the mind as well as those of the body." Adverse by nature to political extremes and public disorder, Hume admitted in an essay on journalistic freedom that "the unbounded liberty of the press" was one of the evils of mixed forms of government, but he said that a suitable remedy would be difficult if not impossible to find. "The spirit of the people must frequently be roused in order to curb the ambition of the court, and the dread of rousing this spirit must be employed to prevent that ambition," he stated. "Nothing so effectual to this purpose as the liberty of the press, by which all the learning, wit, and genius of the nation, may be employed on the side of freedom and everyone animated to its defense."[13]

Whether Americans turned to English opposition ideology, to their own revolutionary Enlightenment, or even to a cool, relatively conservative skeptic like Hume, they were admonished to be wary of government and to understand that a free people needed a free press in order to preserve their liberty. The press was considered, in Bishop Hayter's words, "a new missive weapon" and its users could think of themselves as either warding off oppression or stirring up popular resistance. Montesquieu explained in the preface to his *The Spirit of Laws,* a book censored in France and placed in the Papal Index, that he thought enlightening the minds of the people was important because it had a direct effect on those exercising authority. "In a time of ignorance they have committed even the greatest evils without the least scruple," he remarked, "but in an enlighten'd age they even tremble, while conferring the greatest blessings."[14]

Montesquieu was, however, like Hume, a philosopher affected by the skeptical tradition of Montaigne and Bayle and a moderate satisfied with admiring the British Constitution and with objecting to the eighteenth century's more obvious social ills. Writing in his chateau at La Brède, Montesquieu hoped to free men by gently humanizing them. Hume was content to live the comfortable life of a scholar, librarian, and diplomat.

Others—such as Samuel Adams—were less detached and were anxious to exercise the power of the press which the great minds of the age had merely recognized. The enigmatic, stern Adams sought to liberate a country by fostering a mood of noble indignation. His arts were relentless propaganda and political organization. Using dozens of pen names, Adams helped to fill the radical *Boston Gazette* with essays and news stories carefully designed to provoke public discontent. He was not burdened by intellectual doubts or swayed by connections with an aristocracy he detested. While celebrating the refusal of grand jurors to indict *Gazette* journalists in 1768, he complimented the printers of the paper for having "sounded the alarm" with their press. "It has pointed to this people, their danger and their remedy," he wrote. "It has set before them Liberty and Slavery; and with the most perswasive and pungent language, conjur'd them, in the name of GOD, and the King, and for the sake of all posterity, to chuse Liberty and refuse Chains." Adams and his fellow patriot polemicists were, as they realized, using the press as an instrument of revolution.[15]

III

Praise for the press was not limited to its patently political function. In addition to stressing what Connecticut's *Middlesex Gazette* called "the greatest of its Excellencies, that it is absolutely necessary for the Preservation of Freedom in a Republican Government," journalists maintained that their publications served to raise the quality of individual life and thought by being repositories of insight and experience. Daniel Fowle established his *New-Hampshire Gazette* in 1756 with a typical editorial salutatory saying that he intended to uphold freedom of expression while not encouraging divisive, immoral, or scurrilous contributions. He also warned that "Fondness of News may be carried to an extreme" and said the paper would "contain Extracts from the best Authors on Points of the most useful Knowledge, moral, religious or political Essays, and other such Speculations as may have a Tendency to improve the Mind, afford any Help to Trade, Manufactures, Husbandry, and other useful Arts, and promote the public Welfare in any Respect." Newspapers fulfilled such promises with items as mundane as listings of current prices and with writings as advanced as those of Rousseau.[16]

Assurances did not always seem to match performance, however. Hartford's *Connecticut Courant*'s introductory statement in 1764 said that no art did more for human happiness and civilization than printing and promised that the paper would publish what appeared to be the most authentic and interesting material available. During its first months, the *Courant* published news items on the John Wilkes case and a prayer for tolerance by Voltaire. The paper also included "A Surprizing Account of those Spectres called VAMPYRES" and opinions on whether students at Yale were "deeply sunk in debauchery." Readers of the first issue of the *Middlesex Gazette* were told in 1785 that a well-edited newspaper "furnishes a rational Entertainment for the Moments of Relaxation from Business or Labour; that it facilitates and enlivens Commerce; that it is beneficial to Agriculture and Manufactures; that it is favourable to Morals, Virtue and Literature." Two months later, a correspondent complained that a harsh piece the paper had printed on the propriety of prayer before

military exercises was a malevolent, scurrilous, pedantic, and im-
potent invective. The paper responded nonchalantly with an excerpt
from Bishop Hayter's paean to the press.[17]

Still, despite shortcomings and difficulties, writers proudly claimed
central roles in what they perceived to be the Enlightenment's general
expansion and refinement of men's minds. James Ralph put it bluntly
in *The Case of Authors:* "Knowledge is the Light of the World:
Authors have been the Dispensers of it." Joseph Addison and Richard Steele were less brazen in the *Spectator,* the periodical which did
more than any other to establish the buoyant, reasonable tone and
urbane style of eighteenth-century literary journalism. As Addison
explained it, they hoped to bring "Philosophy out of Closets and
Libraries, Schools and Colleges, to dwell in Clubs and Assemblies,
at Tea-Tables, and in Coffee-Houses." Less than two weeks after the
publication began in 1711, Mr. Spectator used his printer's circulation figures to estimate that his "Morning Lectures" on manners and
morality were reaching 60,000 people a day. Among those who read
the periodical and its subsequent reprintings were Cotton Mather,
who considered sending in his own contributions, and Voltaire, who
used it to improve his command of English. "Since I have raised to
my self so great an Audience," Mr. Spectator said, "I shall spare no
Pains to make their Instruction agreeable, and their Diversion useful." Similarly, American editors routinely pledged to make their
newspapers "useful and entertaining." In 1770, the "Poets Corner"
in John Holt's *New-York Journal* offered verses on "The Newspaper" which began:[18]

> 'Tis truth (with deference to the college)
> News-papers are the spring of knowledge,
> The general source throughout the nation,
> Of every modern conversation.

The pedagogic pretensions of periodical writers fit the Enlightenment's view of mankind's potential. Locke's rejection of "innate
ideas" and of inevitable human depravity, as well as Montesquieu's
declaration that man was a "flexible being," capable of laying aside
prejudices, suggested that given adequate intellectual stimulation,
people could improve their condition. "Of all the animal Creation,
Man is, indeed, the most dependent by Nature, and stands in continual Need of the Aid of his fellow Mortals, to maintain a comfortable Existence," said a *New-York Mercury* essay on freedom of
the press in 1755. "This seeming constitutional Defect, is, however,

fully repaired by his communicative Faculties and Disposition." The essayist, who described the mind of a new-born infant as "a perfect Blank, capable of receiving any Impressions," gave credit to the press for quickening the pace of scientific achievements and for furnishing "each Individual with the Sentiments, not only of the wisest Members of the Community, but even of the Sages of the whole World." The author of "On the Utility of Newspapers," published in the *Newport Mercury* in 1790, noted that most people had not even learned to read before the development of printing. "Their minds were therefore obliged to remain in their original barbarous state, torpid and indifferent with regard to all useful information," the writer said. "In such a state of society there would have been no means to give operation to our late glorious struggle for freedom; but we must have remained the abject slaves of distant, proud, and unfeeling masters."[19]

Ultimately, defenders of free expression were able to argue, press constraints demonstrated contempt for human dignity and divine wisdom. He who kills a man, Milton wrote in *Areopagitica,* "kills a reasonable creature, Gods Image; but hee who destroyes a good Booke, kills reason it selfe, kills the Image of God, as it were in the eye." Saying that God had decreed the beginning of "the reforming of Reformation it self" and that the liberty achieved during the civil war had "rarify'd and enlighten'd our spirits like the influence of heav'n," Milton admonished Parliament not to take action against the press that would obstruct further progress in religious and political wisdom. "We can grow ignorant again, brutish, formall, and slavish, as ye found us," he said, "but you then must first become that which ye cannot be, oppressive, arbitrary, and tyrannous, as they were from whom ye have free'd us."[20]

When Matthew Tindal revived themes of *Areopagitica* for his 1691 pamphlet on press freedom, he said that the press was needed to expose the designs of arbitrary power and to encourage the arts and sciences. "The greatest Enjoyment that rational and sociable Creatures are capable of, is to employ their Thoughts on what Subjects they please, and to communicate them to one another as freely as they think them," Tindal observed, "and herein consists the Dignity and Freedom of humane Nature, without which no other Liberty can be secure." He stated flatly that the Reformation was wholly accomplished by the press and that the only question with regard to printing restraints was whether to be free protestants or slavish papists. Tindal correlated the degree of control to the amount of ignorance, superstition, and bigotry to be found in a country and supposed that the development of printing represented divine providence at work.[21]

The idea of a heavenly sanction for the press was also embraced by eighteenth-century printers and polemicists. Early in 1733, Thomas Whitmarsh's *South Carolina Gazette* presented a front-page essay on the history of printing, followed by a poem including the lines:

> HAIL, PRINTING! hail thou thrice illustrious ART!
> Which clear'd the Head, and which reform'd the Heart,
> Bless'd with new Light a superstitious Age,
> And purg'd the Relicks of barbaric Rage.
> From thee celestial Streams of Learning flow,
> And to thy Pow'r we pure Religion owe.

A correspondent in the fifth issue of James Parker's *Connecticut Gazette* asked for the publication of religious essays and welcomed the appearance of the paper, saying that God had made printing possible and that with the press "our Notions of Religion and the Deity, receive continual Improvements, and proceed in a Progressive State towards Perfection." England's vitriolic Junius remarked in the preface to a collection of his newspaper writings that it was unreasonable to expect a free press to be clear of abuse and that to think otherwise was, in effect, to "arraign the goodness of providence." In 1799, James Madison wrote that the press restrictions of the Sedition Act of 1798 had committed the "double sacrilege" of putting even religious opinion in danger and of "arresting reason in her progress towards perfection."[22]

Libertarian thought from Milton to Madison placed freedom of expression firmly on the side of political and religious advancement. Accordingly, an anonymous essayist in Andrew Bradford's *American Weekly Mercury* could advise Philadelphians in 1732 that all men had been born free, that liberty was a gift from God and an unalienable right of mankind, that governments ought to exist for the good of society and be subject to constitutional checks and restraints, that free inquiry had produced the Reformation and Glorious Revolution, and that the right to publish freely gave Englishmen the "Opportunity of being useful or beneficial to their Country." The writer began the piece, however, by saying that in all countries "where liberty only reigns, every Man hath a Privilege of declaring his Sentiments upon all Topicks with the utmost Freedom; provided He does it with proper Decency, and a just Regard to the Laws."[23]

The *Mercury*'s essayist thus acknowledged the existence of press restraints, but did not then identify which specific laws, if any, could be compatible with his subsequent statements that he would simply leave ridicule of religion for the world to judge and that those trusted with discretionary power in a free government "must Answer for that Discretion to those that trust them."[24] Like many others writing in a libertarian vein, the unnamed writer was content with enunciating general principles and did not spell out how and under what circumstances the right of expression might be justifiably curtailed. Those who did attempt to place precise boundaries on freedom of the press differed substantially in their reasoning and in their choice of legal restraints and defenses.

PART TWO

Political and Legal Questions

IV

Sovereignty and Seditious Libel

In 1803, Samuel Miller, a Presbyterian minister in New York, published *A Brief Retrospect of the Eighteenth Century,* a book subtitled, *A Sketch of the Revolutions and Improvements in Science, Arts, and Literature, During that Period.* Commenting on what he thought had been remarkably rapid development of American journalism, the author observed that the country's newspapers had become "immense moral and political engines, closely connected with the welfare of the state, and deeply involving both its peace and prosperity." He also noted that they had been "pronounced by travellers, the most profligate and scurrilous public prints in the civilized world." On one hand, as Miller analyzed it, newspapers disseminated useful information, exposed political corruption, and promoted unity and the love of freedom. On the other, they could lacerate private character, be obscene and impious, and generate party violence.[1]

Having witnessed, like other Americans, ten years of rabid journalistic warfare between Federalists and Republicans, Miller said that unless public outrage would stifle the "growing evil," the country could expect a crisis when freedom of the press would be abridged or all social bonds would be disrupted. As a scholar considering both sides of a perplexing intellectual issue, he wondered about the practical consequences of having all classes of society quickly and inexpensively agitated by vicious "directors of public opinion." Writing in the aftermath of a presidential election in which the winner, Thomas Jefferson, had been denigrated as an atheist, radical, coward,

57

libertine, and thief, Miller feared that journalism would finally consume "the best feelings and noblest charities of life, in the flame of civil discord." The press had become, he believed, "one of the great safeguards of free government" as well as "one of its most threatening assailants."[2]

The question of the compatibility of a free government and a free press was not a new one, but it had been given an extraordinary amount of attention only a few years before Miller's book because of a singularly dramatic outbreak of press prosecutions—one which illustrated how much and how little legal doctrines had advanced by the end of the eighteenth century. In 1798, during the war hysteria which followed the XYZ Affair, the Federalist majority in Congress passed a Sedition Act making it a crime to publish false, scandalous, and malicious statements about President Adams, Congress, or the national government. The supporters of the act argued that it was a necessary part of preparations for hostilities with France and that liberty of the press meant the absence of the prior restraints of licensing and censorship, not the right to publish writings which would undermine authority. From 1798 through 1800, as many as twenty-five people—almost all of them Republican journalists and printers—faced federal or state sedition charges for expressing their political opinions.[3]

The Sedition Act not only helped to mobilize Republicans for the "revolution" of 1800, but also prompted fresh expressions of libertarian thought on the legal freedom of the press. The issues of press law were debated in Congress and brought before the public to an unprecedented extent. In speeches and protests, newspaper essays and pamphlets, Republicans depicted the Federalists' action as unconstitutional and unnecessary. They also agreed with Madison's Virginia Resolutions of 1798 which said that the Sedition Act was "levelled against the right of freely examining public characters and measures . . . which has ever been justly deemed the only effectual guardian of every other right."[4]

The positions of both parties were well rehearsed by the time petitions for repeal began to reach Congress early in 1799, and three Federalists and two Republicans were appointed to a select committee of the House to review the matter. Reporting for the Federalist members of the committee, Chauncey Goodrich of Connecticut said they preferred to justify the law on the ground of national defense. He said, however, that libels against national authorities had a direct tendency to stir up sedition which Congress had authority to punish.

The First Amendment's guarantee of freedom of the press, Goodrich insisted, was justly, legally, and universally defined as freedom from prior restraint and was not a liberty to make false, scandalous, and malicious publications against the government.[5]

The Republicans' answer was presented by select committee member John Nicholas of Virginia. Facing loud talk, laughter, and coughing from Federalists trying to drown out his speech, he declared that the "monarchical" standards used by the Federalists had been "greatly softened in practice, by public opinion" in England and that the law of libel against magistrates was "a dead letter" and inconsistent with government in the United States. The First Amendment prohibited all federal legislation on the subject of the press, Nicholas said. A resolution to retain the Sedition Act passed by a vote of fifty-two to forty-eight and the law was allowed to expire as scheduled in 1801 when Jefferson took office and issued pardons to those convicted under the statute.[6]

The contest over the passage and continuation of the Sedition Act was fought almost exclusively along party lines, but the episode demonstrated the existence of two distinct and conflicting interpretations of the First Amendment within a decade of its ratification. The full airing of opinions displayed the Federalists' outmoded views of government and reliance on British precedents, although the Sedition Act itself had disregarded these precedents by making truth a defense, requiring malicious intent, and allowing the jury to rule on the law itself in addition to the fact of publication. As a result, Representative Goodrich found himself in the embarrassing position of telling the House that the Sedition Act—a measure to restrict journalists—had actually liberalized the common law regarding the press. Republicans meanwhile firmly upheld what they said was a long-established freedom to criticize government, but awkwardly excused state laws written during the Revolution to restrain loyalists. Representative Nicholas defended a Virginia law against British sympathizers, saying that it had been one of the expedients of a war fought for republican self-government and that "for a time, personal rights were compelled to bend before public necessity."[7]

Yet, as willing as the Federalists and Republicans were to adjust their principles in specific applications, each side articulated a comprehensive doctrine of press freedom that effectively denied the legitimacy of the other. Both parties claimed to be using the one valid, legal definition of a right which had been evolving for centuries. Their fundamental disagreement involved the questions of how far the meaning of liberty of the press had advanced by the time of the Bill of Rights and the extent to which free expression fit in the political system created by the United States Constitution.

I

Expression was restricted to some extent from the very beginning of English law. The slander of one individual by another could be punished in local or ecclesiastical courts. The concept that words might harm government was advanced as early as 1275 in a statute approved by Parliament which came to be known as *De Scandalis Magnatum.* "It is commanded," the statute said, "That from henceforth none be so hardy to tell or publish any false News or Tales, whereby discord, or occasion of discord or slander may grow between the King and his People, or the Great Men of the Realm; and he that doth so, shall be taken and kept in Prison, until he hath brought him into the Court, which was the first Author of the Tale."[8]

De Scandalis Magnatum, purely statutory in nature, was Edward I's reaction to the unrest and uncertainties which bedeviled medieval rulers. The idea of a common law of seditious libel arose not from legal custom, but rather from Sir Edward Coke and his report of a decision of the Court of the Star Chamber in 1606. Lacking actual precedents in English cases, the Star Chamber relied on Roman law and ruled in *De Libellis Famosis,* a case concerning verse written about two prominent bishops, that libellers could be punished at common law or in the Star Chamber whether their defamatory statements were true or false. Libels against private men were said to have a tendency to incite revenge and therefore lead to a breach of the peace. Libels against magistrates and other public persons were deemed a greater offense because they not only involved breach of the peace, "but also the scandal of government; for what greater scandal of government can there be than to have corrupt or wicked magistrates to be appointed and constituted by the King to govern his subjects under him?"[9]

Instead of dying with the abolition of the Star Chamber in 1641 or with the Glorious Revolution, such logic was subsequently held by English authorities to be entirely valid, and the precedent was applied in cases involving the growing and increasingly troublesome periodical press. "If people should not be called to account for possessing the people with an ill opinion of the government, no government can subsist," Chief Justice John Holt said at the seditious libel trial of newspaper publisher John Tutchin in 1704. "For it is very necessary for all governments that the people should have a good opinion of it."[10]

The chief justice's dictum came at a time when, after a century of intermittent constitutional crises, England was beset by political instability and ideological confusion. Following the Glorious Revolution, the threat of despotic monarchy had diminished, but the fury of parties had intensified. As Tories and Whigs split over matters of religion, defense, and succession, parliamentary elections became frequent and sharply contested. Swift, Defoe, and other polemicists of the Augustan Age sought to sway the electorate as party battles raged in a profusion of newspapers and pamphlets. With the power of Parliament apparently established and the excesses of the Stuarts and Puritans bitter memories, neither the passive obedience preached by the Tories nor the active resistance associated with the Whigs seemed entirely satisfactory positions. Criticism of a government that was presumably fending off both arbitrary rule and mob violence could be treated as an attempt to weaken the basis of a just and desirable authority. The press, then, seemed to remain in essentially the same theoretical position it had occupied before the civil war. By the first years of the eighteenth century, however, it had gained a secure foothold in the affairs of the nation through its attachment to parties.[11]

Economic prosperity, the pragmatic political system of Walpole, and a temporary easing of some national and international conflicts helped stabilize the government in the decades following the Hanoverian succession. The concept of seditious libel had nevertheless become fixed in seventeenth- and eighteenth-century precedents and was accordingly described in William Blackstone's *Commentaries on the Laws of England* (1765–1769) as being "necessary for the preservation of peace and good order, of government and religion, the only solid foundations of civil liberty." Liberty of the press meant "no *previous* restraints upon publications," Blackstone asserted. Once published, however, "dangerous or offensive writings" judged to be "of a pernicious tendency" were punishable. In this way Blackstone sought to draw a line between the "liberty" and the "licentiousness" of the press.[12]

Blackstone's *Commentaries* was widely appreciated for its systematization of British law, but it insisted upon a nearly mystical acceptance of current doctrine and institutions. In Blackstone's description, the legal and constitutional structure of eighteenth-century England—however intricate, absurd, or inexplicable it might appear—

became interdependent, inevitable, and in harmony with the divine plan. When its definition of freedom of the press was later cited as authoritative by America's Federalists during the Sedition Act controversy, Republicans argued that Blackstone had simply presented a theory which rationalized existing judicial practice. According to the *Commentaries,* the press had become "properly free" with the expiration of licensing at the end of the seventeenth century. It had remained subject to criminal prosecution for true or false statements made about public officials because of "the tendency which all libels have to create animosities, and to disturb the public peace." This, Blackstone maintained, allowed freedom for private thoughts while correcting the crime of disseminating "bad sentiments, destructive of the ends of society."[13]

Convenient in justifying prosecution for any criticism of government, the Blackstonian concept of press freedom was used time and again against the opponents of English oligarchy. The distinction between the "liberty" and the "licentiousness" of the press was an old one, having been used as early as 1712 by Bolingbroke while he was pursuing printers as secretary of state. Lord North and Chief Justice Hutchinson of Massachusetts were among those attempting to exploit this semantic distinction during the upsurge of British and American radicalism which occurred early in the reign of George III. Both warned of the impact licentious writings would have on a credulous and volatile populace. North asserted in Parliament that attacks on courts of justice made by the likes of Wilkes and Junius would "prove fatal to the law itself." Hutchinson told grand jurors that the libels of Boston newspapers threatened "the Subversion of all Rule among us." Liberty of the press, Hutchinson solemnly declared, meant no more than a freedom to print without a license.[14]

The most sustained promulgation of Blackstonian doctrine came from England's Lord Chief Justice Mansfield, a suspected Jacobite who championed policies of coercion against American colonists. Mansfield earned the enmity of the populace and of many members of Parliament as he presided in seditious libel cases involving John Wilkes (1763–1770), printers and sellers of Junius' "Letter to the King" (1770), John Horne (1777), and the Dean of St. Asaph (1784). Mansfield held the public in low esteem, and the London mob expressed its dislike for him by burning and looting his house during the Gordon riots of 1780. American writers placed him in the same despised category as Lords Bute and North and as Chief Justice Hutchinson whose home was sacked by a Boston mob in 1765.

Although Mansfield recognized that his legal opinions on seditious libel were unpopular and were rejected by juries, he did not relent. "The *liberty of the press* consists in printing without any previous license, subject to the consequences of the law," he insisted during proceedings against the Dean of St. Asaph. "The *licentiousness* of the press is *Pandora*'s box, the source of every evil."[15]

II

To the defenders of the status quo, the press seemed as ominous and unmanageable as the chronic civil unrest of the seventeenth and eighteenth centuries. Like mobs, journalists could arraign authority and seek justice outside of the established governmental system. Both riotous behavior in the streets and angry diatribes in publications might therefore attain legitimacy as means of protecting the public. Accordingly, oligarchs attempted to discredit the press as dangerous to the political order, while their antagonists discounted the damaging effects and emphasized the beneficial aspects of journalistic freedom. Advocates of liberty of the press argued that the real threat to stability was the kind of bad government that liberty of the press would help to prevent. By exposing wrongdoing, they reasoned, the press might upset the ambitions of some individuals, but would preserve the well-being of the state.[16]

Libertarian thought tended to follow the direction of Trenchard and Gordon's Cato who stated that license only rarely resulted in baseless discontent and that the benefits of free expression outweighed the disadvantages. People preferred to live in peace and were subject to the bribes and terrors of the powerful, Cato observed, and it was "certainly of much less Consequence to Mankind, that an Innocent Man should be now and then aspersed than that all Men should be enslaved." So-called libels, Trenchard and Gordon wrote, "undoubtedly keep great Men in Awe, and are some Check upon their Behavior, by shewing them the Deformity of their Actions, as well as warning other People to be upon their Guard against Oppression."[17]

In saying—as Molesworth had suggested in his highly regarded *An Account of Denmark* (1694)—that it was the slumber rather than the suspicions of the people that was truly dangerous, Trenchard and Gordon helped to popularize a radical Whig theme which gained wide acceptance during the eighteenth century. Newspaper and pamphlet writers preached the necessity of popular vigilance and journalistic surveillance. " 'Tis the Duty of every Free People to be con-

stantly upon their Guard," said an *American Weekly Mercury* essay
on liberty of the press in 1734. "History hath furnished us with mel-
ancholy Proofs, that the Stability of a State cannot always be secured
even by the wisest Provisions and the most wholesome Laws: So
much is *human Malice* an over-match for *human Wisdom.*" A free
press preserved liberty, but was hated by those whose treachery it exposed, the author of the piece continued. The guilty talked of *"curb-
ing the License of the Pen, and teaching the Rascals (that is the
People) good Manners"* and proclaimed that "the Pen which is not
emploied in their Service sheds Epidemical Poison." In a subsequent
letter, echoing Cato at several points, the essayist sought to distinguish between the liberty and licentiousness of the press. He said he
understood liberty to be not the license of traducing the conduct of
governors who behave well, but rather the right "of attacking Wickedness in high Places, of disintangling the intricate Folds of a wicked
and corrupt Administration, and of pleading freely for a Redress of
Grievances."[18]

Writers concerned about public wrongdoing made short work of
the argument that a free press made governments weak and unstable.
Gordon, Hume, Hayter, and Junius were among those who declared
that the press actually protected rulers by warning them of unrest and
thereby allowing them to change their conduct before it was too late.
Freedom of expression was an indication and an effect of good government, Cato wrote. "The best Princes have ever encouraged and
promoted Freedom of Speech; they know that upright Measures
would defend themselves, and that all upright Men would defend
them." Explaining the concept of seditious libel to the readers of the
New-York Mercury in 1755, an anonymous essayist noted that law
books said truth was not a defense for the defamation of public officials since it might stir up sedition or a breach of the peace. The mis-
management of a state could mean its ruin where timely notice of the
danger was not given, the writer countered. "And if a People can be
presumed to have a Right in any Instance to oppose the undue Measures of an arbitrary Ruler, when they strike at the very Vitals of the
Constitution, they are certainly justifiable, in opposing them not only
with the Pen, but even with the Sword," he said. "And then, what becomes of the Reason upon which the above Law, relating to Libels,
is founded?" In the same year, James Parker told prospective contributors to his *Connecticut Gazette* that he did not wish to publish
anything in his paper that would undeservedly disturb the peace and
order of the colony. However, proclaiming the press one of the great

bulwarks of liberty, he declared that it was "better to be alarmed falsely twice, than by one fatal Security suffer a real Harm."[19]

Radical Whig ideology thus conceived of a free press as a lash for government and a prod for the people. A product of seventeenth-century perceptions of human weakness and official iniquity, the radical Whig's world view was harsh, didactic, and distrustful. Its militant, confrontational rhetoric on press freedom did not always suit eighteenth-century editors and Enlightenment thinkers, who sometimes attempted to soften the image of aggressive journalism by speaking of its limits and its advantages. The *Connecticut Gazette* and other papers contended that journalistic excesses were essentially self-correcting when discussion was open to all sides. Montesquieu assumed that while freedom of expression allowed countless points of view in a nation, liberty fortified and improved thought. Indulging in one of his speculations about the influence of climate, he theorized in *The Spirit of Laws* that it was the gloomy weather of England that made the British tense and unruly, traits that worked to their advantage since they were anxious to preserve their freedoms. "Slavery is ever preceded by sleep," Montesquieu wrote. "But a people who find no rest in any situation, who continually explore every part, and feel nothing but pain, can hardly be lulled to sleep."[20]

David Hume, who, along with Montesquieu, taught the authors of the United States Constitution to take an empirical approach to government, said in his essay on liberty of the press that the threat of publications exciting upheavals was negligible. Hume maintained that people read "alone and coolly" and were therefore not likely to be carried away by contagious passion. English experience had shown that civil liberties could be safely maintained in spite of some ferment, he said, "and it is to be hoped that men, being every day more accustomed to the free discussion of public affairs, will improve in their judgment of them and be with greater difficulty seduced by every idle rumor and popular clamor." According to Hume, the republican part of England's mixed form of government—with its concern for general and fixed laws—had come to dominate the monarchical part and could continue to do so only as long as the press could warn the people of the encroachments of arbitrary power.[21]

Junius spoke for the radicals of the 1760s and 1770s when he portrayed the press as an essential restraint for bad men and impediment for bad measures. "In that state of abandoned servility and prostitution, to which the undue influence of the crown has reduced the other branches of the legislature," he wrote in the preface to a collection of his published letters, "our ministers and magistrates have in reality little punishment to fear, and few difficulties to contend with, beyond the censure of the press, and the spirit of resistance, which it excites among the people." Answering the charge that licentious political journalism had caused dissension throughout the empire by blackening the reputations of the nation's leaders, Junius remarked that the public evils he and others complained of lay not in the description of government officials, but in their character and conduct. The press, by giving those with power the opportunity to choose between their duties and the surrender of their reputations, he said, could affect their actions even if it did not work miracles upon their hearts.[22]

Libertarian thought in this way regarded a free press as a practical mechanism for enforcing political virtue and thereby promoting public tranquility. In Parliamentary debate held during the public outcry over the Wilkes and Junius cases, voices were heard questioning the reasonableness of the law of seditious libel and asking whether, in fact, press prosecutions did more damage to the government than the writings in question did. Still, reform was slow in coming. To acknowledge a right to criticize government was to recognize a legitimate power and majesty of the people which England's ruling oligarchy typically denied. Law was a relationship between the superior who commanded and the inferior who obeyed, according to Blackstone. In his reactionary view, sovereignty, the ultimate authority in the nation, rested not in a people who gave their consent to be governed, but rather in the legislative power of the king, Lords, and Commons. The people elected members of the Commons, but were otherwise relegated to a state of submission.[23]

III

In a century which began with some sentiment remaining for the divine right of kings and for licensing the press, the Blackstonian positions on seditious libel and Parliamentary sovereignty represented one step away from arbitrary monarchy and simple suppression. Another step was taken by libertarian theorists in England and America who spoke the language of *vox populi, vox dei*. Radicals and reformers made little headway with England's entrenched elite, who ordinarily held the populace in contempt and did not care to have their use of power scrutinized. Across the Atlantic, however, where colonists had experienced a considerable degree of political autonomy in provincial matters and yet lacked representation in Parliament, the situation was different. Pronouncements from London and the maneuvers of royal appointees could seem manifestly anachronistic and unjust to a mid-century Bostonian who could pick up a copy of his city's *Gazette* week after week and read radical Whig essays declaring that government existed to serve a free people and could only be maintained with their consent and criticism.[24]

Radical Whig doctrine was clear on the relationship between the press and the government. "The Administration of Government, is nothing else but the Attendance of the Trustees of the People upon the Interest and Affairs of the People," wrote Cato in an essay on freedom of expression. "And as it is the Part and Business of the People, for whose Sake alone all publick Matters are or ought to be transacted, to see whether they be well or ill transacted; so it is the Interest, and ought to be the Ambition, of all honest Magistrates, to have their Deeds openly examined, and publickly scann'd."[25]

As Americans embraced the idea of social contract expressed in the Declaration of Independence and ratified a Constitution which left the ultimate authority to the people, they reiterated the traditional themes of libertarian press theory in the context of new political realities. "Great is the importance, in infant governments, raised on the basis of freedom; and where every freeman is himself a ruler," said Philadelphia's *Freeman's Journal* in 1781, "that the most unrestrained and impartial channel of intelligence be open to the citizens at large; that they be made acquainted with the *real* state of their affairs, and that the characters of their public servants, both *individually* and *collectively,* be made manifest." A correspondent in Boston's *Herald of Freedom* wrote in 1788 that Americans wished to preserve liberty of the press as the "inestimable jewel" of light and knowledge that led to the country's independence and federal Constitution. Journalistic freedom, the essayist said, protected the people from tyrants, sycophants, mock patriots, unprincipled demagogues, aristocratic juntos, and overbearing democratic majorities. A free press would transmit political knowledge, virtue, and patriotism to future generations, the writer continued, and would produce freemen, heroes, and statesmen until the end of time.[26]

Nine of the eleven revolutionary-era state constitutions specifically declared either that press freedom ought not to be restrained, or that it should be inviolably preserved. In one analysis of what such provisions meant, William Cushing, chief justice of Massachusetts, wrote to John Adams in 1789 that their state's 1780 declaration of rights—with its assertion that liberty of the press was essential to the secu-

rity of freedom in a state and therefore ought not to be restrained—
was at odds with the Blackstonian definition of press freedom as the
absence of prior restraint. The right to make truthful statements
about an administration could not be denied, Cushing said. "Without
this liberty of the press could we have supported our liberties against
british administration? or could our revolution have taken place?" he
asked. "Pretty certainly it could not, at the time it did. Under a sense
and impression of this sort, I conceive, this article was adopted."[27]

When the Constitutional Convention of 1787 failed to include a
bill of rights with protection for freedom of expression and other
civil liberties in the document it offered to the nation, Antifederalists
objected fiercely. A proposal to write a bill of rights was unanimously
defeated at Philadelphia and a subsequent motion to insert a press
clause by itself failed seven states to four. Supporters of the Constitution argued during and after the convention that enumerating rights
was both unnecessary, since the powers of the federal government
were clearly limited, and unwise, since it would appear that liberties
not included were not secured. Antifederalists, on the other hand,
complained bitterly that their opponents had too little regard for
hard-won freedoms and that a free press was essential to a free people. "And in regard to the *liberty of the press,* we renounce all claim
to it forever more. Amen," said an acerbic "Address to the Low-
born" in Philadelphia's *Independent Gazetteer.* "And we shall in future be perfectly contented if our *tongues* be left us to lick the feet of
our wellborn masters." Nothing in the Constitution, Antifederalists
said, exempted the press from licensing, taxation, or libel prosecutions. The Federalists, able to count on most newspapers being sympathetic to ratification, campaigned on the basis of a dire need for the
Constitution, whatever its defects, and made effective use of boycotts
and other tactics to harass printers who did not share their point of
view. Still, the ratifying conventions of two of the most populous
states, Virginia and New York, demanded a press amendment and
were joined by North Carolina, which refused to approve the Constitution until a bill of rights was provided.[28]

Debate on safeguarding the press left some of the new nation's
best legal and political minds defensive and somewhat perplexed.
Encountering hostility over the issue at the Pennsylvania ratifying
convention, James Wilson, a signer of the Constitution and a determined critic of the Blackstonian concept of sovereignty, attempted to
argue that the federal protection for the press was better than that of
the states since states might still try individuals for seditious libel.

Wilson did not endorse such trials but said that freedom of the press could be defined as freedom from prior restraint and that states might still prosecute the authors of attacks on government. "Now I would ask," he said, "is the person prosecuted in a worse situation under the general government, even if it had the power to make laws on this subject, than he is at present under the state government?" Wilson answered charges that Congress could make any laws it wished against the press by saying that it could only pass legislation necessary and proper for executing the powers it had been given in the Constitution.[29]

As one of the authors of *The Federalist* papers, Alexander Hamilton offered the standard argument that a bill of rights was not only unnecessary but also dangerous, because it would imply that liberties not mentioned were not protected. A bill of rights, he contended, made no sense where a constitution was founded on the power of the people who retained all rights. Hamilton cynically added that liberty of the press depended on public opinion whatever constitutional declarations were made. "What is the liberty of the press?" he asked the readers of *The Federalist*. "Who can give it any definition which would not leave the utmost latitude for evasion?" Thomas Jefferson, who was soon to become Hamilton's great rival in the affairs of the nation, admitted that finding acceptable wording for a bill of rights might be difficult. Yet, he told Madison, it would be better to establish liberties such as freedom of the press "in all cases" rather than not to do it in any.[30]

More of a democrat than Hamilton and less of a radical Whig than Jefferson, Madison was a pivotal figure in the controversy. He initially took the position of Hamilton, his collaborator on *The Federalist,* that the people retained what was not granted to the government and that to enumerate some rights was to suggest that others were not protected. Swayed by Jefferson and the fears expressed about the Constitution, Madison introduced the Bill of Rights to the First Congress in 1789 with a speech pointing to the need to secure the liberties "respecting which the people of America are most alarmed." He observed that the British Bill of Rights was a defense against the crown but did not protect the English people from a Parliament with indefinite powers. He said, contrary to Blackstone, that "freedom of the press and rights of conscience, those choicest privileges of the people" were "unguarded" in the collection of laws, traditions, and institutions that made up England's unwritten constitution. Madison told his fellow members of the House of Representatives that a bill of rights, although difficult to write and thought by many unnecessary in a limited government, would tend to prevent abuses of power, would satisfy the public, and would contribute to political stability.[31]

Madison proposed that the amendments state "[the] people shall not be deprived or abridged of their right to speak, to write, or to publish their sentiments; and the freedom of the press, as one of the great bulwarks of liberty, shall be inviolable." He also offered a provision forbidding state violations of press freedom, a stipulation which he successfully guided through the House against the objection that the states would resent interference in their affairs.[32]

As Congress worked on the Bill of Rights, the Senate, debating behind closed doors and keeping only brief records of its proceedings, made two decisions of considerable importance to the press. One was to reject a motion which by saying the press should be protected "in as ample a manner as hath at any time been secured by the common law" would have effectively established Blackstonian standards. A second action, one of several taken by the Senate in apparent reaction to fears about losses of state autonomy, was to vote down an amendment forbidding states to infringe on the freedom of the press and speech, the equal rights of conscience, and the right to trial by jury in criminal cases. Madison had called this "the most valuable amendment in the whole list" before it was passed by the House.[33] Nevertheless, the final version of what later became the First Amendment said only that "Congress shall make no law" respecting an establishment of religion or abridging the freedoms of speech, press, assembly, and petition. This amendment was ratified by the state legislatures with little recorded discussion.

IV

Madison's attitude toward a federal bill of rights was both optimistic and pessimistic. "Repeated violations of these parchment barriers have been committed by overbearing majorities in every State," he wrote to Jefferson in 1788. He added, however, that the "political truths declared in that solemn manner acquire by degrees the character of fundamental maxims of free Government, and as they become incorporated with the national sentiment, counteract the impulses of interest and passion." As a student of the radical Whigs, Montesquieu, and Hume, Madison was able to draw on a century of thought on how liberties could be preserved. He believed that nations relying on popular sovereignty had to preserve liberty by consciously dispersing political power and to maintain stability by effectively distributing the shocks of clashing interests. The governmental system he dispassionately envisioned in the tenth *Federalist* was designed to protect minority rights and to provide "a Republican remedy for the diseases most incident to Republican Government." Introducing the Bill of Rights in Congress, he remarked that both supporters and opponents of the Constitution had perhaps used some political cunning on the question of amendments. He said that "paper barriers" against majority power would have the "salutary effect" of settling rights in public opinion in a way that would be difficult to ignore.[34]

Four days after the First Amendment became part of the Constitution in 1791, Madison published an essay on "Public Opinion" in Philip Freneau's *National Gazette,* a paper founded with the patronage of Jefferson to espouse republican principles in the developing partisan conflicts of Washington's administration. Considering the implications of having a government with public opinion as the "real sovereign," Madison discussed the interactions that the press and other means of communication made possible. He observed that while public opinion, however formed, set bounds to a government, government could also influence public opinion. This, he suggested, would settle debates over the respect the government should give to the sentiments of the people. It was also apparent, he continued, that the Bill of Rights would become part of public opinion and would require that the people be in a position to influence government.[35] Thus, rather than merely accepting the unalloyed radical Whig image of the press as the scourge of tyrants, Madison realized from the experience of the eighteenth century that the press would not only expose bad administration, but could also be used to make a democratic system function properly.

Madison's thought on the connection between self-government and the press was, like that of Jefferson, an amalgam of English libertarian theory and Enlightenment philosophy. Madison's Virginia Resolutions, which were written to condemn the Sedition Act of 1798, recognized that a law intended to silence the press would destroy a proper check on government. To explain the Resolutions, he composed his *Address of the General Assembly to the People of the Commonwealth of Virginia,* which declared that the Federalists were overwhelming "the best hopes of republicanism" under the pretext of meeting a French threat. Adopting radical Whig rhetoric, he warned that "the possessors of power, who are the advocates for its extension, can ever create national embarrassments, to be successively employed to soothe the people into sleep, whilst that power is swelling, silently, secretly, and fatally." The Sedition Act, he said, relied on "the exploded doctrine 'that the administrators of the Government are the masters, and not the servants of the people' " and exposed America "which acquired the honour of taking the lead among nations towards perfecting political principles, to the disgrace of returning first to ancient ignorance and barbarism."[36]

The Sedition Act confirmed the fears of the Antifederalists that Congress would pass laws against the press. Federalists had said that no such power was given to Congress, but the Federalists of 1798 thought otherwise. Apparently realizing that federal common law jurisdiction in criminal cases was highly questionable, the majority party passed a seditious libel statute, using the justification that any government had a right to preserve itself and that the First Amendment's protection for freedom of the press meant freedom from prior restraint. Madison's *Address* was one of the Republican responses which denounced the Federalists' reasoning for effectively allowing Congress unlimited power and converting the First Amendment into a means of abridging rather than preserving freedom. The federal government was given no authority over the press, he maintained, and the First Amendment, which was "designed to quiet every fear," was being made "the source of an act which has produced general terror and alarm."[37]

In his justifications for the Bill of Rights and his subsequent attacks on the Sedition Act, Madison expressed regret that partisan spirit had interfered with fundamental matters of political theory. The disappointing and often hostile Federalist response to his Virginia Resolutions prompted him to write his sweeping *Report on the Resolutions* which was approved by the General Assembly in 1800. The Virginia *Report,* which Jefferson arranged to have distributed to other states, repeated points made in the legislature's earlier *Address* but also set down forceful criticisms of the concept of seditious libel. The Constitution supposed that the president and members of Congress would not always discharge their trusts and consequently provided for elections and, in grave cases, presidential impeachment, Madison reasoned. It was therefore "natural and proper, that, according to the cause and degree of their faults, they should be brought into contempt or disrepute, and incur the hatred of the people." Citizens had a duty to control officials through public opinion, Madison wrote, and had a right to compare candidates for the public trust on equal terms. Returning to the kind of analysis he presented in introducing the Bill of Rights, he pointed out that the common law standards might be logical in British politics, where the king in theory could do no wrong and the largely hereditary Parliament was omnipotent, but did not apply where sovereign peoples created governments "elective, limited, and responsible in all their branches." Even if journalistic freedom seemed to be abused to some degree, Madison said, the world was indebted to the press "for all the triumphs which have been gained by reason and humanity over error and oppression."[38]

V

Demands, Defenses, and Distinctions

Eighteenth-century conflicts over freedom of the press were, of course, not confined to broad, philosophical questions. As the larger issues were being debated, lesser, more technical matters of libel law became perennial topics among journalists and lawyers and at times entangled and overshadowed basic libertarian principles. The crude Blackstonian distinction between the liberty and licentiousness of the press—labeled "sophistry" in Madison's *Address*—was easy to disdain, but difficult to reject altogether. Madison and other defenders of the press repeated the contention of *Cato's Letters* that some degree of abuse was inevitable and was, in fact, inseparable from the exercise of freedom.[1] Nevertheless, few conceived of the press as completely free. Although libertarians slashed away at the law of seditious libel, they also advocated safeguards for private reputation.

I

Opposition to the presence of seditious libel in Anglo-American law took various forms. One approach was to condemn it for its severity and for its origins in the defunct and discredited Court of the Star Chamber. When the printer of the *Craftsman*, Richard Francklin, was prosecuted for seditious libel in 1731, the paper complained that all its government antagonists wanted to be printed were "Panegyricks and Encomiums on all *ministerial Schemes.*" Any expressions of doubt about official actions, wrote Bolingbroke and his editor, Nicholas Amhurst, could be considered *"seditious,* and even *traiterous Libels,"* however decent and well-intended. The *Craftsman* charged that the government had long used improper methods to prosecute printers and maintained that any authority arising from Star Chamber decisions was "null and illegal."[2]

Americans also used the issue of dubious precedents for seditious libel. At Zenger's trial, Andrew Hamilton repeatedly scorned Star Chamber law as dangerous and arbitrary. In a defense of a journalist in 1804, Alexander Hamilton described the abolished court as a "tyrannical and polluted source." Another American lawyer, William Bollan, provided a tedious account of Star Chamber suppression in *The Freedom of Speech and Writing Upon Public Affairs, Considered,* a work published in London in 1766. Others took a more lighthearted approach. In 1768, after publishing a philippic against Governor Francis Bernard, the *Boston Gazette* was characterized by the Massachusetts Council as subversive to all order and necessary subordination. The *Gazette* drolly footnoted Coke's report of *De Libellis Famosis* in an ostensibly defamatory exchange between "Libellus Famosus" and "Famosus Libellus." One offered "A Libel on a Lobster": "I Hope none will be offended; but I really prefer a *Crab* to a *Lobster."* The other replied with "A Libel on Crabs": "I Care not a Farthing who is offended; I would not give one Lobster for Ten Crabs."[3]

Another type of argument, one which was used by Cato, among others, was to point out differences in the application of the law brought about by changes in political power. New York lawyer James Alexander, who relied heavily on Cato when discussing freedom of the press, used this tactic in recalling the famous *Case of the Seven Bishops,* the unsuccessful seditious libel prosecution which was one of the principal events leading to the Glorious Revolution. "Every Body knows what has been called Lybeling in one Age has met with different Treatment in another," he wrote in Zenger's *New-York Weekly Journal,* "in King Jame's Time the Petition of the seven Bishops was called a Libel: But after the Revolution a Godly and pious Petition." In defense of the writings in Zenger's newspaper, Alexander added, "Make our Adversarys the Judges; I don't well know what will not be a Libel; and perhaps, if we be the Judges it will be as Difficult to tell what will." During the debates on press law held in Parliament in 1770, Alexander Wedderburn concluded that defamation changed like a chameleon and depended on public opinion. "There is no other standard, by which it can be measured or ascertained," he said.[4]

In France, Robespierre used this argument in a speech before the National Assembly which was translated and reprinted in Freneau's *National Gazette* in 1791. Robespierre discussed liberty of the press as a check on arbitrary power, noting that only three years earlier Rousseau's *Social Contract* had been condemned as a treasonous work. He remarked that "time and situation alone determine whether an author shall be persecuted or be crowned with honour." Although his treatment of journalists during the Reign of Terror would later belie his words, Robespierre, "The Incorruptible," tied the fact of changing standards to an additional libertarian proposition, "that there is an essential difference between *criminal acts* and the *offences of the press*." As William Walwyn, Philip Furneaux, Jeremy Bentham, Thomas Jefferson, and a number of others had done before him, Robespierre distinguished between actions which could be judged according to established rules and procedures, and "mere opinions" which were pronounced meritorious or criminal depending on shifting circumstances. "There is no freedom of the press where the author of any piece is liable to arbitrary prosecution," he insisted.[5]

Montesquieu had already stated the argument plainly in *The Spirit of Laws,* where he criticized the standards used in making expression equivalent to treason against the state. "Words do not constitute an overt act," he said, "they remain only in idea." Montesquieu thought mere statements were too subject to interpretation to be made into high crimes. "Wherever this law is established," he observed, "there is an end not only of liberty, but even of its very shadow."[6] Thus, in place of Blackstonian logic which assumed words critical of authority had a bad tendency, libertarian thought began to offer a sedition test which judged behavior rather than expression.

Some of the strongest statements discriminating between words and actions came in a widely heralded British pamphlet written by an author who used the pen name "Father of Candor." Printed in successive editions during the years of the Wilkes and Junius cases, the pamphlet pointed to Sir Edward Coke as "the introductor, fosterer, maturer and reporter of the present star-chamber doctrine about libels." It declared that libel prosecutions since the reign of Charles I had generally arisen from and were pursued with "a spirit of party-revenge." Saying that the law should attempt neither to impose "downright passive obedience" nor to prevent the press from being a check on bad actions and an incentive to good ones, Father of Candor stressed that a libel was not an actual breach of the peace. He endorsed the idea that sedition was commited by violent, public action rather than by words. "The notion of pursuing a libeller in a *criminal* way at all, is alien from the nature of a free constitution," he wrote. "Our ancient common law knew of none but a *civil* remedy, by special action on the case for damage incurred, to be assessed by a jury of his fellows. There was no such thing as a public libel known to the law."[7]

II

This distinction between public and personal libel was the most significant and most widely advocated libertarian conception of the legal freedom of the press. The argument that seditious libel lacked proper precedents and the contention that ideas could be separated from actions may not have had much appeal in an age of religious decay and fanaticism, mob activity, and revolution, but differentiating between individual and societal matters presented an attractive principle. From this perspective, criticizing government could be seen as a necessary act of political frustration or of patriotism, whereas disparaging private character could be understood as an invasion of personal rights. As eighteenth-century writers and lawyers attempted to apply this principle, however, differences emerged over the extent of protection needed for the reputations of public persons.

Addison and Steele's *Spectator,* one arbiter of Enlightenment morality, declared that stabbing a private reputation was barbarous and cautioned that wit had to be tempered with virtue and humanity. As individuals as different as Cato, Hutchinson, Smollet, and Junius would later do, Addison asked if it was not as reasonable to guard character as property. Still, even if the *Spectator* stood for journalistic rectitude and seemed calculated to offer some relief from the party broils of its time, Addison shrugged off any cares about the abuse of prominent persons, saying that posterity would determine their greatness. He agreed with Swift that censure was the tax that men paid for being well-known. "It is Folly for an eminent Man to think of escaping it," he observed, "and a Weakness to be affected with it." Addison also remarked that they received not only reproaches they did not deserve, but also praise they did not merit.[8]

Others found the questions of public versus private matters more difficult to resolve. Although acknowledging that expression might be legally punished when sedition was clearly intended, Cato defined

libel as "a Sort of Writing that hurts particular Persons, without doing Good to the Publick." He commented that people would always
deal freely with the characters of their superiors when they were improperly governed. He loyally professed a belief that libels acquired
more "Malignity" the closer they reached to the monarch, but then
said that it was scarcely possible for a free country to make general
laws against defamation that would not make all writing unsafe. Cato
admonished his readers to distinguish between the liberty and licentiousness of the press, but explained that what he disliked was the
uncovering of personal failings which did not affect society. "Ignorance and Folly may be pleaded in Alleviation of private Offences; but
when they come to be publick Offences, they lose all Benefit of such
a Plea," he wrote. Cato did allow that the personal reputations of
governors ought to be protected as long as their private vices did not
enter into their public administration. He half-seriously suggested,
however, that in addition to libels against officials and private persons, a third category be created in the law for "Libels against the
People" to punish questioning the liberties of the governed.[9]

In practice, writers critical of government often pointed to the
public-private distinction as the touchstone of their behavior. The
Craftsman prided itself on its intention to judge Walpole the politician rather than Walpole the man and asserted that it entered into
personal altercation only when insults and provocations by ministerial writers made it a matter of self-defense. One of the *Craftsman's*
correspondents nevertheless protested that it was justifiable to examine the characters of those entrusted with the protection of liberty
and property since *"private Passions* influence *publick Actions."* Still,
a paper such as the *Champion* could denounce Walpole for using
state power against the press and then ask, "In case of a Libel, is not
the Law at least as open to a Minister, as any private Person?" A
belligerent journalist like Junius was prepared to recognize that the
remedies of action or indictment were open to an individual whose
reputation had been injured, but said that circumstances were different when "strictures upon the characters of men in office and the
measures of government" were involved. "As the indulgence of private malice and personal slander should be checked and resisted by
every legal means," he wrote, "so a constant examination into the
characters and conduct of ministers and magistrates should be equally
promoted and encouraged."[10]

Like their English counterparts, eighteenth-century American journalists did not always agree on where to draw the line when discuss-

ing how the press should deal with public reputations. In 1778, for instance, Boston's *Independent Chronicle* asserted that its press was free for "Animadversions on public Characters," but not for "Attacks on private Reputations." On the other hand, George Hough, printer of the *Concord Herald* in New Hampshire, announced in 1790 that press freedom would be "sacred" in his paper for "decent remarks on publick measures, calculated to *reform* government," but that he would not accept "invectives or anecdotes to the injury of publick or private characters." Another tack was to say, as a contributor did in Boston's *Massachusetts Centinel* in 1785, that liberty of the press meant arraigning official conduct, but not private character and actions, "unless they have a tendency to injure the community."[11]

Attorneys made the distinction in their courtroom defenses of writers and publishers. During Zenger's trial, immediately after denying that *De Libellis Famosis* was still law, Andrew Hamilton stated that it was "base and unworthy" to defame anyone. "But when a ruler of a people brings his personal failings, but much more his vices, into his administration, and the people find themselves affected by them, either in their liberties or properties," he continued, "that will alter the case mightily, and all the high things that are said in favor of rulers, and of dignitaries, and upon the side of power will not be able to stop people's mouths when they feel themselves oppressed, I mean in a free government." Hamilton argued that a free people had a natural right to complain when suffering under arbitrary power and "to put their neighbors upon their guard against the craft or open violence of men in authority."[12]

At the trial of Henry S. Woodfall, the first to print Junius' letter to the King, Serjeant John Glynn told the jury that "private personal abuse was wrong, but the public acts of government often demanded public scrutiny." According to the report of the case, Glynn said that if they found the letter "was not written with intent to villify the person of the king, but freely to canvass the acts of government, they would consider the publisher as having done his fellow-subjects essential service, and acquit him." Unlike the Zenger case, where the defendant was simply pronounced not guilty, Woodfall's jurors stood up to the presiding judge, Lord Mansfield, by finding the defendant "Guilty of printing and publishing only"—a verdict which implied Woodfall had broken no law. A new trial was ordered but never held.[13]

Commentaries on seditious libel cases also brought up the public-private distinction. In a lengthy newspaper essay, James Alexander championed Hamilton's interpretation of legal doctrine at Zenger's trial by saying that robbing a person of his reputation was worse than stealing his money, but he then asked if magistrates should have the power to punish words abusing officials for their actions. "Upon the whole, To suppress inquiries into the administration is good policy in an arbitrary Government," he observed, "But a Free Constitution and Freedom of Speech have such a reciprocal dependence on each other, that they cannot subsist without consisting together." After noting that Augustus Caesar had made character defamation subject to the penalties of treason against the state, Alexander sarcastically speculated that when the emperor Caligula made his horse a consul, calling it a stupid animal would have been considered a capital crime likely to stir up its family to acts of revenge.[14]

Bishop Hayter's essay on press freedom made the point that it was the responsibility of the government to act against treason and sedition, but that personal defamation was the concern of individuals. "It is the Wisdom of our Laws in particular, to remind the Party aggrieved, that his Injury is only Personal: for the Law confines the Reparation to the Damage he has sustained," he wrote. "This Damage may be magnify'd by his public Character, but it is only magnified to himself; for the Reparation is made to himself, not to the Public." Analyzing the development of defamation law, Father of Candor later said the problem was that personal and public libel had been confused. "The liberty of exposing and opposing a bad Administration by the pen, is among the necessary privileges of a free people, and is perhaps the greatest benefit that can be derived from the liberty of the press," he wrote. "But Ministers, who by their misdeeds provoke the people to cry out and complain, are very apt to make that very complaint the foundation of new oppression, by prosecuting the same as a libel on the State."[15]

III

Libertarian theorists before 1798 devoted comparatively little thought to the abstract issue of whether a state could be criminally assaulted by words alone—perhaps because they simply dismissed seditious libel as Star Chamber law or because the prosecutions they saw obviously involved one individual's journalistic attack on another. While government officials sought to turn criticism of their behavior into state libel, advocates of press freedom could regard the same statements as justifiable efforts to uncover public wrongdoing. A libertarian essay could, as one in the *Boston Gazette* did in 1755, survey the history of government libel prosecutions and decide that "the true Definition of a Libel" is that "nothing is punishable by Law, but what is maliciously intended to injure particular Persons." Another, like the pamphlet published in Boston by "A Friend to Harmony" in 1789, might go further and argue that any law against libels endangered freedom of the press and that individuals whose reputations have been damaged should enter the journalistic fray rather than subject themselves and others to the expense and delays of the courts.[16] Still, the reality of official attempts to punish opposition writers forced lawyers to use defenses which had a chance of working in the existing legal system.

The libertarians' public-private distinction may have made sense to juries and journalists, but it did not fit in the ideology of the politically powerful. The oligarchy's objection to the concept was stated in a ministerial pamphlet directed against the contributors to the *Craftsman*. "By their Descriptions and Definitions of Liberty, Injuries done to a Nation by Writing are not criminal, nor ought to be accounted for," complained one of Walpole's chief defenders, William Arnall, "the Publick hath not the Right of a private Man, and a Minister's Fame is in a worse Condition than that of the meanest Subject; any defamatory Lies may be circulated against him, any odious Designs falsely laid to his Charge."[17]

In America, Chief Justice Hutchinson equated written attacks on officials with licentious abuse of government and stated that the libel of a ruler was "infinitely more mischievous" than the defamation of a private person. "Shall a Man print that, of the First Ruler of a State, which he will not speak of any one Man in the Community?" he asked grand jurors in 1768. "Shall our first Magistrate be thus slandered with impunity in an *infamous* Paper?" Hutchinson, as well as Chief Justice Mansfield in England, said that public officials could be tried in courts if they were actually guilty of any offenses—an idea which libertarians found impractical for the most part.[18]

Such sentiments had a basis in Star Chamber precedent. In the case *De Libellis Famosis,* the libel of *"a magistrate, or other publick person"* was considered a "greater offence" than the defamation of a private individual since it involved the scandal of government. Because both kinds of libels tended to incite quarrels and breaches of the peace, the court declared, the truth of a publication was always immaterial. The Star Chamber doctrine of libels, or parts of it, were recited by English prosecuting attorneys and judges for most of the eighteenth century. The right to plead truth therefore became a primary libertarian contention and figured prominently in a number of seditious libel trials including, most notably, the Zenger case in 1735. Conservative jurists including Blackstone were, however, eventually willing to concede one opening for the truth defense. Defining libels as "malicious defamations of any person, and especially a magistrate," Blackstone said that truth could be a defense in civil actions since the plaintiff received no private injury when truth was spoken, but that "in a criminal prosecution, the tendency which all libels have to create animosities, and to disturb the public peace, is the sole consideration of the law."[19] In other words, truth could be a defense when one person sued another, but not when government prosecuted an individual for defaming someone else.

Libertarians endeavored to reverse the thrust of this doctrine. Cato asserted that the truth defense only failed to apply when the topic was purely personal and that the exposure of a "public Wickedness" could therefore never be a libel. He maintained that England had "good laws" to punish those who would "calumniate their Superiors, or one another" as long as the laws were properly enforced. An individual who speaks falsely of someone else needs to be punished, Cato said, but scurrilous defamations were "certainly the most harmless and contemptible" kind and it was better that "many Libels should escape, than the Liberty of the Press should be infring'd." He advised journalists to write about their superiors "as modestly as can be consistent with making themselves understood" and corrupt men to realize that the "best Way to escape the Virulence of Libels, is not to deserve them." Serjeant Glynn, speaking in Parliament after appearing for defendants in the Junius trials, remarked that truth was a highway everyone had a right to walk and observed that there were "many more plausible reasons to be given why private truths should not be spoken, than those which relate to the public; for what concerns all, all ought to know."[20]

With courts refusing to accept truth as a defense in government prosecutions, one alternative seditious libel defendants had was simply to rely on juries to return favorable verdicts. In spite of routine instructions from the bench that they could decide only the fact of publication and not the broader question of guilt or innocence under the law, juries rebelled often enough to make prosecutions risky at best. In one such case, the seditious libel trial of bookseller William

Owen in 1752, Charles Pratt, later Lord Camden, argued that a free people had a right to complain about government and that libel was a matter of intention—a fact for the jury to decide. Although Owen had evidently published the pamphlet in question, a criticism of the House of Commons, he was found not guilty. The verdict was a personal blow to William Murray, the future Lord Mansfield, who had argued for the government that the jury was only to determine publication. For reiterating his views on the jury's role while presiding at the Junius trials two decades later, Mansfield was presented with a series of embarrassing questions from Lord Camden in the House of Lords and with the publication of a stinging tirade by Junius. Liberty of the press was the palladium of English freedoms, Junius thundered, and the right of a jury to return a general verdict in all cases was "an essential part of our constitution."[21]

Mansfield held his position through the proceedings against the Dean of St. Asaph in 1784. In his defense of the Dean, Thomas Erskine urged that a jury was better equipped to judge the danger of a libel and the intention of a writer since the court could only decide "blindly and indiscriminately upon all times, circumstances, and intentions." Claiming that judges were "totally independent," Mansfield denounced such effrontery as "puerile rant and declamation." The law could not be left to any twelve men who happened to make a jury, he said. They would be unpredictable, subject to no control, and "under all the prejudices of the popular cry of the day." The issue was not settled until Fox's Libel Act, passed by Parliament in 1792, declared that juries could give general verdicts in libel cases. Parliament did not recognize truth as a defense in criminal proceedings until the passage of Lord Campbell's Act in 1843.[22]

IV

Court trials for seditious libel were seldom attempted in America between the Zenger case in 1735 and the Sedition Act of 1798. Slander cases were fairly common in early America and personal libel suits—some of which involved public persons—occurred from time to time.[23] A more serious threat to the freedom of political expression came from legislatures. In at least twenty instances before the Revolution, individuals were brought before an upper or lower house to answer for critical statements they had published. Patterning their actions on authority sometimes exercised by Parliament, American legislatures occasionally jailed journalists briefly for "contempt" or "breach of legislative privilege" if they refused to apologize or give satisfactory answers. Provincial efforts to use this power were, however, typically capricious, confused, and futile. Printers and writers, who insisted that such proceedings violated due process and freedom of the press, proved difficult to intimidate, and the legislators themselves were often at odds over the issues raised by breach of legislative privilege.[24]

By 1798, when the Federalists were anxious to find a truly effective means of choking political dissent, they decided to pass a sedition law, as Britain's Parliament had done three years earlier in reaction to the radicalism inspired by the French Revolution. Under Republican pressure, the initial version of the American Sedition Act (which even Alexander Hamilton thought was too glaringly repressive for his enemies) was toned down to include the truth defense, the requirement of malice, and the right of juries to return general verdicts. Once prosecutions began under that statute, however, defendants found that their juries were packed, their malice assumed, and their right to use truth limited by their having expressed opinions which were not subject to final proof one way or another.[25]

Although they had little firsthand experience with seditious libel trials, defenders of the press in America were prepared by a century of libertarian thought to make cogent responses to the majority party's maneuver and to reject emphatically the Blackstonian position on freedom of expression which the Federalists used. On the floor of Congress and in their publications, Republicans contended that free governments needed criticism and that matters of personal reputation could be settled in state courts. Representative Edward Livingston of New York told the House that the government ought not to have any power to protect itself from defamation except the force of reason. "The principles of the law of political libels," said Republican leader Albert Gallatin, could be found in the decisions of the Star Chamber and "the rescripts of the worst Emperors of Rome." In his report on the Sedition Act, Representative John Nicholas declared that the government should have no authority "to restrain animadversions on public measures" and that "for protection from private injury from defamation, the States are fully competent."[26]

Outside of Congress, the subject was treated at greater length. Madison's *Address* argued that cases of calumny arose between individuals and that every libelous writing could be punished in state courts "whether it injured public officers or private citizens." The

Sedition Act, he said, opened "the hideous volumes of penal law" and let loose the legal inventions of malice and ambition, "which, in all ages, have debauched morals, depressed liberty, shackled religion, supported despotism, and deluged the scaffold with blood." Criminal statutes, Madison later wrote in his *Report on the Resolutions,* shielded public characters and conduct from the exposure they may deserve. The First Amendment, he said, restrained the federal government from legislating against the press, but those with injured reputations were able to seek a remedy "under the same laws, and in the same tribunals, which protect their lives, their liberties, and their properties."[27]

In *A Treatise Concerning Political Enquiry, and the Liberty of the Press,* a book published in 1800, New York Republican Tunis Wortman insisted that the interests of government never demanded the criminal suppression of libel. Virtuous governments were secure and the people's liberties were maintained, he contended, as long as truth was disseminated and falsehoods were detected. "Civil prosecutions, at the suit of injured individuals," he said, "are a sufficient restraint upon the licentiousness of the Press." Wortman stated that the character of all individuals was "equally sacred" and that public or private persons deserved the same opportunity to seek damages from an impartial jury of citizens.[28]

Virginia lawyer George Hay published two works, both titled *An Essay on the Liberty of the Press,* which denied that press law should punish anything but private injuries. The second, published in 1803, suggested that public officials would be cautious about initiating personal libel actions since printers would have ample opportunities for revenge in the course of their work and the public resented attacks on press freedom. Statements about any public matter could be made with total freedom, Hay wrote, but the author of a false, malicious defamation of an individual's private character was "amenable to that individual, by an action, and to the public, by indictment."[29]

Wortman, Hay, and other libertarians denied that a truthful publication could be a libel, even if it defamed a private reputation. As opponents of the Sedition Act realized, however, the problem with the truth defense was that critical opinions were—by definition—neither provably true nor false. Gallatin observed during Congressional debate that a person declaring the sedition statute an unconstitutional party measure could be found guilty of expressing an ungrounded sentiment by a jury friendly to the administration. Madison

noted in his *Address* and his *Report* that opinions could not be subject to the kind of factual proof that would be needed in a court of
law.[30]

Indeed, journalists were convicted under the Sedition Act for expressing mere political opinions. Defending a writer prosecuted for
portraying the Adams administration as "one continued tempest of
malignant passions" and the president as a "professed aristocrat,"
George Hay argued that it had become necessary "to do what had
never been done perhaps before, to draw a line of discrimination between fact and opinion." The sedition law, Hay told a hostile judge
and packed jury, must have been meant for "fact falsely and maliciously asserted" rather than opinion which could be endlessly debated. Not surprisingly, Hay and his fellow defense lawyers—Virginia's Attorney General Philip Norborne Nicholas and House Clerk
William Wirt—lost the case, but Hay reaffirmed what he had already
set forth in his first *Essay on the Liberty of the Press*—that the truth
defense by itself provided no criterion for distinguishing between
fact and opinion and did not prevent the suppression of political
thought. "I contend therefore, and it appears clear, that if the words
freedom of the press, have any meaning at all," he wrote, "they
mean a total exemption from any law making any publication whatever criminal."[31]

V

The position Hay and his fellow Republicans stated was new only in
the extent to which it acknowledged the inadequacy of safeguards
continually sought under the British legal system and the necessity
of explicitly disposing of the concept of seditious libel in a democratic system where the people were sovereign. For decades, libertarians dealing with British courts had faced constitutional realities
which precluded any realistic expectation of eliminating seditious
libel prosecutions. They had spoken out against the central idea of
seditious libel—that mere criticism of government was dangerous and
had to be punished. If some libertarians did not press for an end to
all trials for defamation initiated by the state, even after the Sedition
Act, it was presumably because it had long been admitted that the
author of a personal libel could be subject to either a civil suit for
damages or a government prosecution. Still, both the Republican demand that defamation be left to the state courts and, to a large
extent, the libertarian movement for libel reforms rested on the as-

sumption that, as Cato put it, "most Libels are purely personal; they fly at Men rather than Things." At the seditious libel trial of John Tutchin in 1704, the defense attorney argued that there could be no libel where no person was named. "A libel that points at nobody in particular, is like a shot at random, that seldom does any mischief," he said. A "national reflection" would not "stir up the people."[32]

Libertarian thought thus might disregard or dismiss seditious libel—an individual's defamation of government—while recognizing that legal action could be taken when a person published certain statements damaging another's reputation. The position, as plain as it appeared, however, was not without difficulties. Nothing in the doctrine or proposed safeguards gave precise indications of how fact was to be separated from opinion or how the private character of public persons was to be separated from their official conduct. As Father of Candor pointed out, the public and private kinds of defamation had often been confused historically and then prosecuted as libels on the state.[33] Libertarians usually intended to extend protection only to the reputations of individuals, but this by itself could mean that journalists might suffer legal consequences for legitimate criticism of politicians.

Libertarians often did accept the view that truth—whatever its shortcomings as a defense, was a necessary boundary for expression. Although recognizing both the difficulty of proving truth and the political nature of prosecutions, Andrew Hamilton remarked at Zenger's trial that no allowances should be made for false charges against public officials. "Truth," he said, "ought to govern the whole affair of libels." In England, Father of Candor wrote that the public had as much right to complain about the misconduct of ministers as it had to reject candidates in an election. "Now," he added, "the merit or demerit of these publications must arise from their being true or false; if they are true, they are highly commendable; if they are wilfully false, they are certainly malicious, seditious, and damnable." Yet, like Hamilton, Father of Candor disdained "public libel" and so was reduced to arguing that the whole matter in each case should be determined by "that security of Englishmans rights, a Jury."[34]

Defenders of journalistic rights might then say—as a correspondent wrote in a Pennsylvania newspaper in 1785—that the press offered citizens the "power to scrutinize, with *candour,* the characters of men in office." Quoting Cato and disparaging Blackstone, Chief Justice Cushing of Massachusetts told John Adams in 1789 that the liberty of making truthful observations about the conduct of an administration helped to secure freedom in a state. On the other hand, he thought, freedom of expression did not mean damaging characters and the press could be "restrained from *injuring* the public or individuals by propagating falsehoods." Cushing asked if the Massachusetts Declaration of Rights did not "comprehend a liberty to treat all subjects and characters freely, within the bounds of truth." Adams answered that the press served to make the characters and conduct of officials known to the people and that "it would be safest to admit evidence to the jury of the Truth of accusations, and if the jury found them true and that they were published for the Public good, they would readily acquit."[35]

Since Cushing still appeared to accept the idea of public libels and Adams made the truth defense contingent on "the Public good," their views corresponded with a cramped version of libertarianism which would later be championed by Alexander Hamilton. St. George Tucker, a Virginia jurist, spelled out a less restrictive position as clearly as he could in his republicanized edition of Blackstone's *Commentaries* published in 1803. Tucker voiced the obligatory Republican derision of the Star Chamber and Blackstone and articulated a Madisonian understanding of the inapplicability of British precedents in a nation with popular sovereignty. Freedom of the press meant a right to publish sentiments on government measures without restraint or punishment, he said, but the state courts were open for the redress of "injuries done the reputation of any person, as *an individual.*" Writers were bound to truth in stating facts, Tucker maintained, and were required to "do justice" to the reputations of officials. "The right of character is a sacred and invaluable right," he explained, "and is not forfeited by accepting a public employment."[36]

VI

Among those who approved of Tucker's work on the *Commentaries* was the third president of the United States, Thomas Jefferson, who more than once decried what he saw as the "honeyed Mansfieldism of Blackstone." Jefferson held fully evolved libertarian views on the role of the press in criticizing government, but insisted on a legal limit to press attacks on personal character. His concern for reputation manifested itself as early as 1776 in his drafts of the Virginia Constitution where he wrote: "Printing presses shall be free, except so far as by commission of private injury cause may be given of pri-

vate action." In a list of essential rights he composed nearly fifty
years later, he included freedom of the press "subject only to lia-
bility for personal injuries."[37]

During his public career, however, Jefferson continually expressed
concern about what he felt were deliberate lies manfactured by news
writers. In his draft of a Virginia Constitution written in 1783 and
his correspondence with Madison on a federal Bill of Rights in 1788,
he stated that printers should be held legally responsible for false
statements of fact. Soon he combined his concerns about personal
libel and false facts into a single formula. Discussing the federal Bill
of Rights in 1789, he suggested a fairly broad area of restriction by
saying that the people should have a right "to publish any thing but
false facts affecting injuriously the life, liberty, property, or reputation of others or affecting the peace of the confederacy with foreign
nations." Yet, in the same year, he sketched out a charter of rights
for France which included a provision that printers should "be
liable to legal prosecution for printing and publishing false facts injurious to the party prosecuting: but they shall be under no other
restraint." Jefferson's most refined statement of his position came in
his "Notes for a Constitution" written about 1794: "Printing presses
shall be free except as to false facts published maliciously either to
injure the reputation of another, whether followed by pecuniary
damages or not, or to expose him to the punishment of the law."[38]

During the Sedition Act controversy and when he was president,
Jefferson made known his contempt for seditious libel prosecutions
as well as his acceptance of legal actions taken by individuals in response to defamation. His Kentucky Resolutions declared that the
First Amendment prevented the federal government from making
laws against the press, that the Sedition Act was therefore "void, and
of no force," and that it was up to the states to determine how far
press licentiousness could be abridged without lessening press freedom. "While a full range is proper for actions by individuals, either
public or private, for slanders affecting them," he explained to his
attorney general in 1802, "I would wish much to see the experiment
tried of getting along without public prosecutions for *libels*."[39]

Jefferson did write to Governor Thomas McKean of Pennsylvania
in 1803 to say that he thought "a few prosecutions" would have a
"wholesome effect in restoring the integrity of the presses" in his
state, but he presumably meant the prosecution of personal libel
cases by individuals. The states, he told Abigail Adams in 1804, had
the exclusive authority over freedom of the press. "They have ac-

cordingly, all of them, made provisions for punishing slander," he said, "which those who have time and inclination, resort to for the vindication of their characters." The truth of allegations, he added, should be a defense. Jefferson made a similar pronouncement in his second inaugural address in which he said that public servants should use state laws against falsehood and defamation, but that public duties made greater demands on their time. Jefferson became increasingly frustrated with the performance of the press during his presidency and yet did not abandon his belief that the press was to keep government honest and to be honest itself. He stopped the prosecutions and punishments being carried out under the Sedition Act when he took office and later ordered—somewhat tardily—an end to a series of seditious libel prosecutions attempted by Connecticut Republicans.[40]

Jefferson's doctrine on press freedom offered a comparatively simple solution to a complex problem, but the courts of the states were not easily cleansed of political chicanery or old precedents. Confusion over standards for libel continued well into the twentieth century. One of the reasons was a prosecution Jefferson never took notice of, a seditious libel case tried in 1803. The defendant was Harry Croswell, an obscure Federalist editor in Hudson, New York, who was indicted by a grand jury for stating that the president had paid a journalist to defame Washington and Adams. The use of truth as a defense became the central issue. Croswell's lawyers, who spoke favorably about the Sedition Act, admitted that truth might not be a justification in private libels, but they said it could be given in evidence where the charge was a "public libel, or a libel on government, attacked in the person of its highest officer." Not allowing truth as a defense, they argued, would be repugnant to a republican government where the people are sovereign.[41]

Convicted after being denied an opportunity to use truth as a defense, Croswell took his case to the New York Supreme Court where he was represented by Alexander Hamilton. Having supported the Sedition Act and criminal libel trials, Hamilton did not take the position that such prosecutions had no place in American law. Instead, he advanced standards which were compatible with the Sedition Act, a law which, he told the court, did not deserve the scorn it had received. "The Liberty of the Press consists, in my idea," he said in his argument, "in publishing the truth, from good motives and for justifiable ends, though it reflect on government, on magistrates, or individuals." He also expressed admiration for Lord Mansfield as a "truly great man," but said that juries should be allowed to judge intent as well as law and facts.[42]

Hamilton lost the appeal, but his superficially libertarian stance—one which still accepted the idea governments could be defamed—impressed others. The New York legislature quickly passed a statute on criminal libel which allowed juries to determine the law and fact and defendants to plead truth published with good motives and for justifiable ends. The supposed safeguards—which made truth dependent on motives and ends—were eventually incorporated into the state constitution. A number of other states followed the lead of New York and placed similar language in their statutes and constitutions.[43]

In the nineteenth and twentieth centuries, state courts gradually became less satisfied with standards which required that statements about persons in government be strictly true. Increasing numbers of judges began to accept the position that even false statements about public officials should be protected if they were made without malice and with reason for believing that they were true. Other courts, however, recognized a privilege for opinions based on facts, but not a protection for facts that were not strictly true. Finally, in 1964, the United States Supreme Court sought to resolve the matter in the case of *New York Times v. Sullivan.* Repeatedly quoting the reactions of Jefferson and Madison to the Sedition Act of 1798, the Court stressed the importance of robust and open political debate. Public officials should be prohibited from recovering damages for a defamatory falsehood related to their official conduct, the opinion said, unless they could prove the statement was made with " 'actual malice'—that is, with knowledge that it was false or with reckless disregard of whether it was false or not."[44]

The *New York Times* decision came in a civil libel case. Eight months later the U.S. Supreme Court held in *Garrison v. Louisiana,* a case involving criticism of judges' conduct, that its *Times* rule would also apply to criminal libel prosecutions. Noting that such prosecutions had all but disappeared, the Court observed that they were based on obsolete notions about personal defamation provoking individuals to a breach of the peace. The opinion rejected the Hamiltonian qualifications on truth as a defense where public affairs were discussed and said that constitutional protections applied to any statements—personal or otherwise—touching on an official's fit-ness for office. Although three concurring opinions argued for an even wider freedom for the press in treating public matters, the Court concluded that it had taken a position which would safeguard the nation's paramount interest in the people having a free flow of information about their servants in government.[45] The *New York Times* and *Garrison* rulings thus set a national standard consistent with centuries of development in libertarian press theory.

PART THREE

The Ideology in Practice: The Case of Franklin and His Partners

VI

The Colonial Journalist:
Good Humour'd Unless Provok'd

In the summer of 1798, at the height of the Sedition Act frenzy, Samuel Smith, a Republican congressman from Maryland, cut out a newspaper article and mailed it to Vice President Thomas Jefferson. The article accused Jefferson of having recently been *"closeted"* with several people, including the editor of the Philadelphia *Aurora,* Benjamin Franklin Bache, who was then awaiting trial for seditious libel. Noting that his movements were watched by his political opponents, Jefferson wrote to Smith that Bache, the country's most militant Republican journalist, was a man of ability and of principles favorable to liberty and the American form of government. "Mr. Bache has another claim on my respect," Jefferson added, "as being the grandson of Dr. Franklin, the greatest man & ornament of the age and country in which he lived."[1]

Jefferson frequently used hyperbole, but his assessment of Benjamin Franklin, who had been dead for eight years, was a reasonable one. In addition to his many contributions to science, literature, and everyday life, Franklin was a prominent participant in virtually all of the major American political developments of his time. He, along with Jefferson, stood at the pinnacle of the American Enlightenment. During their public careers, however, both Franklin and Jefferson were denounced in print as being weak, devious, immoral, and incompetent. Neither ultimately wished to see personal attacks go unpunished, but both believed that free expression, whatever its difficulties, was essential for maintaining a free and uncorrupted government.

Jefferson and Franklin, both poor speakers, relied heavily on their superb writing to account for their actions and explain their ideas. Both indulged in righteous anger but generally avoided purely scurrilous remarks about individual political opponents. Still, their approaches to political communication differed. Jefferson, although he understood the power of the press and declared that it would be the "engine" in his party's drive for power in 1800, confined himself almost exclusively to the relatively aloof activities of producing public documents and private letters. Franklin, on the other hand, was a printer by trade and not above the tasks and risks of competitive journalism. His writing ability, he observed in his autobiography, was "of great Use to me in the Course of my Life, and was a principle Means of my Advancement."[2]

Franklin, along with his relatives and business associates who were printers, pursued vigorous journalism at an early point in the development of the American press. They also demonstrated that libertarian press theory could be easier to defend in principle than to put into practice. They found that assertive journalism enraged powerful individuals and that personal libel flowed all too readily from the pens of writers. Efforts to promulgate Enlightenment ideals could lapse into mere propaganda and personality contests. Yet early American journalism operated at a level of sagaciousness and intensity that made it all but impossible to restrain.

I

Benjamin Franklin had an early introduction to disputes over freedom of expression. Raised in Boston, where defamation suits and licensing controversies had already been occurring for decades before his birth in 1706, he was able to witness repeated attempts to suppress the opinions of church and government factions. One of the pieces he read in his youth was *A Looking Glass for the Times* which was written in 1676 by his grandfather, Peter Folger, to castigate the Massachusetts Puritans for persecuting religious sects. Folger, who was a Baptist living on the island of Nantucket, congratulated himself in the work for not being a libeller, but admitted his surprise that his polemic had been able to "pass the Press." Folger's plea for tolerance impressed his grandson as having been "written with a good deal of Decent Plainness & manly Freedom."[3] Anxious to develop his own skill as a writer, Franklin managed to achieve a clear, self-confident prose style during his youth, but found that decency was difficult to maintain and that strong opinions were not always appreciated.

At the age of twelve, Benjamin Franklin had both a "Bookish Inclination" and a "Hankering for the Sea," as he recalled in his memoirs. His Puritan father, Josiah, who had already lost one son at sea, did not want him to become a sailor. He took Benjamin on walks through Boston to observe tradesmen at work and to find an occupation that would keep an intellectually curious boy on dry land. Benjamin was at length apprenticed to his twenty-one-year-old brother James, a printer who had recently returned from his own apprenticeship in England. Benjamin quickly demonstrated proficiency in the work, but the two older Franklins were soon at odds in advising him about writing. James encouraged him to write news ballads for the two of them to print. Hawking the first one in the streets, Benjamin was proud to see that copies sold well. Josiah, who was giving his son suggestions on style, nevertheless ridiculed the verses and warned him that poets were generally beggars. Franklin, who regarded his father as a man of sound judgment, then began to practice writing prose with the *Spectator* as his model. He was, he later remembered, "extremely ambitious" to become "a tolerable English Writer."[4]

James Franklin, meanwhile, was using a brash, entrepreneurial spirit he had acquired in England to compete with Boston's five other printers. In 1719 he helped postmaster William Brooker start the *Boston Gazette,* the second continuously published newspaper in Boston and the second in the American colonies. A new postmaster, Philip Musgrave, took over the newspaper in 1720 and chose another printer, Samuel Kneeland. Undaunted by this turn of events, Franklin started his own newspaper, the *New-England Courant,* in 1721. In addition to titillating its readers with stories of crime and sex, the *Courant* accused Musgrave of being inept and dishonest as postmaster. The paper also spewed forth abuse of local Puritan clergymen—Increase and Cotton Mather in particular—for advocating inoculation during an outbreak of smallpox. While charging the ministers with recklessly encouraging a dangerous medical procedure, the *Courant*'s writers depicted Musgrave as a "Butter-headed Churl" who stole money from letters and made himself an "Intolerable Grievance which the People Groan under." A policy statement in the second issue of the paper had promised that nothing would be

published reflecting on the clergy or government or lacking in "Decency or good Manners." The next item, however, was a piece of
black humor on "A Project for reducing the Eastern Indians by
Inoculation."[5]

A writer in Boston's oldest newspaper, the *News-Letter,* found the
Courant "full freighted with Nonsence, Unmannerliness, Railery,
Prophaneness, Immorality, Arrogancy, Calumnies, Lyes, Contradic-
tions, and what not, all tending to Quarrels and Divisions, and to
Debauch and Corrupt the Minds and Manners of New England."
Using a reference to an outlawed group of devil worshippers in
England, a defender of the ministers used Musgrave's *Gazette* to
portray Franklin's correspondents as "the *Hell-Fire Club* of *Boston.*"
In an announcement in the *Gazette,* Rev. Increase Mather warned
the public not to read the "Wicked Paper" and lamented the absence
of effective restraints. "I can well remember when the Civil Govern-
ment could have taken an effectual Course to suppress such a *Cursed
Libel!*" he fumed.[6]

James Franklin could remain serene in the face of such outbursts
because the government appeared incapable of controlling the press
as Mather had so bluntly suggested. Licensing, a formality largely
disregarded by Boston printers for years, no longer seemed a threat.
On March 15, 1721, Governor Samuel Shute reminded the General
Court that the king had given him authority to license publications
and asked the legislators for a law to use against "Factious & Scandalous papers." The House, which cared little for the governor or
his prerogatives, refused to comply, citing the "innumerable inconveniencies and dangerous Circumstances this People might Labour
under in a little time."[7]

The Council, which agreed with the governor on the need for a
press law, was meanwhile finding it foolish to depend on the courts.
In February the Council had ordered the attorney general to prosecute bookseller Benjamin Gray for publishing a pamphlet on currency problems in the colony. Acting in contempt of the Council,
Gray advertised that he sold "all" recent pamphlets and in May a
grand jury refused to indict him. During the episode James Franklin
printed and Gray sold Daniel Defoe's *News From the Moon,* a masterful burlesque of public officials attempting to punish their critics.[8]

After he started publishing the *New-England Courant* later in
1721, Franklin had the opportunity to spell out some of the principles of libertarian press theory. He calmly dismissed complaints
about his newspaper's editorial content, saying that he practiced a

lawful trade and that he and his correspondents had a right to speak out in self-defense. "And the Law of Nature, not only *allows,* but *obliges* every Man to defend himself against his Enemies, how great and good soever they may appear," he declared. For good measure, he reprinted recently published essays by Trenchard and Gordon's Cato on freedom of expression and on the need for the people to jealously guard their liberties. Cato defined libel as writing that hurt particular persons, without doing good to the public, and stated that governments were instituted for the people. The exposing of public misdeeds, Cato told the readers of the *Courant,* could never be a libel.[9]

Although he printed little in favor of the *Courant*'s adversaries, Franklin continually maintained that he was an impartial editor who was simply "publishing the different Opinions of Men." This, he insisted, was the only reasonable policy. "Even Errors made publick, and afterwards publickly expos'd," he wrote, "less endanger the Constitution of Church or State, than when they are (without Opposition) industriously propagated in private Conversation." In an essay on the proper role of an editor, one of his contributors, a Mr. Gardner, praised Franklin for his courage and impartiality and told him that no newspaper publisher could please everyone. "Indeed the whole managery of such an Affair, requires the greatest Prudence imaginable," he said. "A Man had need exercise as much Caution, as if he were to fall between the perilous Rocks of Scilly and the fatal Quick-sands of Carabdis, that so he may keep the middle Channel between all Parties, and only press either Side to pursue the publick Interest, at least preferrably to their private Prospects."[10]

James Franklin thus set out to be a champion of free expression and of the people's interests and as long as he crusaded against smallpox inoculation, he had a safe issue. When the epidemic erupted in the summer of 1721, the Massachusetts House, Boston's town selectmen, and all but one of the city's physicians had gone on record opposing the practice. As half of the city's 12,000 residents contracted the disease and more than 800 died, Franklin cheerfully reported his subscription gains. He warned the Mathers, who were busy condemning the paper, that he could say of the *Courant* and himself what a Connecticut trader once said of his onions: *"The more they are curs'd, the more they will grow."* Rumors being spread that the government was about to suppress the paper, Franklin observed, only brought in new customers with "an Itch after the Novelty of the Subject that should cause such a Report."[11]

The editor's only serious bout with remorse came when he printed a story by John Checkley, a militant Anglican who was one of the *Courant*'s initial contributors. Checkley charged that one of the writers defending the ministers, Reverend Thomas Walter, a nephew of Cotton Mather, was inspired by rum and entertained in the bed of "two Sisters, of not the best Reputation in the World." After a scolding from his own pastors, Franklin announced he would accept no more of Checkley's articles and promised to publish in the future only pieces that were "innocently Diverting" and "free from malicious Reflections." Franklin's resolution did not last long, however. In subsequent months, as the smallpox epidemic took its toll and finally ended early in 1722, Franklin published essays recalling the ministers' participation in the Salem witchcraft trials and employing vicious wit to depict the Mathers as deranged hypocrites. Cotton Mather confronted James Franklin in the street at one point and lectured him on the consequences of serving the Devil. Franklin reported the incident in the *Courant* and stated that he was acting only as an impartial printer and was inviting pieces written with "Freedom, Sense and Moderation."[12]

II

Benjamin Franklin imbibed the spirit of the *Courant* writers and in 1722 became one of its contributors. From April through October, the sixteen-year-old apprentice published fourteen comic and often bitingly satirical letters on Harvard, hoop-petticoats, funeral elegies, drunkenness, and other topics. Signing his essays with the pen name "Silence Dogood" and placing them under the door of the printing house at night, he had the satisfaction of hearing the Hell-Fire Club praise the pieces without knowing who wrote them. When he revealed his authorship, the *Courant*'s writers expressed their admiration. In the second Dogood letter, Benjamin followed the paper's editorial slant by proclaiming himself "a mortal Enemy to arbitrary Government & unlimited Power" and saying that he had a natural inclination and ability for criticizing others. "I speak this by Way of Warning to all such whose Offences shall come under my Cognizance," he told his readers, "for I never intend to wrap my Talent in a Napkin." Franklin did not plan to be always severe, however. He was, he explained, "good-humour'd" unless "first provok'd."[13]

Franklin did proceed in a jocular tone until a serious provocation actually occurred in the summer of 1722. At the time of the colony's spring elections, the *Courant* had needled particular candidates for attempting to intimidate or improperly influence voters. James Franklin had also published a pointed but anonymous pamphlet advising the public to elect representatives who could remain uncorrupted, revive the economy, and support freedom of the press against misguided efforts by some members of the Council to restrict it. Such impertinence did not go unnoticed. When, in June, a *Courant* news item sarcastically announced that the Massachusetts government was ready to dispatch a ship to pursue a band of pirates "sometime this Month, if Wind and Weather permit," the Council summoned James Franklin to its chambers. The editor, as he later admitted, acted with "Indiscretion & Indecency" before the legislators, and both houses agreed to imprison him until the end of the session for breach of legislative privilege. Benjamin Franklin was also questioned, but, as he recalled in his autobiography, "did not give them any Satisfaction." While the older Franklin was confined, the Council took note of the *Courant*'s insults "boldly Reflecting" on the government, churches, and college and voted to place the publication under the censorship of the secretary of the province. The House, which had its own conflicts with the Council and with Governor Shute's administration, rejected the measure.[14]

During the month that James Franklin was in jail, his younger brother took charge of the *Courant*. Benjamin wrote in his memoirs that he "resented a good deal" the legislature's action and "made bold to give our Rulers some Rubs." Benjamin began cautiously, however, by inventing a cool, urbane, and curiously revealing persona for himself as editor. "Janus" described himself as a lover of truth who sought desirable knowledge and avoided extremes in conversation and behavior. "I converse with all sorts of Persons," Franklin wrote, "and know how to adapt my Discourse to the Company I am in, be it Serious, Comical, or anything else; for I can screw my self into as many Shapes as there are different Opinions amongst Men." Observing that he often joked and that some of his female companions considered him a fool, a sharp fellow, or a wag, the maturing Franklin stated that he had arrived at "such a firm and equal Temper of mind" that he could hear good and bad opinions about himself and value or despise them as he pleased.[15]

Janus, who purported to "appear in the Town towards the Dusk of the Evening, to make Observations," was perhaps too mysterious and self-conscious a version of Addison and Steele's Mr. Spectator to be an immediate success in Boston. To deal with the legislators and others the *Courant* had angered, Franklin reverted to his Silence Dogood pseudonym and issued a policy statement saying the *Courant* did not attempt to please everyone and would look with "Pity and Contempt" on those who reproached it while it promoted virtue and worthy actions. Mrs. Dogood used a lengthy quotation from Trenchard and Gordon's Cato to respond to the jailing of the *Courant*'s publisher. Cato contended that officials were only trustees of the people and that freedom of expression was essential to free government. The only limit on this liberty, Cato said, was where one individual injured the right of another. Dogood's next essay roundly condemned hypocrisy in religion and government. James Franklin appreciated his brother's efforts, but Benjamin found that others—apparently including his father—"began to consider me in an unfavourable Light, as a young Genius that had a Turn for Libelling and Satyr."[16]

Once James Franklin was released, he took his case to his readers. He published statements pointing out that he had been denied due process of law and questioning the authority of a provincial government to imitate Parliament by using breach of legislative privilege. He also printed a poem supposedly *"Thrust into the Grate by an unknown Hand"* which decried his paper as seditious and defamatory and complained that the *Courant* was "prais'd and priz'd by some above the Bible." In response, James Franklin claimed he never published anything to affront the government, but he then asked if it was "a greater Crime in some Men to discover a Fault, than for others to commit it." Franklin brought his arguments to a conclusion in September with a long, front-page poem parodying his appearance before the Council and ridiculing its members for their reaction to honest criticism. "Some Crime . . . You are afraid should thus be shown," the verse said, "And to your injur'd Country known."[17]

A second confrontation with the legislature occurred when the *Courant* of January 14, 1723, carried a slashing essay on Puritan pretentiousness as well as brusque letters advising the House on how to conduct itself in its relations with the governor. Citing the paper's habit of mocking religion and affronting the government, both houses of the legislature voted to forbid James Franklin to publish the *Courant* without the prior approval of the secretary of the province. Franklin disregarded the order—which passed the House by only one vote—and placed in his next issue a psalm from the Bible which began:[18]

O Thou whose Justice reigns on high,
And makes th' Oppressor cease,
Behold how envious Sinners try
To vex and break my Peace!
The Sons of Violence and Lies
Join to devour me, Lord;
But as my hourly Dangers rise
My Refuge is thy Word.

The Council issued an order for his arrest, but the undersheriff reported back the same day that he had been unable to find Franklin during a "Diligent Search." The *Courant,* however, continued to appear and to convey its indignation. In the first *Courant* published while the printer was in hiding, Franklin was given a ludicrous set of rules on how to be "pleasant and agreeable" and was wryly cautioned that he should neither condemn any persons nor risk damnation by resisting rulers who governed by divine right. He was also told to pay particular attention to Boston's emerging political machine—those "Men of Power and Influence" who were "scoffingly call'd, *The CANVAS CLUB."* Letters in the following issue noted that Franklin had broken no law and was being punished without an opportunity to defend himself. One of the correspondents addressed Judge Samuel Sewall, a member of the Council, and reminded the public of his role in the Salem witchcraft trials. "If this *Printer* has transgress'd any Law," the writer said, "he ought to have been presented by a Grand Jury, and a fair Tryal brought on." In Philadelphia, Andrew Bradford's *American Weekly Mercury* commented that the Massachusetts legislators appeared to be "oppressors and bigots."[19]

When James Franklin reappeared in early February, he was required to post a one-year, £100 bond, and his case was scheduled for grand jury action. Acting on the advice of his Hell-Fire Club, the editor took the precaution of changing the name of the printer of the *Courant* to Benjamin Franklin, so that he would not be guilty of further infractions of the legislature's order that James Franklin not print the paper without permission. The younger brother, who considered the change of name a "very flimsy Scheme," was accordingly released from his apprenticeship, but was required to sign new, secret indentures. The nominal editor then proceeded to announce that his brother had quit the paper and that Janus, a man of good temper and sound judgment, had taken over. "No generous and impartial Person then can blame the present Undertaking, which is designed purely for the Diversion and Merriment of the Reader," Benjamin wrote. "Pieces of Pleasancy and Mirth have a secret Charm in them to allay the Heats and Tumors of our Spirits, and to make a Man forget his restless Resentments." In the same issue was a notice concerning advertisements which stated that the circulation of the *Courant* was "far greater" than its competitors and that it was "more generally read by a vast Number of Borrowers."[20]

For several months, the *Courant* did confine itself to witty essays and poems addressed to Janus. Not until the week that the grand jury was to decide on Franklin's case did the paper make another play for public support. Three of the four pages of the issue of May 6, 1723, were devoted to a letter from "PHILO-DICAIOS" which defended the printer. The correspondent objected to the wording of the legislature's order and showed how the procedures used against Franklin had not allowed him due process of law. He then offered a hypothetical dialogue between a barrister and a juryman on the subject of whether a bishop who complained about instances of judicial misconduct should be indicted on the charge of having uttered false and scandalous words about government and the administration of justice. The juryman stated flatly that he would pronounce the bishop not guilty and that the words in themselves were "not Criminal, nor reflecting on any particulars." The barrister agreed and remarked that the situation was like that of the Spanish Inquisition when Protestants were dressed in garments painted with devils. Innocent men should not be condemned, the barrister said, "for Words or Matters harmless in themselves, and possibly very well intended, but only rendered *Criminal* by being thus hideously dressed up, and wrested with some far-fetch'd, forced and odious Construction."[21]

The next issue of the *New-England Courant* was able to report that the grand jury had refused to indict James Franklin for violating the legislature's order. Franklin did not bother to comment on his victory, but did insert a news item from a London paper which he thought would be "entertaining" for his readers. Appearing with a Boston dateline, the story gave an account of the legislative proceedings against Franklin and said that the author of the *Courant* was believed to be a member of the "diabolical Society" known as the Hell-Fire Club.[22]

III

While employed at his brother's printing house, Benjamin Franklin learned the advantages of being able to manipulate appearances, to maintain composure, and to argue shrewdly and boldly in journalistic confrontations. Schooled in radical Whig doctrine, he spent his free hours reading works of logic, deism, and philosophy. Through his reading he became a "real Doubter" in religion and a vegetarian. He also began to use the Socratic method "continually" and "grew very artful & expert in drawing People even of superior Knowledge into Concessions the Consequences of which they did not foresee, entangling them in Difficulties out of which they could not extricate themselves. . . ."[23]

Franklin's quickly developing talents and intellectual positions served him well enough as Silence Dogood and Janus, but at the same time he saw his relationship with his master and others deteriorate. James Franklin, who concluded that Benjamin's successes had made him vain, sometimes struck his younger brother for being insolent. With only a covert apprenticeship agreement holding him, Benjamin made up his mind to go to another printer, but neither his father nor his brother would let him. After considering that he had made himself "a little obnoxious, to the governing Party" and had been "pointed at with Horror by good People, as an Infidel or Atheist," Benjamin decided to run away from Boston, where he thought he would be likely to get into "Scrapes" like the "arbitrary Proceedings" against his brother. He sold some of his books for money and boarded a ship for New York, the nearest city with a printer. Not finding a job there, he went on to Philadelphia, where he found work in the printing shop of Samuel Keimer. In the September 30, 1723, issue of the *New-England Courant,* an advertisement said: "James Franklin, Printer in Queen Street, wants a likely lad for an Apprentice."[24]

James Franklin published the *Courant* for three more years, but without further success. He continued to print droll essays and verse and to identify Janus as the editor and Benjamin Franklin as the printer. The amount of original material declined, however, and the number of advertisements was never satisfactory. From time to time the paper reported on press freedom issues as they arose in England and America, and letters occasionally made economic or political comments, but correspondents often settled into protracted literary and religious bickering. Although Janus at one point asked the participants in a religious debate to "suspend their red hot Zeal," Franklin sometimes allowed the tone of the *Courant* to sink to mere invective. Still presenting himself as an innocent, impartial printer, he professed a casual attitude toward personal defamation, something he had promised to avoid during the inoculation controversy. Detraction should be heeded if true, Franklin said, and could be ignored if it was not. "As no man is accounted guilty in the Law till he is Found so upon Tryal," he maintained, "so all Reports are to be look'd upon as false, till they are prov'd otherwise."[25]

Facing depressed economic conditions in Boston, James Franklin discontinued the *Courant* in 1726 and prepared to leave for Newport, Rhode Island, a city half the size of Boston, but without any printer. Before leaving Boston, Franklin composed and published a verse pamphlet titled *The Life and Death of Old Father Janus, The Vile Author of the Late Wicked Courant.* He explained in the poem that he might have been considered a "Public Pest" and a "thriftless Fool," but had felt the necessity of pleading for truth, justice, liberty, and common sense even if the paper's "pois'nous Arrows" made enemies. "With your own Rules your Practice interfer'd," he admitted to himself. At the end, he wrote:[26]

> Thus, vext with Fleas, the *Fox* to save his Blood,
> Contrives Deliv'rance from some neighb'ring Flood:
> Softly he sails from Shore, then gently dives,
> And on a Woolly Ark, the rav'nous Vermin leaves.

With its relatively high degree of freedom, Rhode Island had long served as a refuge from Puritan theocracy. After arriving in Newport, James Franklin celebrated the liberty of his new home in a poem on the ghost of Samuel Gorton, a Rhode Island religious and political radical who had been banished from Massachusetts ninety years before. He also printed the colony laws, religious tracts, and his own "Poor Robin" almanacs, a publication of lively and sometimes coarse humor which took a facetious approach to astrology and served as a model for his brother's "Poor Richard." As Poor Robin, Franklin spoke out against partisanship and damage to personal reputation:[27]

> The Faults of my friend I'd scorn to expose,
> And detest private Scandal, tho' cast on my Foes. . . .
> No Man's Person I hate, tho' his Conduct I blame.
> I can censure a Vice without stabbing a Name.
> To no Party I'm Slave; in no Squabble I join,
> Nor damn the Opinion that differs from mine.

The subject of attacks on private character also came up in the *Rhode-Island Gazette,* another forum for wit and occasional political commentary which Franklin published for eight months beginning on September 27, 1732. Correspondents in the first issues of the short-lived paper repeatedly disavowed any patience with the defamation of individual reputations. One recommended that Franklin provide plain discussions of the "true Principles of Liberty" and reject both *"Personal Scandal"* and the "insipid Affectation of fine Writing and Politeness, that has made some Folks so ridiculous." Accordingly, in a poem in a subsequent issue, "Will Rusty" lamented:[28]

> HE that to *Wit* has no pretence,
> May lawfully make use of *Sense:*
> Yet *Sense* offends as much as Wit,
> If any Mark it chance to hit. . . .

A week after Will Rusty's performance, Franklin apologized for publishing a newspaper that was too often *"dull and flat"* and blamed his health and the newness of the undertaking. "Self Interest, which is at the Bottom of most of the Actions of Life (altho' gilded over with other Pretences) prompted me to exceed my Brother News-writers in every Point," he said of his efforts to start the paper. He said he still intended to "soar a little higher" and *"lay open the Malignity and Folly of several Practices that are very Prevalent."*[29]

A notice in the *Gazette* of January 11, 1733, asking for more punctual payments and more subscriptions apparently went unheeded, however, and the paper was discontinued by the end of May. Benjamin Franklin, who was becoming established as a printer in Philadelphia, visited Newport in the autumn and had a "cordial and affectionate" meeting with his brother. "He was fast declining in his Health," Benjamin wrote in his memoirs, "and requested of me that in case of his Death which he apprehended not far distant, I would take home his Son, then but 10 Years of Age, and bring him up to the Printing Business." James Franklin died on his thirty-eighth birthday, February 4, 1735. His widow, Ann, and their two daughters continued to operate the press. His son, James Franklin, Jr., after completing an apprenticeship with his uncle in Philadelphia, returned to Rhode Island where in 1758 he founded the *Newport Mercury,* which he published until his death in 1762. Samuel Hall, a printer who married one of Ann Franklin's daughters and received financial help from Benjamin Franklin, took over the *Mercury* and eventually became one of the most notable patriot editors of the American Revolution.[30]

VII

The Enlightened Printer:
Virtue and Vituperation

In his autobiography, Benjamin Franklin recalled how the Quakers of Pennsylvania were periodically embarrassed by their highly publicized pacifism and went along with subterfuges invented to allow them to contribute to defense preparations. He observed that he found much more prudent the conduct of a sect of German Baptists—the "Dunkers"—who refused to print any declaration of their faith for fear that they would feel bound to it and would be unwilling to receive further light from God. Franklin remarked that such modesty was perhaps unique in the history of religion since other sects supposed themselves to be in possession of all truth and thought that those who differed were just so much in the wrong. "Like a Man travelling in foggy Weather," Franklin wrote, "Those at some distance before him on the Road he sees wrapt up in the Fog, as well as those behind him, and also the People in the Fields on each side; but neer him all appears clear—Tho' in truth he is as much in the Fog as any of them."[1]

The mature Franklin often commented on the futility of theological debate and subscribed to only a minimum set of religious beliefs, at the same time stressing the importance of moral conduct. He found the doctrines of his father's Puritan faith either doubtful or unintelligible and yet seemed to appreciate the emphasis on independent, upright behavior. While serving as his brother's apprentice, he read in the evenings and spent his Sundays studying books instead of going to church. He was moved by the benevolent spirit of Defoe's *Essay on Projects* and Cotton Mather's *Essays to Do Good.* His reading of Locke, Shaftesbury, and Collins turned him toward deism. In 1725, while living in London where he had gone to buy printing equipment for himself, he wrote his first pamphlet, *A Dissertation on Liberty and Necessity, Pleasure and Pain.* This "little metaphysical Piece," as he later described it, "concluded that nothing could possibly be wrong in the World, & that Vice and Virtue were empty Distinctions." The prominent London printer who employed him, Samuel Palmer, found the pamphlet "abominable" and argued with him about it. Contemplating some of his own personal failings and mistreatment he had received from several other freethinkers he knew, Franklin soon made up his mind that although his necessitarian logic "might be true," it "was not very useful." He grew convinced, he stated in his memoirs, that good behavior was by nature beneficial and that *"Truth, Sincerity & Integrity"* were of the utmost importance in achieving happiness in life. "I had therefore a tolerable Character to begin the World with," he wrote. "I valued it properly & determin'd to preserve it." Deciding that his pamphlet had an "ill Tendency," he burned all but one of the remaining copies.[2]

Accordingly, Franklin returned to the course he had taken as Silence Dogood, that of a self-proclaimed "Enemy to Vice, and a Friend to Vertue," but he did so with a heightened moral sensibility. While sailing back to Pennsylvania at the age of twenty, he composed a plan of future conduct intended to correct a life which had been "a confused variety of different scenes." After listing resolutions on frugality, truthfulness, and industry, he put down a final one which stated his intention "to speak ill of no man whatever, not even in a matter of truth." Once in Philadelphia, where he again went to work for Samuel Keimer, Franklin began to put his plan into effect. He developed his personal "Articles of Belief and Acts of Religion," a private liturgy which prayed for help in "eschewing Vice and embracing Virtue," and mentioned in particular the faults of "Calumny and Detraction." He also started a "Project of arriving at moral Perfection" in which he studiously compared his daily actions to a list of thirteen virtues that included silence, justice, moderation, tranquility and humility.[3]

Franklin wanted to publish his self-help scheme in a book. He waited, however, until the age of seventy-eight to include it in the second part of his memoirs, where he wrote that he had fallen far short of perfection in his life but had reaped benefits from the self-discipline he did achieve. In the third part of his autobiography,

written at the age of eighty-two, Franklin said that he had not found
time to form a "Society of tne *Free and Easy*" to promote his method.
He nevertheless considered his annual *Poor Richard's Almanack* "a
proper Vehicle for conveying Instruction among the common People" and so filled it "with Proverbial Sentences, chiefly such as inculcated Industry and Frugality, as the Means of procuring Wealth
and thereby securing Virtue, it being more difficult for a Man in
Want to act always honestly." He informed the readers of his memoirs that he considered his *Pennsylvania Gazette* "another Means of
communicating Instruction, & in that View frequently reprinted in it
Extracts from the Spectator and other moral Writers." In editing his
newspaper, he wrote, he "carefully excluded all Libelling and Personal Abuse."[4]

Imbued with the righteous zeal of the Puritan, the republican spirit
of the radical Whig, and the idealism of the Enlightenment philosopher, Benjamin Franklin brought to his journalism a potent and pervading sense of the utility and justice of virtuous behavior. In an essay on literary style that he wrote for the *Pennsylvania Gazette* in
1733, he offered it as a maxim *"That no Piece can properly be called
good, and well written, which is void of any Tendency to benefit the
Reader, either by improving his Virtue or his Knowledge."*[5] Franklin's desire to succeed in business, however, could interfere with his
resolutions. As an ambitious young printer, he occasionally let practical considerations override his high-minded commitments.

At times, Franklin also violated what he recognized in his autobiography as his habit of expressing himself "in Terms of modest
Diffidence," a tactic which he believed made it easier for him to
carry his points. "And as the chief Ends of Conversation are to *inform*, or to be *informed*, to *please* or to *persuade*," he wrote, "I wish
well meaning sensible Men would not lessen their Power of doing
Good by a Positive assuming Manner that seldom fails to disgust,
tends to create Opposition, and to defeat every one of those Purposes for which Speech was given us." George Whitefield, he noted
in the memoirs, was an effective preacher, but lost much of his following when he opened himself to severe criticism by publishing unguarded and erroneous opinions. In his autobiography, Franklin reported that he did not enter into published debate on his own electrical
experiments, preferring instead to let the papers "shift for themselves."[6]

Franklin did not demand thorough consistency of himself. He was
ultimately more committed to achievable goals than to any abstract

notions of dispassionate journalistic goodness or prudence. As a result, he could prove to be a shrewd opponent. "So convenient a thing it is to be a *reasonable Creature,*" he wrote in his memoirs, "since it enables one to find or make a Reason for every thing one has a mind to do."[7] Franklin always found reasons to justify his own freedom of expression and sometimes to oppose the same right for others.

I

When Benjamin Franklin arrived in Philadelphia for the first time, he was a hungry, disheveled, runaway apprentice with "a Dutch Dollar and about a Shilling in Copper" in his pocket. He went to work in the shop of Samuel Keimer, a printer he described as "an odd Fish, ignorant of common Life, fond of rudely opposing receiv'd Opinions, slovenly to extream dirtiness, enthusiastic in some Points of Religion, and a little Knavish withal." Keimer made use of Franklin's trade skills and business sense, but, finding his wages too high, quarrelled with him and eventually drove him to establish his own printing office in 1728. Once in business for himself, Franklin generally followed advice he had received from his father on how to conduct himself in Pennsylvania. According to Franklin's autobiography, Josiah had warned him to behave respectfully, to obtain the general esteem, and to be industrious and prudent with money. Franklin also noted that his father, who had witnessed his forays as Silence Dogood, told him to "avoid lampooning & libelling to which he thought I had too much Inclination."[8] The young printer's propensity for disparagement, a bent he had resolved to control, could nevertheless come through when he was faced with journalistic competition or controversy.

Soon after setting up his shop in 1728, Franklin quietly laid plans to begin a newspaper to rival Andrew Bradford's *American Weekly Mercury*. Although the *Mercury* was a profitable publication, Franklin thought it was "a paltry thing, wretchedly manag'd, no way entertaining." Keimer, hearing of Franklin's scheme, decided to preempt him by announcing that he would start publishing a newspaper he called the *Universal Instructor in all Arts and Sciences; and Pennsylvania Gazette*. Keimer issued a handbill denouncing the *Mercury* as "not only a Reproach to the Province, but such a Scandal to the very Name of Printing, that it may, for its unparallel'd Blunders and Incorrectness, be truly stiled *Nonsence in Folio,* instead of a Serviceable News-Paper." When the *Universal Instructor* appeared, it invited criticism by offering columns full of articles from Chambers' *Cyclopaedia* in alphabetical order. When an entry on abortion appeared, Franklin, using female pseudonyms, wrote letters to Bradford's *Mercury* expressing mock horror and suggesting that Keimer give up his publication if he had nothing better to print.[9]

Franklin then began a series of "Busy-Body" essays in the *Mercury* in which he promised to serve impartially as a "Terror to Evil-Doers" and to inculcate the principles of virtue. "But as I know the Mob hate Instruction, and the Generality would never read beyond the first Line of my Lectures, if they were usually fill'd with nothing but wholesome Precepts and Advice," he wrote, "I must therefore sometimes humour them in their own Way." Busy-Body derided Keimer as "Cretico," the "sowre Philosopher," and advised him to let his "musty Authors" gather dust on his shelves. An "N.B."—perhaps added by Bradford—claimed that Cretico lived in another province, but Keimer recognized himself and published an essay on the "Odiousness of *Defamation* and *Scandal*." Following the kind of logic his brother James had used, Franklin defended himself in the *Mercury* by asserting that a man could not claim a right to his good name if he had acted to forfeit it, that only the public could judge reputations, and that when bad characters were drawn, they could only fit those who deserved them. Busy-Body agreed that attacking a person's reputation was detestable, but said that it was ridiculous for anyone to complain about being defamed when the statement was true. Keimer's *Instructor* then dropped its benign, intellectual tone and belittled Franklin as "Not one but every Ape's Epitome." Keimer pointed to his writing style as an imitation of the *Spectator* and pictured him as never more than "an Understrapper to a Press" until promoted by "that Prodigy of Wit, Mr. B———d."[10]

Bradford evidently welcomed Busy-Body's carping at Keimer, but he did not appreciate Franklin's taking advantage of his absence from Philadelphia on business to submit an addition to the eighth Busy-Body essay. Berating and challenging the province's opponents of paper money, the new section was printed in the March 27, 1729, issue of the *Mercury*. But "upon a seasonable Admonition of a certain Gentleman," Bradford explained a week later, the printer's wife, Dorcas, "took up all the Copies she could find, and suppress'd the Printing of it." A second edition of the March 27 paper appeared without the addition. In the ninth Busy-Body, Joseph Breintnall, a friend of Franklin's who took over the series, remarked that he could not see in the piece "any Thing so criminal as to deserve the Flames" and observed that the few copies which did reach the public were "more generally read than it would if there had been no such Endeavours used to destroy it."[11]

With the *Mercury* openly protecting the opponents of a popular point of view and Keimer vainly thrashing in anger, Franklin had cleverly maneuvered his two competitors into embarrassing positions during the first months of 1729. Still, he was not prepared to start his own newspaper. In September, during the fall election campaigns, Breintnall's Busy-Body advocated rotation in office as a means of preserving liberty. Seeing this as an insult, the provincial Council jailed Bradford briefly, but the next issue of the *Mercury* carried an even bolder political essay from Busy-Body. At the same time, Keimer, who had not managed to obtain more than ninety subscribers, was being pressed by creditors. Franklin, although struggling financially himself, was able to buy Keimer's *Instructor* for a "Trifle," as he put it in his memoirs. Franklin took over with the issue of October 2, 1729, and quickly revamped the publication. He shortened its name to the *Pennsylvania Gazette,* dropped the encyclopedia articles, and pledged to make the paper "as agreeable and useful an Entertainment as the Nature of the Thing will allow." He soon attracted what he later called "the principal People" as subscribers with articles and commentary on the governor's salary dispute then in progress in Massachusetts. Praising the stand taken by that colony's assembly, he editorialized that the American sons of the mother country were retaining "that ardent Spirit of Liberty, and that undaunted Courage in the Defence of it, which has in every Age so gloriously distinguished BRITONS and ENGLISHMEN from all the Rest of Mankind."[12]

Yet, while popular politics and lively prose proved to be as successful for the *Gazette* as it had been for the *Courant,* Bradford remained in a commanding position since he was the local postmaster and did the province's public printing. Shortly after his addition to the eighth Busy-Body was suppressed, Franklin noticed that Bradford, who he thought had become "rich & easy" in his trade despite being "very illiterate," had printed an address of the Assembly to Governor Patrick Gordon in a "coarse blundering manner." Franklin reprinted the address in a correct and more elegant form, distributed a copy to each member, and, with the help of friends he was gaining in the legislature, was given the Assembly's official printing beginning in 1730. Franklin also wrote and published an anonymous pamphlet on paper currency which was, he said in his memoirs, "well receiv'd by the common People in general; but the Rich Men dislik'd it." His arguments, he believed, helped to promote paper money legislation and hence the profitable work of printing new currency. "This was another Advantage gain'd by my being able to write," he noted in his autobiography.[13]

Bradford's hold on the postmastership appeared to be a more difficult problem. The public, Franklin later observed, assumed that the postmaster's paper had better access to news and was able to offer better distribution of advertisements. Franklin did, in fact, have to bribe postriders to carry his *Gazette,* since Bradford had ordered them not to take it. Resenting the postmaster's action, Franklin taunted Bradford from time to time in the *Gazette* for publishing stale or inaccurate news. An opportunity for revenge came in 1737, when Bradford was removed from his position as postmaster for negligent accounting and Franklin was named to replace him. Satisfied at seeing that his competitor's paper "declin'd proportionably," Franklin did not retaliate. The deputy postmaster general, however, lost patience with Bradford's continuing failure to settle his final accounts and in 1739 directed Franklin to sue Bradford and to deny free postage to the *Mercury.* Franklin did not prevent his riders from accepting the *Mercury* on their own, a practice which either he or they apparently stopped in 1740. At that time the two printers were publishing mutual recriminations and ridicule as they engaged in an acrimonious race to publish America's first magazine. The prospective editor of Bradford's *American Magazine,* John Webbe, publicly accused Franklin of having declared at one time that his forbearance on the delivery of the paper was intended to keep Bradford *"under his Thumb."* Webbe, the lawyer Franklin had chosen to sue Bradford, speculated in the *Mercury* that the publisher of the *Gazette* might have given the deputy postmaster general, Alexander Spotswood, false information leading to Bradford's dismissal. Franklin did not take notice of the charges, but when he was later appointed joint deputy postmaster general for North America, he tried to eliminate some of the uncertainties publishers faced by setting uniform requirements for the distribution of newspapers through the mails.[14]

Franklin's sometimes harsh treatment of competing printers conflicted not only with his private resolutions, but also with the spirit of the "Junto," a club for discussion, service, and self-improvement which he set up early in his Philadelphia career. Members were required to respect each other, to acknowledge that no one should be harmed in name or otherwise for "mere speculative opinions," and to love mankind in general and truth for truth's sake. Small fines were imposed for indulging in positive opinions or direct contradiction. As part of a list of "Standing Queries" composed by Franklin for use at each meeting, members were asked whether their reputations had fallen under any attack and whether they had defended the character of fellow members.[15]

The Junto lasted for several decades and helped Franklin refine and execute his many civic projects from the Library Company to the Academy and College of Pennsylvania. As he later explained in his autobiography, he also customarily used pamphlets and his newspaper to promote philanthropic ventures such as the Pennsylvania Hospital. The physician who had first proposed the hospital, Franklin recalled in his memoirs, did not find enough support but at length "came to me, with the Compliment that he found there was no such thing as carrying a public Spirited Project through, without my being concern'd in it."[16]

II

The position Franklin achieved in Pennsylvania, was indeed one of importance and influence, and was augmented by his being appointed clerk of the Assembly in 1736. He nevertheless realized that his personal reputation was not beyond reproach. At about the time of his marriage to Deborah Read in 1730, when Franklin was indulging in what he later described as frequent "Intrigues with low Women," he fathered his illegitimate son William, who later became royal governor of New Jersey. Franklin's raising of William presumably engendered gossip, which in turn may have caused him to publish several essays on detraction in the *Gazette*. In 1732, Franklin printed a piece which depicted the free use of "CENSURE" as an effective restraint on the practices of powerful, "ill-designing" persons as well as on the actions of private men. In the next issue, however, Franklin decided to make a point about personal scandal. Writing as Alice Addertongue, he offered to help the paper double its list of subscribers with news accounts of "4 *Knavish Tricks,* 2 crackt M——n—ds, 5 *Cu—ld-ms,* 3 *drub'd Wives,* and 4 *Henpeck'd Husbands.*" Responding as editor, Franklin said he would not publish the articles since they were "in Reality no News at all." Ten months later he wrote a paragraph for his paper which compared persons who enjoyed malicious talk to flies that feasted on sores.

In 1734 the *Gazette* published two essays from the *Spectator* on maligning character. Franklin introduced one by suggesting that those who thought that all around them was tainted were probably doing so "from some Corruption in themselves, and possibly from their own Stench." The *Spectator* essay which followed stated that attacks on the names of particular persons were "the Marks of an evil Mind, and highly criminal in themselves" even when supported with the appearance of truth.[17]

Franklin's responses to published attacks on his character were either to remain silent or to issue detailed denials. He did not respond, for instance, when a *Mercury* correspondent caustically addressed him as "pious Mr. F———" and "religious Mr. F———" and castigated him for "running violently on the side of the Populace" in Pennsylvania's chancery court controversy of 1735 and 1736. On the other hand, he published affidavits and a point-by-point rebuttal in 1738 when the *Mercury* brought his name into a murder case involving a young man who was killed during a mock initiation into the Masons.[18]

Franklin did not always insist on taking himself seriously, however. As he began to gain positions of responsibility and to become Philadelphia's leading citizen, he demonstrated an ability to use light humor to preempt competitors and disarm opponents. Having made an embarrassing mistake in setting the type for a news story in 1730, for example, he produced an entertaining piece on printers' errors for the next issue, in which he managed to contrast his usual correctness with Bradford's repeated slips. A year later he described himself in a *Gazette* news item as a "Boo bee" for accidentally stepping into a barrel of tar on a Philadelphia wharf.[19]

Franklin's self-effacing wit was nowhere more evident than in his annual Poor Richard almanac. Although he pictured himself as a humble dispenser of common wisdom, Poor Richard was a shrewd observer of human foibles and was skillful at cleverly ridiculing rival almanac makers. Franklin sold nearly ten thousand of his almanacs a year, but his most masterful triumphs in humor came in his hoaxes. The hoaxes typically exposed religious or political injustice, but at least one had an autobiographical dimension. In the widely reprinted "Speech of Miss Polly Baker," Franklin advanced the positive side of illegitimate children being born to conscientious women and suggested that laws punishing such women were unreasonable. Not surprisingly, the Polly Baker piece did not appear in the *Gazette* and

Franklin did not make his authorship known until thirty years after its earliest known appearance in London's *General Advertiser* in 1747.[20]

Convinced that practicing right behavior was more important than having particular spiritual beliefs, Franklin readily mixed humor with religious topics in the early years of his business. He also expressed a willingness to publish all sides of theological debates. In July of 1730 he reprinted a series of *London Journal* essays on primitive Christianity which, Franklin then reported, "some worthy and learned Men" among the *Gazette*'s readers thought contained "sundry false, heretical and pernicious Positions and Opinions." He offered to print answers refuting the arguments "without putting the Authors to one Penny Charge." No answers appeared, but Franklin soon concocted his "Witch Trial at Mount Holly" hoax, a news item which portrayed fearful residents of New Jersey testing accused witches by placing them individually on one side of a scale and the Bible on the other. They found, the *Gazette* said, "the Lumps of Mortality severally were too heavy for Moses and all the Prophets and Apostles."[21]

A more difficult situation developed in 1731 when a bit of levity directed at Anglican clergymen appeared in an advertising handbill he printed. This, Franklin noted in the *Gazette,* caused "Several good Men" to announce a boycott of his business and to accuse him of "abundant Malice" against religion. Franklin countered with an "Apology for Printers" in the *Gazette* which listed twenty-two logical reasons for his conduct. He insisted that he had refused to print many things that might "promote Immorality" or include "Party or Personal Reflections," but that very little would be published if those who practiced his trade would try to please everyone. "Printers are educated in the Belief," he wrote, "that when Men differ in Opinion, both Sides ought equally to have the Advantage of being heard by the Publick: and that when Truth and Error have fair Play, the former is always an overmatch for the latter." Franklin thus used the notion of impartiality and the marketplace of ideas concept, but did not actually say that he believed in either. In fact, a few sentences later he blamed the "viciously and corruptly educated" public for making it attractive for printers to publish "vicious or silly things not worth reading." Franklin repeated the marketplace argument—saying only that it was "a Principle among Printers"—in 1740 when he was accused of being biased toward evangelist George Whitefield. On two separate occasions in that year, Franklin introduced letters against

Whitefield supporters by admitting that they contained personal invective, but excusing the letters as vindications of conduct that had been publicly discussed and as proof of his impartiality as a printer.[22]

Although Franklin from time to time published satiric pieces consistent with his religious outlook, he did not demonstrate how far he was willing to go in religious brawling until Samuel Hemphill, a young clergyman, was tried for heterodoxy by the Presbyterian Synod in 1735. Appreciating the stress on virtue rather than doctrine in Hemphill's sermons, Franklin joined an animated journalistic debate on the case by writing three pamphlets in his defense. Franklin's views were summarized shortly before the trial in the *Gazette* where he wrote that "it little becomes poor fallible Man to be positive and dogmatical in his Opinions" and that a "virtuous heretick shall be saved before a wicked Christian." The printer had no hope of preventing Hemphill's suspension, however, once it was revealed that his sermons were plagiarized. He used the last of his three pamphlets to refer to the clergyman's opponents as *"Rev. Asses"* and to show how they were seeking "to stamp an Appearance of Sanctity upon Animosity, false Zeal, Injustice, Fraud, Oppression."[23]

After the Hemphill debacle and the heated outpourings of the Great Awakening, Franklin's combativeness on religious issues diminished. "Talking against Religion is unchaining a Tyger," Poor Richard remarked in 1751, "The Beast let loose may worry his Deliverer." Franklin observed in his 1757 almanac that making statements against another's faith resulted in anger "which no Man of common Sense would hazard for a lively Expression; much less a Person of good Breeding, who should make it his chief Aim to be well with all." In the same year he advised a correspondent to burn a manuscript questioning religious doctrine so as to avoid making enemies and undermining the basis of whatever morality most people had. "He that spits against the Wind," Franklin cautioned, "spits in his own Face."[24]

In the decades before the American Revolution, Franklin started to emphasize tolerance and the utility of public worship. He wrote his "Parable against Persecution" and worked on a revision of the Lord's Prayer and an abridgment of the Anglican Book of Common Prayer. Although he rarely attended church services, Franklin solemnly admonished his daughter, Sarah, "Go constantly to Church whoever preaches." He later wrote in his memoirs that he remembered an innkeeper named Brown who had written a travesty of the Bible which "set many of the Facts in a very ridiculous Light, &

might have hurt weak minds if his Work had been publish'd." Franklin stated in his autobiography that even the worst faith "had some good Effects" and that he had decided "to avoid all Discourse that might tend to lessen the good Opinion another might have of his own Religion."[25]

By the end of his life, Franklin was ready to forget that he had ever written anything questioning or ridiculing conventional beliefs. In a letter sent to Ezra Stiles a month before he died in 1790, he said he expected to enjoy an afterlife and that the morals and religion of Jesus were "the best the World ever saw or is likely to see." He admitted having doubts about the divinity of Christ, but remarked that he would soon know the answer to the question without having "to busy myself with it now." He said that he saw no harm in its being believed if it made Christ's teachings more respected and better observed. "I have ever let others enjoy their religious Sentiments," he claimed, "without reflecting on them for those that appeared to me unsupportable and even absurd."[26]

III

Benjamin Franklin became less interested in taking up religious matters as he gradually grew more entangled in politics and political journalism. He identified himself with the cause of individual freedom as early as the time of his apprenticeship in Boston, but like other radical Whigs, he assumed that virtuous, public-spirited libertarians remained independent of corrupting party politics. In his "OBSERVATIONS on my reading History in Library," a paper he wrote in 1731 and included in his autobiography fifty-seven years later, he blamed self-interested parties for the world's confusion and put forth the idea of an international "Party for Virtue." Accordingly, the *Pennsylvania Gazette* was not as deeply involved in political altercations as it might have been. Franklin wrote in his memoirs that he refused to print libels in his paper because he had contracted with his subscribers "to furnish them with what might be either useful or entertaining." He explained that he did not want responsibility for spreading defamation, but that he would "print the Piece separately if desired, and the Author might have as many Copies as he pleased to distribute himself." A newspaper, he said, was not like a stagecoach where everyone who paid was entitled to a place.[27]

A portion of his pamphlet publishing was controversial. In 1730, for instance, he printed *The Mystery of Iniquity,* an anti-slavery tract

written by Ralph Sandiford, a Quaker merchant. Although threatened with prosecution, Sandiford distributed free copies of his work.
"And whereas some Persons would not apply for his Books *Gratis*,"
Franklin drolly announced in the *Gazette,* "the Printer having Leave
from the Author, has them ready for Sale at 12d. a-piece, at the *New
Printing-Office* near the *Market.*" A decade later Franklin was willing
to publish a speech given to a grand jury by Samuel Chew, chief justice of the Lower Counties, to justify self-defense in war. As a result
of the speech, Chew was expelled from the Society of Friends. Franklin published a second speech to the grand jury on the same subject,
but when Chew tried to use the pages of the *Gazette* to protest his
expulsion, he found Franklin less cooperative. Noting that one Philadelphia printer "postpon'd it for prudential Considerations" and the
other simply declined it, the chief justice finally published his protest
in a supplement to the *New-York Post-Boy,* the paper edited by
Franklin's partner, James Parker. In his introduction to the protest,
Chew vented his suspicion that the Quaker party had managed to
suppress its publication in Philadelphia.[28]

Franklin's reluctance to make his paper a vehicle of partisan diatribes in Pennsylvania politics received its severest test in 1733 when
Bradford's *Mercury* began a long campaign to villify Andrew Hamilton, the powerful speaker of the Assembly. Hamilton had helped
Franklin obtain the public printing and had been a member of the
Council before he realigned himself against the governor and proprietors. The *Mercury,* which tended to favor proprietary interests, used
personal invective and innuendo against Hamilton and justified its
actions on the basis of freedom of the press. The *Gazette,* while its
publisher was on a seven-week trip to Boston and Newport, responded
with a lengthy poem against party malice and a mocking treatment of
Bradford and one of his contributors. When Franklin returned, he
announced in the *Gazette* of October 18 that anything published during his absence which could be "construed into Personal Reflection"
was printed without his knowledge or approval and had to be "ascribed
to the Inadvertance of those who carried on his Business."[29]

Franklin's attempt to calm matters did not accomplish its purpose.
The *Mercury* of the same date carried a letter which characterized
Hamilton as a dangerous demagogue who dominated the province's
loan office, courts, and Assembly. A month later the *Gazette* responded in the form of an interview with a relaxed, rational Hamilton who presented himself as a protector of the common man's rights.

This "Half-hour's Conversation with a Friend" began with Franklin observing that the anonymous accuser provided no particulars. Even some of Hamilton's enemies did not believe all the charges, Franklin added, but they did agree with "that old Saying, *Throw Dirt enough, and some will stick.*" Hamilton defended himself masterfully. "The People of Pennsylvania are too wise to be cheated into an Opinion that a Man is to be destroy'd because his Superiors and a few of their Creatures apprehend that he stands in their Way," he remarked. "No, they know a Man can lose neither Life, Liberty, nor Estate, but by the Judgment of twelve Freemen of Pennsylvania."[30]

Two years later, Hamilton successfully appealed to a New York jury at the seditious libel trial of John Peter Zenger. Franklin sold James Alexander's *Narrative* of the case published in 1736 and was the first to publish Alexander's lengthy defense of Hamilton's arguments at the trial in 1737. The essay, which appeared in four parts, used the marketplace of ideas concept, identified freedom of expression as a natural right and pillar of free government, and chronicled the suppressive tactics of despots who "constantly encouraged prosecutions for words."[31]

The *Mercury* sourly denied that Hamilton had any right to pose as a sincere friend of freedom of the press and continued to criticize him. In 1741, however, both newspapers printed Franklin's glowing obituary of Hamilton in which he was remembered as "no Friend to Power" and as "the Poor Man's Friend." The obituary made a point of identifying Hamilton with "the Cause of Liberty" and attempted to excuse his "free Manner of treating Religious Subjects" and lack of adherence to any particular church. "He lived not without Enemies," Franklin wrote. "For, as he was himself open and honest, he took pains to unmask the Hypocrite, and boldly censured the Knave, without regard to Station or Profession."[32]

In the following decades, Franklin, in effect, assumed Hamilton's role as Pennsylvania's foremost popular politician, and the number of his original contributions to Philadelphia journalism declined. Some of the audacious pieces the *Gazette* might have published in the 1740s—such as Samuel Chew's protest and the "Speech of Miss Polly Baker"—appeared elsewhere. At least one composition, a humorous essay on choosing a mistress, which Franklin wrote in the form of a letter in 1745, remained discreetly hidden from the public. As an increasingly important figure in government and philanthropy, and as a man gaining a reputation for his inventions and experiments with electricity, Franklin was acquiring stature in the world and was less inclined to take unnecessary risks. "Little Strokes," Poor Richard observed at this time, "Fell great Oaks."[33]

Still, journalistic writing continued to serve Franklin and his causes when he chose to employ it. His 1747 pamphlet *Plain Truth* had, as his memoirs related, "a sudden & surprizing Effect" in promoting defense measures after French and Spanish privateers appeared near the mouth of the Delaware, and the Quaker-dominated Assembly failed to take action. Practicing the arts of propaganda, he warned Pennsylvanians that they would be "subject to the wanton and unbridled Rage, Rapine and Lust, of *Negroes, Molattoes,* and others, the vilest and most abandoned of Mankind." The way to preserve peace, he wrote, was to be prepared for war. Franklin's views ran counter to the doctrine of the Quakers as well as the opinion of their opponents, the "Gentlemen's Party," but he dealt carefully with the two groups. "Tho' *Plain Truth* bore somewhat hard on both Parties here," he reported to Cadwallader Colden in New York, "it has had the Happiness not to give much Offence to either." Franklin let it be known that he would print all essays on the subject without charge, either in the *Gazette* or in pamphlets delivered with the paper.[34]

Although pressured to resign as clerk of the Assembly, Franklin was convinced that a majority of Quakers objected only to offensive combat, and so he did not hesitate to devote himself to the business of organizing, financing, equipping, and training volunteers. Franklin's popularity rose as fear over the French and Spanish ships gradually abated. Seeing his activities as a threat to his proprietary prerogatives, however, Thomas Penn wrote to the provincial secretary, Richard Peters, to express his dread of Franklin as a "dangerous Man" with a "very uneasy Spirit" and perilous political doctrine. "However as he is a Sort of Tribune of the People, he must be treated with regard," Penn warned.[35]

In the midst of the crisis, Franklin turned over the daily affairs of his printing business to a new partner, David Hall, freeing himself for other endeavors. In 1748 he was elected to Philadelphia's Common Council and in 1751 he took a seat in the Pennsylvania Assembly where he was busily employed in drafting petitions, reports, and public documents. "And I conceived my becoming a Member would enlarge my Power of doing Good," Franklin later said of his election to the legislature. "I would not however insinuate that my Ambition was not flatter'd by all these Promotions. It certainly was." He stated that these were "spontaneous Testimonies of the public's good Opinion" of him and that he was elected and reelected for years without ever asking for a vote.[36]

As Franklin emerged as a leader in Pennsylvania politics, his reputation was also growing in other colonies. In 1753 he accepted honorary degrees from Harvard and Yale and an appointment as joint deputy postmaster for North America. In 1754 he concerned himself with the need for colonial cooperation in the face of French and Indian attacks on the frontier and played a principal role in the drafting of the Albany Plan of Union. He also created a political cartoon which was revived during the American Revolution—a dismembered snake, representing the colonies, with the motto "JOIN, or DIE."[37]

VIII

The Prerevolutionary Printer:
The Ideal of Impartiality

During his career as a provincial tradesman, Benjamin Franklin built a loosely structured network of fellow printers that spanned the colonies. Most of his associates had little of his ability for using journalistic artifice, and none attained anything close to his prestige, but several did hold local offices and the majority were capable publishers. They were typically his former employees and often became postmasters through his appointment. He shipped them Poor Richard almanacs and shop supplies and periodically advised them on financial and political matters. Some of his business relationships with printers were short-lived—such as those he established in attempts to start a German-language paper in Pennsylvania. Others—like his efforts to help his troublesome nephew Benjamin Mecom—involved intermittent attention to family duties. Franklin's principal partnerships were with Lewis and Peter Timothy in Charleston, James Parker in New York and New Haven, and David Hall in Philadelphia. As newspaper publishers, they, like Franklin, advocated libertarian press theory and despite apparent anti-authoritarian biases, promised impartiality in their editorial policies. They sometimes discouraged party diatribes and personal defamation, but even as they began to champion the American cause before the Revolutionary War, they remained attached to the ideal of an open press.[1]

I

Franklin's first attempt to set up another printer began in 1731 when he dispatched one of his journeymen, Thomas Whitmarsh, to South Carolina where the legislature was offering a bounty of £1000 to encourage the establishment of a press in the colony. Whitmarsh opened a shop and early in 1732 founded the *South-Carolina Gazette.* In verses Franklin later reprinted while defending Andrew Hamilton, Whitmarsh told the readers of his first issue that he detested personal scandal and that the paper would be neither "High Church, nor Low Church, nor Tory, nor Whig." The poem continued:

> To sift Truth from all Rubbish, I do what I can,
> And, God knows, if I err—I'm a fallible Man. . . .
> Where merit appears, tho' in Rags, I respect it,
> And plead Virtue's Cause, should the whole World reject it.
> Cool Reason I bow to, wheresoever 'tis found,
> And rejoice when sound Learning with Favour is crown'd.

Whitmarsh told potential contributors that party divisions were the "Bane of all Civil Society" and asked them, for the sake of unity in a colony where their numbers were small, to avoid controversies in matters of church and state. Religious and political disputes nevertheless appeared in the *Gazette,* and Whitmarsh, although he had obtained the colony's government printing, published the various sides and informed his readers that he was acting impartially. At one point he adapted and republished Franklin's "Apology for Printers."[2]

When Whitmarsh died unexpectedly in 1733, Franklin replaced him with another of his journeymen, Lewis Timothy. In his first issue of the *Gazette,* Timothy stated that only press restraints "just sufficient to prevent Men from writing either *Blasphemy* or *Treason*" could be justified in a free country. "*The Liberty of the Press,* is the most unlucky Scourge that can hang over the Heads of a *corrupt* and *wicked* Ministry," he wrote, "and when this essential Branch of our Liberties is either *attack'd, abridged,* or *taken away* from us, every Man without any Pretensions to the Spirit of Prophesy, may certainly predict *Slavery* and *Ruin* to his Fellow-Citizens."[3]

Both Lewis Timothy and his son Peter, who took over the paper at his father's death in 1738 and continued to publish it until the Revolution, made the *Gazette* a forum for clashing opinions. In order to justify the publication of controversial writings, the newspaper reprinted essays on press freedom, written by Cato and Hume. As a result of his willingness to print unpopular or controversial views, however, Peter Timothy became the target of several unsuccessful prosecutions. In one such instance in 1747, when an attempt was made to indict Timothy for printing sarcastic remarks about Governor James Glen's efforts to enforce Sunday laws, the members of the grand jury decided in favor of the paper, saying that liberty of the press was a right "so *justly contended* for by our Ancestors" which they hoped would be *"preserved to our latest Posterity."*[4]

Peter Timothy did, however, act cautiously when his contributors indulged in self-interested politics and personal libel. In order to put distance between himself and such writings, he sometimes required that party tirades and attacks on private character be paid for as advertisements. He nevertheless occasionally indulged in wry political commentary himself. After Governor Glen informed the legislature in 1748 that the colony had a "perfect good Understanding" with the Indian nations on the frontier and that there was not an enemy Indian within a thousand miles of Charleston, Timothy reported stories about Indians killing and carrying off South Carolinians. "There are People who say," the printer noted, "that the Distance from *Charles-Town* to the Places where our Enemy *Indians* have done those things, is somewhat *less* than a *Thousand Miles."* Responding later to an angry reader who threatened to cut off his ears for the remark, Timothy wrote in the *Gazette* that his fear of losing his ears had caused him to admit his mistake. The distance, the editor said, was actually one or two hundred miles rather than somewhat less than a thousand. Governor Glen promised to conduct an inquiry and warned that he would bring the writers and publishers to "condign Punishment" if the stories proved inaccurate. Timothy replied with a series of essays from *Cato's Letters* and elsewhere on freedom of the press and the need to expose bad administrations. In 1750 and again in 1751, grand juries refused to indict Timothy for printing a pamphlet critical of Glen's role in frontier affairs.[5]

James Parker, another Franklin employee who became a partner, took a similarly autonomous course of action in New York where he set up a press in 1742 and started printing the *New-York Weekly Post-Boy* in 1743. Continually buffeted by political and religious factions and cheated by a series of unscrupulous business associates, he kept up a morose correspondence with Franklin and helped him keep his American affairs in order until his death in 1770. "When Party-Spirit runs high, poor Printers are in a wretched Condition," Parker told the readers of the *Post-Boy* in 1752. He observed that members of his trade working under such circumstances should be "entirely independent" and that he had often declared his impartiality. Englishmen had a right to speak their sentiments, he insisted, and printers had to print for both sides or starve. "But if one Side only is to be served," he continued, "then adieu to that Liberty and Property, which are the Glory and Boast of *Britons,* and for which our Fore-fathers have so often sacrificed their Blood and Fortunes." Press freedom infuriated even its strongest defenders when they were criticized, he explained, but it was "one of the grand Bulwarks of English Liberty." Parker indicated, however, that he did not wish to be understood as having a completely open press. He said that honorable and patriotic persons despised false or abusive aspersions, and he concluded his statement by requesting that the authors of party letters not ask him to print anything unless they signed their names to it.[6]

Parker's remarks were apparently prompted by his having angered New York politicians several weeks earlier with the publication of complaints about corruption in public affairs. He provoked additional controversy in April, however, when he printed a deistic essay which was published from time to time in the early American press. Replying to a reader who protested the implications of the piece, Parker, who was a lay reader in an Episcopal church, stated that the Christian religion was too strong to be damaged by criticism and that its adversaries could be given a fair hearing. Not lacking enemies in New York politics, Parker was indicted for blasphemous libel. Parker issued a statement reasserting his impartiality and reminding those who were angry with him that they had made use of freedom of the press in the past and might need it again in the future. He also indicated that he no longer wished to accommodate writers who were unwilling to sign their pieces or be named later. Franklin interceded by writing to his friend and fellow scientist, Cadwallader Colden, an influential member of the governor's Council, to request his help in obtaining a *nolle prosequi.* Franklin described Parker as a "thorough Believer" and said that he promised not to give any more offense in religion or politics. He added that stopping the prosecution would best serve the cause of religion since the trial of the printer would only make the piece "1000 times more publick." Despite the fact that some of Parker's publications had reflected badly on his administration, Governor George Clinton issued a *nolle prosequi* and the case ended with the printer paying court costs and pledging to be more careful in the future.[7]

Parker may indeed have felt somewhat chastened by the attempted prosecution, but he was not ready to spurn contentious writers. Later in 1752 he started printing a weekly periodical, *The Independent Reflector,* for William Livingston, a lawyer who began his career in the office of James Alexander. The *Reflector* promoted itself as a nonpartisan publication which would be devoted to liberty and the exposure of corruption and which would not employ "personal Reflections" unless necessary to uncover "public Villainy." Livingston and several associates wrote essays critical of the conduct of New York officials and expounded radical Whig political doctrine, but they also published anticlerical sentiments and angry protests against plans to place the city's new college under Anglican control. Religious debate ensued in the city's newspapers, with Hugh Gaine's *Mercury* publishing only the Anglican side and Parker's paper allowing the *Reflector*'s pseudonymous supporters to answer. Parker began losing *Post-Boy* subscribers, however, and stopped accepting the letters he was offered on the subject. Livingston's friends were thus precluded from using either paper. One of them, William Smith, Jr., responded in the *Reflector* with a blazing essay on the press as a "great Means of Knowledge" and a "grand Security of civil Liberty." He said that secrecy was necessary to protect authors from the guilty public officials they criticized. The press could be used "with Impugnity" to reveal tyranny, he maintained, and should only be limited where it became a "Prejudice to the public Weal" by advocating slavish principles.[8]

In the next issue of the *Post-Boy,* Parker defended his decision. He said that he did not consider himself a competent judge of what ought to be suppressed and thought it his duty to print for all sides when it was possible to do so. He had found, however, that he was only printing one side and that "designing Persons" were trying to make the *Post-Boy* a party newspaper. He explained that he would not place any restraint on what he printed outside of his newspaper if "the Writer will either patronize it, or keep within the Bounds of Law and Justice." Parker then offered his definition of liberty of the press. "If a Man wrongs the community, every Member of that Community has a Right to complain," he wrote. "If the Complaint be false, the Law is open and the Remedy is easy; but if true, the best Remedy is to reform."[9]

All that remained for Livingston and his friends was to produce their own publications. Parker had insisted that the *Post-Boy* remain an impartial paper and had pointed out that false statements about a person in public life could be considered libel, but he announced his willingness to cooperate with them on separate ventures. They did use Parker's press for several more months, but their tactics turned toward levelling personal attacks. One of their efforts, a vitriolic periodical named *The Occasional Reverberator,* appeared only four times before Parker refused to continue it. When the *Reflector* showed signs of adopting a shrill and bitter tone and Parker was threatened with the loss of the public printing because of it, he decided to abandon the publication. The last issue, the fifty-second, appeared in November of 1753. The writers had told him that he could stop printing the *Reflector* if he should "sustain any considerable disadvantage by continuing it," but he failed to honor an agreement that he would print it until at least June of 1754. They then prevailed on another printer, Henry De Foreest, to publish a lengthy "Preface" to the *Independent Reflector.* The preface stated that the publication had been "most tyrannically suppressed" and blamed Parker for failing to print "unpalatable truths."[10]

Still smarting over the episode a year later, Parker placed an essay on the press as a "great Buckler against Oppression" in the *Post-Boy.* He then inserted a statement saying that his experience with Livingston and his associates had shown that articles "fomenting Divisions" in church and state were of no benefit to the public and were useless in a "Weekly Intelligencer." He pronounced himself willing to print such pieces in pamphlets and other forms and then quoted Voltaire's "Advice to a Journalist" which praised the practice of impartiality in editing a newspaper. "As far as lay in his Power, when personal Invective was not visible, he endeavoured to preserve the just *Liberty of the Press,"* Parker wrote of himself, "But must confess, that it has been sometimes his Unhappiness to be made a Tool to crafty designing Men, tho' never with a willing Mind."[11]

II

The ability of American printers to disassociate themselves from factional strife and remain independent declined after mid-century, but the ideal of impartiality in newspaper journalism did not die easily. With increasing competition in the trade, the pressures placed on the colonies by the French and Indian War, and the ideological confrontations of the American Revolution, printers were driven toward making political choices. Yet they often resisted wholesale changes in their conception of what liberty of the press meant. The intensity of debate and the demands on printers did not, for the most part, produce any startlingly new ideas about press freedom, but they did bring some fresh problems and adjusted interpretations.

While printers encountered difficulties with provincial authorities in a number of colonies during the French and Indian War, the conflicts were particularly acute in New York. In 1755 Lieutenant Governor James De Lancey ordered that no accounts of Braddock's defeat be published. Sir Charles Hardy, a new governor who arrived later in the year, found the colony's printers a mixture of "impudence and arrogance" and made known his desire to "crush" them. Parker, who printed several highly controversial pamphlets during the war, was brought before the Assembly in March of 1756 for publishing a letter in the *Post-Boy* charging that the legislature had failed to take adequate defense measures. Having already been voted guilty of contempt before he arrived, Parker provided a reluctant apology, but he and his partner William Weyman were held in custody for ten days.[12]

Parker nevertheless continued to uphold his commitment to press freedom. Later in 1756, a *Post-Boy* correspondent complained that writers were causing disunity in the colonies and expressed regret that there was no expedient to curb liberty of the press which did not infringe on English freedoms. "How common is it to see a Shoemaker, Taylor, or Barber, haranguing with a great deal of Warmth on the publick Affairs?" the writer asked. "He will condemn a General, Governor, or Province with as much Assurance as if he were of the Privy Council, and knew exactly wherein they had been faulty:— He gets his Knowledge from the News-Papers, and looks upon it undoubtedly true because it is printed." The letter argued that complaints in the press should be ignored. Expressing dismay that any Englishman could have such sentiments, Parker and Weyman noted that they had "seen and felt many oblique Strokes at the LIBERTY OF THE PRESS," but none like their correspondent's. They then offered a protracted essay quoting Cato and celebrating the role of the press in advancing learning, religion, and liberty.[13]

When stamp acts were approved in Massachusetts in 1755 and in New York in 1756 to raise money for military expenditures, Parker was one of the provincial printers who protested angrily. His campaign against the tax began in the *Post-Boy* with observations on the financial hardships it imposed on printers and culminated in a 1759 broadside asking "British Subjects and Lovers of Liberty" to consider his plight and raising the possibility that New York politicians had passed the measure to put him out of business. He concentrated most of his argument on the stamp act as an oppressive and discriminatory method of obtaining funds. "Some good Patriots were for dropping this Tax a Year ago," Parker said of a repeal motion in the Assembly, "and 'tis probable would have been joined by others sufficient to have effected it, had proper Information been given." An irritating and ineffective source of revenue, the tax was allowed to expire at the end of 1759.[14]

In Philadelphia, Benjamin Franklin's partner, David Hall, emphasized factual reporting and took a generally neutral direction in Pennsylvania politics. Hall did display pro-American and pro-British sentiments during the French and Indian War, but was initially, at least, content to remain an industrious and unobtrusive businessman. In the early years of the partnership, Franklin was in Philadelphia and able to handle any delicate situations that arose. In 1755, for instance, Governor Robert Hunter Morris ordered the firm not to print in the Assembly's *Votes* two letters he had received from England with instructions on war matters. Franklin put the order before the Assembly, received its answer that only the House could decide what belonged in its minutes, and informed the governor that he and Hall were obliged to obey the legislators as their "immediate Servants."[15]

Not all of Franklin and Hall's difficulties were resolved so easily. For most of 1755 the proprietor's governor and the Quaker-dominated Assembly were in a stalemate over issues related to defending the province and the House's insistence on taxing the Penns' proprietary estates. The result was political confusion in Philadelphia and near panic on the frontier. Frustrated with the conduct of both sides, Franklin tried to act as a mediator but soon turned against Morris and reluctantly assumed a clearly antiproprietary position in the Assembly. "We are all in Flames, as you will see by the Papers," he wrote to one correspondent in August. "Those who caress'd me a few Months since, are now endeavouring to defame me every where by every base Art," he added. "But it happens that I have the means of my full Defence and their effectual Defeat, in my Power, and shall use those means in due time." In Assembly messages and essays in the columns of the *Pennsylvania Gazette,* Franklin masterfully justified the actions he and his Quaker allies took in the legislature to engineer an end to the deadlock and the beginning of an effective military response to Indian raids.[16]

As Franklin took on more political responsibilities, however, he shifted toward a less libertarian stance on press freedom. The chief critic of Franklin and the Assembly was Rev. William Smith, provost of the College of Philadelphia and a truculent propagandist for proprietary interests. Smith entered the fray with *A Brief State of the Province of Pennsylvania,* a pamphlet published in London early in 1755. *A Brief State* charged that the Quakers were failing to protect the province and suggested a number of remedies including restrictions on the printing houses of their political allies, Pennsylvania's German population. Franklin, who served on an Assembly committee that referred to the publication as a "Libel," was one of those who felt the jabs of Smith's pen. Yet, at the end of 1755 when "Humphrey Scourge" published an antiproprietary pamphlet which, among other things, accused Smith of being a Jesuit in the pay of the French, the *Pennsylvania Gazette* carried a statement from the Friends' Monthly Meeting expressing abhorrence of Scourge's *Tit for Tat* as a "virulent, seditious and scandalous Libel." Responding to Quaker concerns a week later, the *Gazette* announced that it wanted "any Pieces of a healing Nature," but nothing containing personal reflections or promoting dissension.[17]

Franklin and Hall thus effectively removed the *Gazette* from the party turbulence that followed. Franklin did use the *Gazette* for a set of questions he composed to embarrass a militia association formed in opposition to a regiment he himself commanded, but the paper then denied his adversaries a chance to reply. The most striking and brutal exchanges during the spring of 1756 took place in William Bradford's *Pennsylvania Journal.* After "Humphry Scourge" denounced Smith for hoping to be named the Anglican bishop of America and Smith berated Franklin for military and political pretensions, a supporter of the Assembly branded Smith "a Minister of the infernal Prince of Darkness" and bemoaned the "Vomitings of this infamous Hireling" against Franklin. Smith, in turn, brought up the birth of Franklin's illegitimate son and said that his ambitions were "to imprint his own corrupt Notions of Government upon the Minds of the People" and to "level all *Distinctions.*"[18]

While Franklin was on a trip to New York in July, the Assembly lost patience with Smith and summoned him to answer for a piece he had published in a London newspaper earlier in the year. When Smith proved evasive and seemed ready to stand on a right not to testify against himself, the Assembly dropped the matter. The clergyman, however, replied with a pamphlet asserting his right to complain. When a member of the Assembly threatened the printer of the pamphlet, James Chattin, with being called before the House, Smith published a second edition to decry the incident as an attempt to interfere with the sacred liberties of the press.[19]

Early in 1757 Benjamin Franklin was appointed to serve as the Assembly's agent in London and to argue for taxation of the proprietary estates. After sailing to England and entering into negotiations with Thomas Penn, Franklin soon acquired a thorough contempt for him as a "low Jockey" in political matters. Angry at a lack of progress in resolving the Assembly's disputes with the Penns, he oversaw the publication of Richard Jackson's *An Historical Review of the Constitution and Government of Pensylvania,* a polemic which he thought would "probably be one of the first Acts of Hostility on our Side, as being necessary to prepare the Minds of the Publick; in which the Proprietors will be gibbeted up as they deserve, to rot and stink in the Nostrils of Posterity."[20]

Not long after Franklin arrived in London, however, the Assembly moved to punish one of its perennial critics, William Moore, by charging him with misconduct as a justice of the peace. The *Pennsylvania Gazette* printed the charges and Moore prepared a spirited reply which he asked David Hall to print in the paper. Apprehensive about the tone of the piece, Hall refused to publish it, but one of Moore's friends complained to him that he would be denying liberty of the press. Fearing that he would be labelled a partisan printer if he did not publish Moore's reply, Hall conferred with three members of the Assembly who agreed with him that he should publish the statement in order to avoid being accused of not maintaining a free and open press. Moore's address appeared in the *Gazette* and, at Smith's direction, was soon reprinted in a German-language newspaper, the *Philadelphische Zeitung.* Finding an opportunity to strike at two adversaries at once, the Assembly early in 1758 ordered the arrests of Smith and Moore for contempt. The reactionary provost struggled to impress his captors with impassioned rhetoric on freedom, but the House voted to confine him until he would give them the satisfaction of acknowledging his journalistic mistakes. Showing little regard for consistency, the Assembly made a point of commending the three members who advised Hall to print the address "for the due Care they had taken at the same time to guard against any Encroachment on so useful a Privilege as the Liberty of the Press."[21]

The charges against Moore were eventually dismissed by the governor, but Smith stubbornly fought the Assembly's action in the *Pennsylvania Journal* and in the *American Magazine,* which he edited, as a violation of due process and liberty of the press. Smith did some of his writing while in custody during the three months following his arrest. He was released when the Assembly adjourned in April, but was rearrested later in the year and imprisoned while the House was in session. Having appealed his case to the Privy Council, Smith fled in December to England where he was able to present himself as a defender of the British Empire and the Anglican Church.[22]

When reports of Smith's confinement reached London, Franklin had qualms about the behavior of his political allies. He wrote to compliment David Hall on having acted prudently, but he feared the Assembly members had gone too far. As their agent, however, he had little choice but to do his duty and help prepare an answer to Smith's petition to the Privy Council. Avoiding mention of the cases of James Franklin and James Parker, Franklin supplied his solicitor with several precedents for breach-of-legislative-privilege arrests by colonial legislatures. He also wrote a point-by-point rebuttal to Smith's petition and guided the lawyer in preparing a brief which concluded that the provost, "a common Scribbler of Libels and False Abusive papers, both against publick Bodies and private Persons," was taken into custody "merely for a Contempt" and would have been released simply "upon a bare submission."[23]

Realizing that Smith had powerful friends in England, Franklin was not optimistic about the outcome. In 1759 the Privy Council ruled that the publication was a libel the Assembly had a right to punish, but that Smith's rights had been violated since he had not defamed the legislature then in session and because he had been improperly denied a writ of habeas corpus. The decision did nothing to abate the feud between the two men. They continued to express disdain for each other as long as they lived. Franklin remarked, however, that he was resigned to having Smith as his adversary since it was "convenient to have at least one Enemy, who by his Readiness to revile one on all Occasions, may make one careful of one's Conduct."[24]

Franklin's enemies grew more numerous and more scornful after he returned from London frustrated with his inability to deal with the Penns and determined to use the press and his position in the Assembly to promote a change from proprietary to royal government in Pennsylvania. Franklin was caricatured as corrupt and ambitious in writings and cartoons, but he was slow to respond in kind. "I bore the personal Abuse of five scurrilous Pamphlets, and three Copperplate Prints, from the Proprietary Party, before I made the smallest Return," he told one correspondent in 1764, "and they begin to think they might continue to affront me with Impunity." Franklin's small "Return" was to suggest in a pamphlet that Thomas and Richard Penn be remembered with a monument inscription he composed describing them as dishonest and depraved tyrants who wanted to reduce the people of Pennsylvania to slavery. When Franklin sought reelection to the Assembly later in the year, an anonymous proprietary writer remembered the Penn inscription and published a blistering mock epitaph for Franklin which summarized allegations then circulating in Philadelphia—that he had taken credit for the scientific discoveries of others, begged and bought honorary degrees, insulted the "highest order of Men," attempted to overturn the government, received provincial funds for services he did not perform, and allowed a woman named Barbara, the mother of his illegitimate son, to starve and be shabbily buried.[25]

Franklin was defeated in the contest, but his party held its majority, and within a month he was chosen for a second time to represent the Assembly in England. Ten members of the Assembly who opposed the appointment printed a protest declaring their dislike for him, his political opinions, and his supposed mishandling of provincial funds during his first mission. In a signed pamphlet published the day he left for London in 1764, Franklin responded to the protest and scolded his accusers saying that such legislative protests should not encumber the minutes and should not be made vehicles of libel and personal malice. He remarked that his reputation was dearer to him than his life, but concluded by announcing that he forgave his enemies.[26]

William Smith, who also suffered a portion of the scurrility generated by the election campaign, reacted with a long, anonymous pamphlet which scathingly attacked Franklin as a liar and incendiary. One of a series of charges that Smith made was that Franklin had made a practice of filling the legislative minutes with his own messages and reports and then charged the Assembly large sums for printing them. Several of Franklin's friends published a statement in two Philadelphia newspapers which decried Smith's "false, malicious and scandalous Invectives" and insisted that the anonymous pamphleteer come forward and identify himself. The statement, signed by John Hughes, asked the writer to agree to give £5 to the Pennsylvania Hospital for every charge against Franklin he could not prove to the satisfaction of arbitrators. Hughes proposed to donate £10 for every accusation that could be substantiated. After an anonymous reply defended unsigned political attacks and derided the offer, Hughes lectured his opponent on the difference between personal libel and allowable discourse on public issues. "Has Politics necessarily any Connection with private Slander, or private Slander with Politics?" he demanded. "Decent *political* Papers are by no Means offensive to the Laws of your Country, tho' slanderous *personal* Writings are, as being manifestly destructive of the public Peace."[27]

III

Although Benjamin Franklin arrived in London in time to make arguments against the American Stamp Act, Parliament passed the measure with little significant opposition. In the colonies, Franklin's associates not only regarded the tax as unjust, but also recognized that it presented a threat to their livelihoods. David Hall and Peter Timothy put black borders on the issues of their papers that greeted the act and both reported on the protests that swept through the colonies. James Parker was, at the time, leasing his *New-York Post-Boy* to John Holt who took a radical editorial direction that brought him the support of the Sons of Liberty. Parker did, however, mail out bundles of the *Constitutional Courant,* an inflammatory anti-stamp paper which appeared only once and which was printed at Parker's New Jersey shop. The printer was a former employee, William Goddard, a Son of Liberty who had a press in Providence, Rhode Island. The *Courant* consisted of two essays that indignantly condemned the Stamp Act but took differing positions on the proper American response. One endorsed using force to demonstrate disapproval of the law and the other maintained that violence injured a good cause.[28]

The stands that Hall, Timothy, and Parker took were nevertheless not radical enough for many of their fellow colonists. Hall angered Philadelphians by failing to join other newspapers in printing fervent essays against the tax. Before the act took effect, Hall lost more than five hundred subscribers who resented his moderation and did not want to purchase stamped newspapers. Franklin advised him not to give up the *Gazette* and told him that he was acting prudently, since irate writings only hurt the American cause in England. Hall decided, however, that the best reply to his antagonists would be "to humour them in some Publications, as they seem to insist so much upon it." On October 31, the last day he could legally print without stamps, he announced that he was suspending the *Gazette* in order to deliberate on ways to elude "the Chains" forged by Parliament. Hall did continue to publish the *Gazette* without interruption, but he did not use his imprint for several months. In January, 1766, he joined his fellow printer William Bradford, a member of the Sons of Liberty, in raising a crowd that prevented a supply of stamped paper from being unloaded in the city. After Parliament passed the Townshend Acts a year later, Hall's *Gazette* took a radical turn and became a leading proponent of nonimportation, but it still remained open to writers on both sides of the issue.[29]

Peter Timothy expressed his disgust with the Stamp Act in his *Gazette* and took a role in mob activities, but announced that his paper would simply raise the price of subscriptions in order to pay the tax. Timothy changed his mind, however, and suspended the paper while the act was in force. Angry with his refusal to print without stamps or to engage in particularly violent opposition, Charleston radicals financed a printing shop and newspaper for Timothy's former apprentice, Charles Crouch. The result, Timothy wrote to Franklin, was that he found himself reduced from "the most *popular*" to "the most *unpopular* Man in the Province."[30]

Timothy soon regained his reputation, however, with strong support for the nonimportation movement and the relentless publication of news and opinion supporting the American cause. He nevertheless continued to insist that both sides of the dispute be heard. When, for instance, South Carolina's Commons House of Assembly rejected a petition against nonimportation without a reading in 1769 and other printers in Charleston refused to publish it, Timothy printed the document and added a statement of his own. He did not accept the arguments of the petition, he said, but had kept his press "*open to all Parties*" for thirty years without letting his interests compete with those of the public. Individual liberty and the preservation of the Constitution, Timothy told his readers, very often depended upon "*free* Access" to the press.[31]

Having leased the *Post-Boy* to John Holt before the Stamp Act, James Parker escaped having to make editorial decisions during the crisis. He did, however, keep Franklin informed on how the "fatal *Black-Act*" was threatening to ruin printers and was making the people "all running Mad." Parker, like Franklin, favored working peacefully for repeal. Still, he admitted that "sometimes the true Old English Spirit of Liberty" rose within him and that he was glad he was not printing in New York where "perhaps the Impetuosity of my Temper would have plunged me deep one way or the other." In 1766, after the Stamp Act was repealed, Holt's lease on Parker's

New York shop expired. Deeply in debt to Parker but having the support of local radicals, Holt started his own newspaper, the *New-York Journal,* on May 29 with the *Post-Boy*'s subscribers. He used the occasion to suggest to his readers that Parker was not a friend of liberty. Already under suspicion for having income from the post office and customs house (which Franklin had arranged and which he could not afford to give up), Parker hesitated to compete with a publication set up by the Sons of Liberty. They were, he reported to Franklin, "the Ruling Party" in New York and were forcing ship captains to deliver mail at a coffee house in violation of postal regulations. "It is surprizing to see the Influence they have," he added, "and the Dread every one is under of Opening their Mouths against them."[32]

After failing to receive a settlement from Holt, Parker resumed publication of the *Post-Boy* in October 1766. He began pursuing Holt through the courts and through the columns of the newspaper. Parker built his list of subscribers to four hundred before his publication of William Livingston's "American Whig" series brought in two hundred more in 1768. Livingston cost Parker seventy subscribers by attacking a proposal for an American episcopate, however, and Holt pirated the series for his own use. Although Parker joined Holt in publishing the Boston patriots' "Journal of Occurrences," distributed in 1768 and 1769, he took a moderate and impartial course overall. He made an effort to obtain an unbiased account of the Battle of Golden Hill and printed a cautious article on the Boston Massacre in 1770.[33]

IV

In Philadelphia, Franklin's political adversaries took advantage of his absence and asserted in the press, the Assembly, and elsewhere that Franklin had abetted the passage of the Stamp Act. His friends denied that he was involved. On the night of September 16–17, 1765, eight hundred supporters posted themselves on the streets to stop a mob that appeared ready to attack his house as well as the home of John Hughes who had been named stamp distributor on Franklin's recommendation. After repeal of the act, the *Pennsylvania Journal* obtained and published letters Hughes wrote to Franklin and the stamp commissioners in 1765 to complain about the public outcry against the tax and to state his wish to carry out his duties. Denying that the letters were authentic, Hughes immediately sued for libel. He asked for £1200 in damages but failed twice to appear in court, and the suit was dropped. William and Thomas Bradford, publishers of the paper, then triumphantly declared in the *Journal* that Americans should have "an honest and generous indignation against the wretch that would attempt to enslave his countrymen by restraints on the press." Freedom of the press preserved constitutional privileges, they wrote, and was an "unrestrained liberty" which every Englishman claimed. A week later they published "An ESSAY, Towards discovering the Authors and Promoters of the memorable STAMP ACT" which placed blame squarely on Franklin.[34]

Franklin took the *Journal's* aspersions calmly and wrote to his closest political ally in Pennsylvania, Joseph Galloway, that they had to console themselves with the knowledge that the accusations were not deserved. "Dirt thrown on a Mud-Wall may stick and incorporate," he said, quoting Poor Richard, "but it will not long adhere to polish'd Marble." Galloway, who had actively opposed the use of violence during the crisis and urged moderation in Pennsylvania's response, was less sanguine. He had assumed the leadership of the antiproprietary party after Franklin returned to London and wanted a newspaper willing to serve his cause exclusively. He was incensed by the proprietary party's use of the *Journal* and resented Hall's insistence on impartiality in the *Gazette*.[35]

Hall traced Galloway's "Malice and Ill-will" toward him to the week before the Assembly election of 1764 when Galloway had asked him to print an attack on John Dickinson, an opponent of the movement toward royal government in the province. Dickinson found out about the piece, asked to see it, and requested an opportunity to reply since the *Gazette* would not appear again before the election. He also warned Hall that if he were not allowed to see it, he would hold him responsible for the defamation. Hall asked Galloway to agree to let Dickinson look at the essay, but Galloway refused. Hall then informed Galloway that he did not think he could print his article. Galloway became angry and accused Hall of being partial. Hall replied that no man on Earth could make him print what he thought was wrong. Three years later Hall related the episode to William Strahan and told him that he only wanted the liberty to print for both sides, but that both parties insisted that he print only for them. "My press is now freely open," he said, "and shall be, and always should have been, if I had had my Will."[36]

Since Hall's independence did not please Galloway, he and Thomas Wharton, another Franklin partisan, formed a secret partnership to

finance a printing shop for William Goddard in Philadelphia. Goddard began publishing the *Pennsylvania Chronicle* early in 1767 and
for the first two months devoted the paper to defending Franklin's
conduct during the Stamp Act crisis and reprinting essays he wrote
at the time for London newspapers. In the third issue, Goddard
printed a piece signed "THE PUBLIC" which hailed the appearance
of a paper that would preserve press freedom and impartiality and
condone the use of anonymous writings. The essay stated that the
press was the bulwark of liberty and that corrupt ministers had attempted to destroy it "by wicked Subtilties, and tortured Construc-
tions" in the law or by "obstructing all the Avenues of Truth" through
"secret Agreements" " with printers. "THE PUBLIC" also explained
that it knew the difference "between private Slanders and personal
Scurrilities, and those Performances which discover the Diseases of
my political Constitution, and prescribe their remedies."[37]

Hall was upset at the arrival of a newspaper which claimed it was
more dedicated to freedom of the press than his own. Although his
partnership with Franklin had expired a year earlier and his relationship with Galloway was cool at best, he was particularly un-
nerved by seeing the *Chronicle* printed at one of Franklin's houses
and on one of his presses. He wrote Franklin to ask for an explanation and Franklin answered that the arrangement with Goddard had
been initiated without his knowledge or participation. Franklin had,
in fact, only learned of the agreement late in 1766, when his son
William wrote that he had let Goddard use the press because Hall
had become "a meer Snake in the Grass" who favored the proprietary party. Hall protested to William Strahan that he gave both parties equal access to his newspaper and that, if anything, he was biased
toward the Assembly cause and against proprietary politicians.[38]

Goddard, meanwhile, was beginning to anger Galloway's opponents.
In the seventh issue of his paper he announced that he had been
threatened with being *"roughly handled"* for maintaining liberty of
the press and declared that he would remain unawed and unbiased.
A week later, however, he offered his readers an explanation for not
printing a piece directed against Galloway and William Franklin. He
maintained liberty of the press, he said, but did not think that meant
printing "all the Trash which every rancorous, illiberal, anonymous
Scribbler" submitted for publication. When the next issue suggested
that William Hicks of the proprietary party was the author of the
rejected piece, Hicks wrote a denial which Goddard also refused to
print because it contained "false Insinuations" about his conduct as

a printer. Hicks had appeared at the door of Goddard's house to demand the name of the writer who had accused him, but Goddard refused to reveal the author. Hicks later threatened to beat him with a cudgel and on April 4 confronted him at a coffee house. Hicks and a group of his friends dragged Goddard out of the building with William Bradford pulling his hair. Goddard described the incident in the *Chronicle* and asked if such behavior did not "tend to destroy the *freedom* of all the Presses in the province, the great bulwark of its Liberty." Goddard also took the opportunity to deny charges made by Hicks in the two other papers that he published under " '*superior* direction'."[39]

Later in 1767, Goddard demonstrated his independence from Galloway by being the first editor to publish John Dickinson's *Letters from a Pennsylvania Farmer.* Franklin thought enough of this argument against the taxation policies of Parliament to prepare his own preface for a London edition, but Galloway still regarded Dickinson as a political adversary and was uncomfortable with the strident tone of the *Letters.* Galloway, who later became a loyalist, attempted to assert control over Goddard's press, but the *Chronicle* joined the *Journal* and the *Gazette* in strongly supporting the nonimportation movement. Goddard soon broke with Galloway and Wharton and revealed the details of his association with them by publishing *The Partnership: or the History of the Rise and Progress of the Pennsylvania Chronicle* in 1770. A year later Goddard denounced Galloway in *A True and Faithful Narrative. . . .* which William Franklin sent to his father. "I cast my Eye over Goddard's Piece against our Friend Mr. Galloway and then lit my Fire with it," Franklin wrote back to his son. "I think such feeble malicious Attacks cannot hurt him."[40]

IX

The Revolutionary Journalist:
The Court of the Press

As a colonial agent and American propagandist in England and later as a diplomat in France, Benjamin Franklin spent all but three years from 1757 to 1785 in Europe. During this time, he routinely used the skill in journalistic argument and satire which he first developed as a printer's apprentice in the 1720s. Commenting in 1773 on two of his better known satires of British government in America, "Rules by Which a Great Empire May Be Reduced to a Small One" and "An Edict by the King of Prussia," Franklin said that they were calculated to expose the mother country's conduct "in a short, comprehensive, and striking view, and stated therefore in out-of-the-way forms, as most likely to take the general attention." Franklin was a skeptical Enlightenment philosopher by education, but a republican in spirit. He concerned himself very little with the mechanisms of government, saying how it was administered—whether or not for the public good—was most important. Observing that vice and virtue were "but a see-saw Game" in individuals, he acknowledged as Poor Richard that few men deserved passionate censure or praise. "Let Satyr blast, with every Mark of Hate," the almanac said, however, "The vain Aspirer, or dishonest Great."[1]

Franklin's approach to political debate was to be highly critical and yet careful and open-minded. His bold journalistic essays, written under the protection of pseudonyms, did more to cleverly undercut opponents' positions than to advocate alternatives. In the portion of his memoirs written in 1784, he stated that he had, early in his career, made it a rule to forbear direct contradiction, which could anger others and prove embarrassing when mistakes were made. "And this Mode, which I at first put on, with some violence to natural Inclination, became at length so easy & so habitual to me," Franklin said, "that perhaps for these Fifty Years past no one has ever heard a dogmatical Expression escape me." Apparently following Montaigne, as he sometimes did, Franklin wrote that he had forbidden himself the use of terms such as *"certainly"* and *"undoubtedly"* and had instead said, *"I conceive, I apprehend,* or *I imagine* a thing to be so or so." In his noted speech at the closing of the Constitutional Convention, he acknowledged having reservations about the document the delegates had produced, but admitted that he had often been forced to change his ideas during his long life and that he was not sure that the new Constitution was not in fact the best they could have. He asked each dissenting member to "doubt a little of his own infallibility" and to allow unanimous approval. "Much of the strength and efficiency of any government, in procuring and securing happiness to the people, depends on *opinion*," he observed, "on the general opinion of the goodness of that government, as well as the wisdom and integrity of its governors."[2]

Franklin was sensitive to the nuances of public opinion and how it was shaped. His success in journalism and politics was due in large part to his ability to remain, like the Janus persona he created in Boston, a detached, multi-faceted "Man of good Temper, courteous Deportment, sound Judgment, a mortal Hater of Nonsense, Foppery, Formality, and endless Ceremony." One of the consequences of his accommodating demeanor was his ability to keep English friends and correspondents ranging from Francis Dashwood and Thomas Paine to Lord Bute and George Whitefield. He disliked confrontation, but was resigned to its necessity. As a young tradesman in Philadelphia, he could, as he did in his "Apology for Printers," insist that he refused to print "Party or Personal Reflections," and yet excuse the publishing of "things full of Spleen and Animosity" since the ideas of mankind varied considerably and printers "naturally acquire a vast Unconcernedness as to the right or wrong Opinions contained in what they print."[3] His good-natured skepticism and habit of being slow to adopt rigid points of view were nowhere more evident than in his approach to the rights of journalists. While he often assessed what he thought was the importance of the press and discussed what he thought were general bounds for its proper use, he never solved the problem of how to limit free expression without losing its advantages and destroying a basic right.

I

While Franklin acted out his roles as philosopher, politician, and propagandist in England, his American associates faced extraordinary tensions in the years preceding the Revolutionary War. James Parker found himself in an awkward position in 1770 after printing a broadside which charged that the New York Assembly—under the direction of the De Lancey faction—betrayed the colony by agreeing to contribute to the support of a garrison of royal troops. Parker was summoned to the Council and questioned on the identity of the author, but he proved evasive. Aware of the power of the colony's patriots, he told the Council that he would be bailed out of jail if he concealed the name and would be "wrecked" if he did not. After Parker withdrew to ponder his predicament, one of his journeymen told the members that Alexander McDougall, a Son of Liberty, had been in the office to correct the proof sheet and had taken delivery of the copies. When Parker returned, he was told about the examination of his journeyman and promised a pardon if he would provide the name. Parker then said that McDougall had ordered the printing, but had not insisted on secrecy.[4]

After McDougall was charged with seditious libel and jailed, Parker's *Post-Boy* delivered a barrage of arguments for press freedom which included Cato, Andrew Hamilton's arguments at the Zenger trial, and even a tirade for liberty from a member of the Council, William Smith. Along with John Holt's *Journal,* the *Post-Boy* hailed McDougall as America's Wilkes and promoted public demonstrations which honored him as a martyr to press freedom. Correspondents denounced the Star Chamber doctrines of seditious libel as absurd and defunct and declared that the performance of public officials could be freely criticized. "Every Officer in the State, is *the Servant* of the Common Wealth; and each Individual is virtually concerned in his Appointment," insisted "Brutus" in the *Post-Boy.* "Hence, therefore, it follows, that a single Member in Community, has an indisputable Right, to arraign at the public Tribunal, the Conduct of Persons in Authority. And how is this to be effected, but by maintaining the *Liberty of the Press?*" Brutus added that he did not approve of public strictures on private characters, but that

"Villains in Office" should be "mounted on the open Scaffold" to justify their conduct.[5]

McDougall's antagonists wanted to see him punished. A friend of the De Lancey faction, James Duane, produced a twelve-part "Dougliad" series for Hugh Gaine's *Mercury* to mock the patriot hero. Duane followed Blackstone in arguing that freedom of the press meant freedom from prior restraint and that government could take action against seditious writers. When McDougall was indicted in April, Parker's *Post-Boy* depicted the action as a blow to press freedom and the American cause. The paper also provided a detailed explanation of how the grand jury had been packed with friends and relatives of Assembly members. The common law seditious libel case against McDougall was hampered when Parker died on July 2, 1770, and thereby deprived the prosecution of its principal witness. The Assembly then took over and simply cited McDougall for contempt in December. "America's Wilkes" was imprisoned until the Assembly was prorogued in March 1771.[6]

Like Parker's *Post-Boy,* the newspapers of Franklin's other primary trade associates began to speak in favor of patriot positions, but remained willing to publish other points of view. When David Hall died in 1772, his sons and their partner, William Sellers, maintained this policy until the war by clearly approving of radical sentiments and yet giving space to at least some loyalist correspondents. In South Carolina, Peter Timothy's editorial impartiality was repeatedly confirmed. While the Commons House of Assembly refused to do business from 1762 to 1764 because of a dispute with Governor Thomas Boone over election procedures, Timothy printed statements on both sides of the issue despite an order from Boone and his Council forbidding all newspaper writings which might appear injurious to government authority. Another legislative deadlock began in 1769 when the lower house insisted on sending £1500 to aid John Wilkes. During the controversy, which lasted until the Revolution, the *Gazette* again published the various views.[7]

In 1772, Timothy was in poor health and turned his business over to partners. In announcing his retirement after thirty-three years, he told his readers that he loved his country and that he had often sacrificed his private interests to his chief concern, "the Public Good." Taking the stance of a classic republican, he said that he was prepared to sacrifice more. Later in the year, however, Timothy realized that he was not prepared financially for retirement and he wrote to Franklin to see if he could arrange an appointment to the post of naval officer at Charleston. Franklin replied that he had become regarded as "too much of an American" in London and could no longer help anyone obtain government positions. He also upbraided Timothy saying that "to leave a good Trade in hopes of an Office, is quitting a Certainty for an Uncertainty, and losing Substance for Shadow."[8]

The *South-Carolina Gazette,* meanwhile, was being printed by Thomas Powell, Charleston's librarian and Timothy's one-time foreman. Powell introduced himself to the readers by acknowledging himself to be a servant of the public and by saying that he hoped the paper would be "both USEFUL and ENTERTAINING." He intended to exclude "all PERSONAL SCANDAL," he explained, but would allow neither promises of reward nor threats of punishment to prevent the paper from exposing "PUBLIC Characters" to public scorn whenever they appeared to deserve it. Powell also promised to avoid partiality as much as circumstances would allow. "If we should however at SOME Periods be found to lean a LITTLE," he added, "we hope it may prove on that Side which will meet with an easy Justification."[9]

Powell's short tenure as the printer of the *Gazette* was nevertheless turbulent. Radical correspondents insulted their opponents and the paper reprinted the writings of English journalists—including Wilkes and Junius—as they attacked Lord North, Lord Chief Justice Mansfield, and other symbols of British oligarchy. In 1773 the Council jailed Powell for printing a protest against its actions, but two members of the Commons House of Assembly issued a writ of habeas corpus to free him. The Commons House endorsed the step taken by its members and awarded Timothy and Powell the exclusive right to print its proceedings. Already at odds over the Wilkes fund and other issues, the Council and Commons House spared no efforts in criticizing each other over the episode. The lower house depicted the use of breach of legislative privilege against Powell as unlawful and oppressive. The *Gazette,* which printed statements on both sides of the controversy, expressed shock at the Council's lack of regard for freedom of the press and reminded its readers that a free press was needed to guard against arbitrary power.[10]

The case went to England, but it was not decided before the Revolution. After Powell quit the paper late in 1773, Timothy returned as printer. In the remaining years of his life, before he died in a shipwreck in 1782, Timothy devoted himself to the American cause. He served in patriot organizations and eventually held positions in the state government. His contribution to political affairs was such that in 1777 he congratulated himself in a letter to Franklin for having single-handedly raised "the Opposition to Tyranny" in South Carolina.[11]

II

During his service in England as a colonial agent from 1757 to 1762 and again from 1764 to 1775, Benjamin Franklin impressed a number of prominent Europeans with his sagacity and wit. "America has sent us many good things, Gold, Silver, Tobacco, Indigo & c.," David Hume wrote to Franklin in 1762, "But you are the first Philosopher, and indeed the first Great Man of Letters for whom we are beholden to her." At the same time, writing under various pseudonyms, Franklin was regularly using London newspapers to present reasoned arguments for American viewpoints as well as piercing satires. He lamented the inaccurate ideas London writers had of the colonies and mocked, among other notions, the theory of biological degeneration, a belief that plants, animals, and people languished when taken to the New World. America had, he wrote in one jocular newspaper essay, sheep so heavy with wool that their tails had to be supported by small wagons.[12]

To those who sympathized with British objectives, Franklin was an unscrupulous propagandist. In his loyalist history of the American Revolution, Peter Oliver remarked that Benjamin Franklin entered his trade as a *"Printers Devil"* and that "by a Climax in Reputation, he reversed the Phrase, & taught us to read it backward, as Witches do the Lords Prayer." He had learned a black art, Oliver continued, "and made it much blacker, by forcing the Press often to speak the Thing that was not." The historian lamented that Franklin's experiments with electricity made him a celebrity with England's foremost citizens and enabled him to join forces with opposition leaders in a way which "gave such a Shock to Government, & brought on such Convulsions, as the english Constitution will not be cured of in one Century, if ever." A bitter aristocrat, Oliver quoted verses published in *Gentleman's Magazine* in 1777 which said:[13]

> Oh! had he been Wise to pursue
> The Track for his Talents design'd,
> What a Tribute of Praise had been due
> To the Teacher & Friend of Mankind?

> But, to covet political Fame
> Was in him a degrading Ambition,
> A Spark that from *Lucifer* came,
> And kindled the Blaze of Sedition.

Franklin was, however, less inclined toward rebellion than Oliver and other supporters of the oligarchy realized or were willing to acknowledge. He long held out hope for a reconciliation between England and the colonies and had a distaste for civil unrest. His ties to British officialdom were initially so strong and his disgust with violently partisan journalism so great, that he could only express approval when the House of Commons voted 273 to 111 that the forty-fifth issue of the *North Briton* was a seditious libel. The House, he told one correspondent, had shown a "just Resentment" for the "seditious Conduct" of John Wilkes. When Wilkes won election to Parliament in 1768 and was hailed on both sides of the ocean, Franklin conveyed his astonishment in letters to his son William, then royal governor of New Jersey. "I am sorry to see in the American Papers that some People there are so indiscreet as to distinguish themselves in applauding his No. 45, which I suppose they do not know was a Paper in which their King was personally affronted, whom I am sure they love and honour," he wrote. "It hurts you here with sober sensible Men, when they see you so easily infected with the Madness of English Mobs."[14]

In the years before the American Revolution, Franklin found fault with both the popular politicians and the ruling oligarchy. When a choice eventually had to be made, he took the side of a people against a government, as he had done earlier in Pennsylvania. Franklin was, after all, most comfortable with a libertarian outlook. While he was an agent in London, he happily consorted with religious and political radicals and he regularly dined with a group of men he called his "club of honest whigs." His contributions to the English press were often attempts to portray Americans as oppressed and yet loyal subjects. "But they are Whigs," Franklin warned in a 1772 essay, "and whenever the Crown assumes Prerogatives it has not, or makes unwarrantable Use of those it has, they will oppose as far as they are able." He expressed regret that the Whig philosophies of the colonists were "now out of Fashion" in Britain. Three years later he complained that the Whiggism of New Englanders had become "an *unpardonable Sin.*" Only by February 1775, when the king had declared Massachusetts to be in rebellion, was Franklin pessimistic about a solution and ready to align himself with what he called "the

Popular or Country Party in America." He wrote to the still loyal Joseph Galloway, who had proposed plans for a new British-American union, that holding America and England together would be like binding the dead and the living. A new union, Franklin said, would be joining "the extream Corruption prevalent among all Orders of men in this old rotten State, and the glorious publick Virtue so predominant in our rising Country."[15]

Franklin turned away from whatever ambitions he may have harbored for being accepted in ruling circles in England and perhaps receiving an appointment as a royal governor like his son. He, in effect, had no choice. He had endured too many insults to himself and the colonies. On January 29, 1774, he was castigated for an hour before a committee of the Privy Council by Solicitor General Alexander Wedderburn. Two days later Franklin was removed from the office of deputy postmaster general for North America. Wedderburn's invectives were ostensibly aimed at Franklin for his having acquired indignant letters sent to England by Massachusetts Governor Thomas Hutchinson and sending them to Boston radicals. Franklin suspected the real reason was that he had exposed British policies "too poignantly" in his journalistic forays.[16]

Franklin reacted calmly to his sinking fortunes in England. Once subjected to what he called "abundant Abuse in the Papers," however, he went to work on a tract explaining his role in the Hutchinson letters episode. He began by explaining that he did not reply to attacks on his public conduct since he assumed that splashes of dirt thrown on his character *"would all rub off when they were dry."* He nevertheless defended himself as a man who sought the welfare of both Britain and the colonies. "Hence it has often happened to me," Franklin wrote, "that while I have been thought here too much of an American, I have in America been deem'd too much of an Englishman." Conveniently forgetting his own attitude toward Wilkes ten years earlier, he also took note of the reports that the administration had been investigating his correspondence with colonial assemblies. "The News Papers have announc'd, that *Treason* is found in some of my Letters," Franklin wrote. "It must then be of some new Species. The Invention of Court Lawyers has always been fruitful in the Discovery of new Treasons; and perhaps it is now become Treason to censure the Conduct of Ministers." Thirteen years later, at the Convention of 1787, Franklin broke his usual silence to speak in favor of the constitutional language defining treason as an "overt act."[17]

After his departure from England, Franklin became absorbed in the business of war and statecraft. He landed at Philadelphia on May 5, 1775, and was told about the battles of Lexington and Concord. The next day the Pennsylvania Assembly appointed him a delegate to the Second Continental Congress. While serving as a member of Congressional committees and eventually as president of his state's Constitutional Convention in 1776, Franklin made use of his writing ability. He edited the Declaration of Independence and revised Pennsylvania's Declaration of Rights. Franklin had no objection to a provision in the Declaration of Rights which said: "That the People have a Right to Freedom of Speech, and of writing and publishing their Sentiments, therefore the Freedom of the Press ought not to be restrained."[18]

Sent to negotiate treaties with France in 1776, Franklin set up a press at his Passy residence and began producing official documents, American propaganda, and casual essays to entertain his French hosts. The propaganda included his grisly "Supplement to the *Boston Independent Chronicle*" hoax which purported to describe hundreds of Indian scalpings of men, women, and children carried out for the British. He also composed his laudatory "Information to Those Who Would Remove to America" essay and wrote to European friends that English newspaper writers spread strange ideas about the new nation in order to discourage trade and emigration. After returning to America in 1785 at age seventy-nine, Franklin helped to advance the careers of several young printers and continued to contribute to periodicals. His last newspaper piece, published a month before his death in 1790, parodied arguments made in support of the slave trade.[19]

In his correspondence at the end of the Revolution, Franklin expressed admiration for the role the press had come to play in national and international affairs. "The facility, with which the same truths may be repeatedly enforced by placing them daily in different lights in *newspapers,* which are everywhere read, gives a great chance of establishing them," he wrote in 1782. "And now we find, that it is not only right to strike when the iron is hot, but that it may be very practicable to heat it by continually striking." A year later he maintained that arbitrary governments were likely to disappear gradually as one of the effects of "the art of printing, which diffuses so general a light, augmenting with the growing day, and of so penetrating a nature, that all the window-shutters despotism and priestcraft can oppose to keep it out, prove insufficient."[20]

Franklin's Enlightenment enthusiasm for the press was tempered in the last decade of his life, however, by persistent concerns about the image of his country and weary reactions to personal defamation. Having been free from neither the ridicule and rumors of loyalist writers nor the suspicions of patriots during the Revolution, Franklin complained to Robert Morris in 1781 that "the Publick is often niggardly, even of its Thanks, while you are sure of being censured by malevolent Cricks and Bug-writers, who will abuse you while you are serving them, and wound your Character in nameless Pamphlets; thereby resembling those little dirty stinking insects, that attack us only in the dark, disturb our Repose, molesting and wounding us, while our Sweat and Blood are contributing to their Subsistence." Franklin told Francis Hopkinson in 1782 that he was dismayed by "the Pieces of Personal Abuse, so scandalously common in our Newspapers" and that he removed "such as would disgrace us" before passing along American papers to French friends. "The Conductor of a Newspaper should, methinks, consider himself as in some degree the Guardian of his Country's Reputation, and refuse to insert such Writings as may hurt it," he wrote. "If People will print their Abuses of one another, let them do it in little Pamphlets, and distribute them where they think proper."[21]

Franklin continued to make his dissatisfactions known after returning to Philadelphia and reentering American politics as president of the Supreme Executive Council of Pennsylvania and as a delegate to the Constitutional Convention. He was particularly frustrated by the journalistic debates over ratification of the federal Constitution and the criticism he received as one of the signers. In 1787, Antifederalist editor Eleazer Oswald published an essay characterizing Franklin as a feeble-minded old fool and Washington as a dupe for supporting the Constitution. The essay appeared first in Oswald's Philadelphia newspaper, the *Independent Gazetteer,* and was widely reprinted elsewhere. In 1788, Franklin accordingly showed little sympathy when Oswald was jailed for contempt of court for publishing comments on a libel suit brought against him by a Federalist editor. In a duel in 1786, moreover, Oswald had seriously wounded Mathew Carey, a young printer who had worked for Franklin in Passy and later emigrated to Philadelphia. Oswald's wife, Elizabeth, nevertheless wrote to Franklin to ask for his advice and for his help as president. "And I do think if you will take the trouble to consider of this affair," she implored, "you will join with me in saying, that he has

been unjustly confined; and that if such things are allowed, they may
be of dangerous consequences." Franklin replied that it would be
improper for him to consider the matter since he might later be asked
to do so officially. He concluded his letter with the wish that her
"prudent Counsels might prevail with him to change that Conduct of
his Paper by which he has made and provok'd so many Enemies."[22]

In the same year he wrote in his memoirs that when he was an
editor he had a policy of refusing to publish personal detraction in
his newspaper, but that he did allow writers the liberty of having
abusive material printed separately at his shop for their own circulation. He lamented that printers had begun to "make no scruple of
gratifying the Malice of Individuals by false Accusations of the fair-
est Characters among ourselves, augmenting Animosity even to the
producing of Duels." Franklin also wrote to the editors of the *Pennsylvania Gazette* in 1788 to observe that there was nothing more
likely to endanger liberty of the press than "the abuse of that liberty, by employing it in personal accusation, detraction, and calumny." He added that the "excesses some of our papers have been
guilty of in this particular, have set this State in a bad light abroad."[23]

Franklin's final statement on press freedom came in "An Account
of the Supremest Court of Judicature in Pennsylvania, viz. the Court
of the Press," an essay he wrote for Philadelphia's *Federal Gazette*
seven months before his death in April 1790. He recognized the
quasi-judicial place of journalism in society, but he treated the institution sarcastically as an example of overgrown power with no legal
restraints. He compared the standards of the press in publishing libels to the procedures used by the Inquisition and wondered what
could be done to protect reputations which would not destroy liberty
of the press. "If by the *liberty of the press* were understood merely
the liberty of discussing the propriety of public measures and political opinions, let us have as much of it as you please," he wrote. "But
if it means the liberty of affronting, calumniating and defaming one
another, I, for my part, own myself willing to part with my share of
it, whenever our legislators shall please so to alter the law, and shall
chearfully consent to exchange my *liberty* of abusing others for the
privilege of not being abused myself." Franklin left the work of
making "an explicit law" defining press freedom to others. What he
did do was to attempt to make clear to his readers the need to protect both reputation, which he said was "dearer to you perhaps than
your life," and liberty of the press, which was a freedom "every

Pennsylvanian would fight and die for: Though few of us, I believe, have distinct ideas of its nature and extent."[24]

III

Beyond making a libertarian distinction between public and private matters, Benjamin Franklin was ultimately unable to set exact boundaries on liberty of the press. Although he occasionally adopted a relaxed attitude toward personal libel as his brother James had done, he disliked calumny—the malicious use of false statements to injure reputation. As a philosopher he appreciated the effectiveness of the press in enlightening and motivating a country, but as a politician he refused to support the likes of William Smith, John Wilkes, and Eleazer Oswald—journalists he thought had improperly attacked private character in their writings on public affairs. Along with Jefferson and Madison, Franklin endorsed a freedom to discuss issues, but stressed a need to protect the reputations of individuals— including public persons—from defamatory falsehoods. The difficulty with this position was that it could restrict the range of allowable political debate. Although it did not favor prosecutions for criticisms of an idea or a government, it did allow cases to be brought for the personal libel of government officials. As such, this approach represented a middle ground between libertarians like Junius who appeared ready to justify virtually any statement about the political conduct of a public person and those like Alexander Hamilton who still accepted the concept of seditious libel of government, but made truth a qualified defense.

As a proponent of the revolutionary Enlightenment, Franklin, in fact, was unsure about laws in general and his position on press cases in particular. Franklin and a number of other Americans were acutely aware of the rigors and shortcomings of the existing legal system. Criminal laws, Franklin told a correspondent in 1783, were in disorder everywhere in the world and were enforced with much injustice. He sometimes imagined, he said, that it would be better "if there were no such laws, and the punishment of injuries were left to private resentment." He applied this notion to journalistic rights in his "Court of the Press" essay. Before laws were made, he observed, people had the freedom to drub others who gave them ill language. He then proposed bringing back "the liberty of the Cudgel" to go along with freedom of the press. Writers who attacked individuals could be waylaid and beaten, he reasoned, and those who affronted the public could be tarred, feathered, and tossed in a blanket. This might disturb the peace, he admitted, but it would preserve "the sacred *liberty of the Press.*"[25]

Still, Franklin's attitude toward the law had changed by the end of the 1780s. "The Opposition given, more or less, in every State, to the propos'd Constitution from a Jealousy of Power, strengthens an Opinion of mine that America is too enlighten'd to be enslav'd," he said in a 1788 letter, "and that the Happiness of its People is less in danger from an *Excess* of Power in the Governors, than from the *Defect* of due Obedience, even to their own good Laws, in the Governed." Franklin, along with many in the United States, had lost much of his radical Whig fervor by the time the federal Constitution was being ratified. The ratification debate's discussion of checks and balances in the parts of government, he said in his "Court of the Press" essay, had made him think about the press and "suspect some check may be proper in this part also."[26]

Franklin did not offer any specific suggestion, but the matter was addressed shortly after his death when Pennsylvania's highly controversial constitution of 1776 was discarded and replaced with a less radical document. The 1776 constitution had simply declared that freedom of the press "ought not to be restrained" and that the press would be "free to every person who undertakes to examine the proceedings of the legislature, or any part of government." The state constitution of 1790, however, said that journalists were not to be restrained by any law made to restrict communications on the proceedings of government, but that they were otherwise responsible for the "abuse" of that liberty. New language said that in "prosecutions for the publication of papers investigating the official conduct of officers or men in a public capacity, or where the matter published is proper for public information" truth could be given in evidence and the jury would determine both the law and facts of the case. Kentucky and Delaware adopted nearly identical provisions for their constitutions in 1792.[27]

Pennsylvania's 1790 constitution, which was written at the time that the First Amendment was being ratified, may have indicated an acceptance of seditious libel with some reforms. Promoted by the state's "Republican" faction as the answer to the perceived democratic excesses of the 1776 Constitution, the new document's press provision may have been designed to suppress criticism of government as dangerous. More likely, the provisions of 1790—which spoke of freedom of expression as "one of the invaluable rights of man"—recognized the "abuse" of the libel of individuals as Franklin had and the fact that either an individual or a government might prosecute such defamation cases.[28] The new language on truth as a defense and general verdicts by juries dealt with the existing problem of how to treat defamatory statements about individual conduct in public life.

The issue had been debated extensively after Eleazer Oswald was twice taken into custody in 1782 for publishing highly derogatory remarks about the judicial behavior of Chief Justice Thomas Mc-Kean. Oswald, a Republican journalist, was a fierce opponent of Mc-Kean and other members of the state's Constitutionalist faction which supported the Constitution of 1776. Apparently reacting to McKean's having said at the time of the editor's first arrest that the defamation in question was "seditious, scandalous, *and* infamous," correspondents in Oswald's newspaper denounced the action as an attempt to introduce the doctrines of the Star Chamber, Blackstone, and Mansfield and to deny the use of truth as a defense. They pointed to a need to scrutinize public men as servants of the people, to the state Constitution's protection for the discussion of the proceedings of government, and to the problems with adopting English precedents in America. The bill of indictment eventually presented to the grand jury was for a "false, scandalous and malicious Libel" of McKean rather than a "seditious" libel, but in any event the grand jury refused to indict Oswald despite repeated urgings from the presiding judge, Thomas McKean. Oswald described the outcome as a victory for a free people and a free press against the encroachments of power. "I here take opportunity to declare," he told his readers, "no tyranny or persecution will ever disuade or intimidate me from printing the most *spirited* pieces, accompanied with truth and decency, which shall be handed me on those public affairs in which we are all so deeply concerned."[29]

Comments on the case in Philadelphia's other newspapers were indicative of the range of opinions about press freedom that existed in Pennsylvania in the 1780s. Writers in Francis Bailey's *Freeman's Journal,* a Constitutionalist organ, defended the prosecution as a proper response to the publication of falsehoods which damaged an individual's reputation. The *Pennsylvania Gazette,* meanwhile, published arguments critical of the action taken against Oswald. "ARISTIDES" credited the members of the grand jury with having resisted "the introduction of that accursed engine of tyranny, the doctrine of

criminal libels into our courts, where it has been hitherto unknown."
"AN UNDISGUISED WHIG" maintained that it was better to allow the publication of scurrility than to have state tyrants destroy the
people. Press restraints were foolish, he continued, because truthful
chastisements helped to prevent further wrongdoing and because those
who did not deserve malicious representations shone in their innocence and belied any scandal with their conduct. "The freedom of
the press injures no man," he stated. Sixteen members of the grand
jury, for their part, published a "Memorial and Remonstrance" in
the *Gazette* to answer assertions by McKean that members of the
grand jury had been biased by party affiliation and had improperly
met with Oswald during a recess. The statement said that they had
maintained "their unshaken zeal for the liberties of their country,"
but it was prefaced by a paragraph which expressed their "abhorrence and detestation of all such defamatory publications, as have a
tendency wantonly to expose public characters to censure or contempt,—or private ones to abuse and obloquy."[30]

The Pennsylvania constitution of 1790, when finally obtained by
the Republicans who supported Oswald, acknowledged that public
officials could be libelled as individuals. It thus accepted what Franklin and like-minded libertarians had concluded. It made truth a defense in such instances and left matters of law and fact to rest on
what the grand jurors in Oswald's case referred to as "the sacred
rights of Juries, which form the bulwark of our civil liberties."[31] The
inadequacy of such safeguards was, of course, demonstrated later in
the decade at the trials of the journalists prosecuted under the Sedition Act passed by the majority party in Congress.

IV

The main target of Federalist wrath in 1798 was Benjamin Franklin
Bache, a man who had been introduced into the printing trade by his
grandfather, Benjamin Franklin. A Jeffersonian editor in Philadelphia, Bache was educated under Franklin's supervision. He became a
doctrinaire proponent of Enlightenment and revolutionary principles—
particularly those of Benjamin Franklin's protégé, Thomas Paine. Unlike his grandfather, who had talents and ambitions in many fields,
Bache made newspaper writing an almost exclusive occupation, as it
was possible to do in the United States by the 1790s. Fully prepared
to see the journalist as one who performed missionary service for
knowledge, justice, and democracy, Bache represented the epitome

of libertarian press theory and practice in eighteenth-century America.

Benjamin Franklin formed an emotional attachment to his grandson years before meeting him. When Franklin's daughter, Sarah, gave birth to the boy in 1769, Franklin was on an extended stay in England. The glowing letters he read about the child in Philadelphia reminded him of his own son Francis who had not been inoculated and had died of smallpox in 1736. "All who have seen my Grandson, agree with you in their Accounts of his being an uncommonly fine Boy," Franklin wrote to his sister Jane Mecom in 1772, "which brings often Afresh to my Mind the Idea of my Son Franky, tho' now dead 36 Years, whom I have seldom since seen equal'd in every thing, and whom to this Day I cannot think of without a Sigh." Among those who kept him informed about the boy's progress was Franklin's wife Deborah who delighted in her grandson's behavior and wrote frequently about her little "Kingbird." The grandfather shipped presents for "Benny-boy" and supplied the latest medical information on inoculation. When Franklin finally returned in 1775, his wife was dead and his son William was ready to side with the British. In 1776, with the colonies at war with England, seven-year-old Benjamin was told that he was to sail to France with his illustrious grandfather.[32]

Bache spent nine years in Europe. French became his language, his manners were refined, and he met an array of famous men. Franklin took him to the aged Voltaire who placed his hands on the boy's head and uttered the benediction: "God and Liberty." Franklin spent generous sums on his schooling, but was otherwise austere and demanding. When the grandfather became wary of Bache's being educated in France, a Catholic monarchy, he sent him off for four years of school in Geneva so that he would live "where the proper Principles prevail." Franklin often made it clear that he wanted Bache to be diligent and obedient. "I shall always love you very much if you continue to be a good Boy," he wrote in one letter to his grandson. Bache trusted and revered Franklin and did what he could to live up to the high expectations. When he returned from Geneva his grandfather arranged for him to receive expert instruction in printing and typefounding. "I have determin'd to give him a Trade that he may have something to depend on," Franklin explained to Bache's father in America, "and not be oblig'd to ask Favours or Offices of anybody."[33]

Bache returned to Philadelphia with his grandfather in 1785 and received his help in starting a printing business. Franklin set up joint ventures in the politically safe areas of typefounding and children's books, but both proved unprofitable. In 1788 they started the Franklin Society, a mutual aid and insurance organization for printers. In 1790, six months after his grandfather's death, Bache began publishing a daily newspaper he named the *General Advertiser, and Political, Commercial, Agricultural and Literary Journal.* The first issue, which appeared a month after the new state Constitution was adopted and a year before the federal Bill of Rights was ratified, summarized the foundations of libertarian press theory:[34]

> *The Freedom of the Press* is the *Bulwark of Liberty.* An impartial Newspaper is the useful offspring of that *Freedom.* Its object is to inform.
>
> In a Commonwealth, the PEOPLE are the Basis on which all power and authority rest. On the extent of their knowledge and information the solidity of that Foundation depends. If the PEOPLE are enlightened the Nation stands and flourishes: thro' ignorance it falls or degenerates.

After three weeks of daily publication, the twenty-two-year-old editor admitted to his readers he was having difficulty finding enough newsworthy information on European affairs for his paper. "As to domestic politics,—no party disputes to raise the printer's drooping spirits; not a legislature sitting to furnish a few columns of debates; not even so much as a piece of private abuse to grace a paper," he said. "Zounds, people now have no spirit in them." Bache found more than enough controversy within a few years as national parties began to form and assail each other. Sustained by early encouragement from Thomas Jefferson and eventually by a loan from James Monroe, Bache became a strident opponent of the Washington and Adams administrations. His grandfather's efforts to direct him into less contentious areas of printing as well as his scorn for the injustices of the "Court of the Press" were ignored. "Public men are all amenable to the tribunal of the press in a free state; the greater, indeed, their trust, the more responsible are they," Bache editorialized in 1794. "It may also with truth be said, that the brighter their virtues are, the fairer their characters will appear after a public investigation of their conduct."[35]

Bache was only one of a number of Republican journalists who espoused such sentiments in the face of Federalist outrage at the opposition press, but he went further than his fellow editors in putting his principles into practice. He published sensitive diplomatic papers—including the undisclosed texts of Jay's Treaty in 1795 and of Talleyrand's letter to the American envoys in 1798—which proved embarrassing to the Federalists. He also reprinted letters forged by the British during the Revolutionary War to discredit George Washington. Washington, who complained bitterly to his friends and cabinet members about Bache's paper, was described regularly as a vain and inept man with monarchical tendencies. Washington planned to devote a portion of his Farewell Address to the abuse he received in the press, but changed his mind. He did, however, spend part of his last day in office writing a lengthy letter for the files of the State Department denying that he had anything to do with the forged letters Bache had published. At the time Washington retired, Bache's paper compared him to George III and complained that he had "debauched" and "deceived" the nation. "Let the history of the federal government instruct mankind," the paper observed, "that the masque of patriotism may be wore to conceal the foulest designs against the liberties of a people."[36]

Bache thus became the country's best-known Republican journalist. To reflect his radical orientation and perhaps his unstinting support for the French republic, he changed the name of his newspaper to the *Aurora*. In announcing the new name, he declared that "neither the frowns of men, or allurements of private interest shall make him swerve from the line of his public duty." The *Aurora* would, he said, seek to dispel ignorance and thereby "strengthen the fair fabric of freedom on its surest foundation, publicity and information."[37]

His opponents saw other motives in Bache's journalistic conduct. Federalist papers accused him of taking money from the French and of indulging in gutter journalism to build circulation. When Bache's initial reaction to the Adams administration was favorable, the president wrote to his wife Abigail that he would "soon be acquitted of the crime" of the *Aurora*'s praise. As Adams and the Federalists responded to a series of naval and diplomatic insults from France by preparing for war, the *Aurora* and other Republican newspapers exploded with invective and were denounced as traitorous in return. War hysteria and partisan aspersions intensified from the beginning of the Adams administration in 1797 through the summer of 1798. Bache was twice physically assaulted and twice had his house menaced by mobs. Federalists excluded him from the floor of the House of Representatives where he and other reporters had taken notes. When a boycott of his business began, Bache watched his finances deteriorate. In the spring of 1798 the majority party began discussing a sedition law to use against Republican newspapers. "Bache's has been particularly named," Jefferson reported to James Madison. In Congressional debate on the Sedition Act in July, the *Aurora* was used as a prime example of a dangerous publication and its editor was pointed to as a close associate of the Republican vice president, Thomas Jefferson.[38]

Bache was not silenced. He depicted the steps taken against him as attacks on freedom of the press and he remained committed to what he regarded as his journalistic duty. In issue after issue, he portrayed the Federalists as warmongers and Adams as unfit for office. Apparently unable to wait for the passage of the Sedition Act, District Judge Richard Peters had him arrested in June on a federal common law charge of seditiously libelling the president and the executive branch of government. Bache published statements interpreting the federal Constitution to mean that only state courts could have jurisdiction in libel cases, but he predicted in his newspaper that his case would be settled on the basis of "THE LIBERTY OF THE PRESS." The day after he made his initial appearance in court, he affirmed in the *Aurora* "that prosecution no more than persecution, shall cause him to abandon what he considers the cause of truth and republicanism." Others were less optimistic about Bache's prospects. "What will be the *issue* of the prosecutions and persecutions cannot yet be determined," commented Thomas Adams, a Republican editor in Boston, "as the term *Libel*, has been so variously defined." The trial was set for October and Bache, with the help of friends, posted $4000 bail.[39]

For the next two months Bache and his correspondents turned their attention to the Sedition Act which was signed by President Adams on July 14. Bache hammered on several themes: that the law was passed for political purposes, that it was a clear violation of the First Amendment's restriction on Congress, and that it conflicted with the principle of popular sovereignty. "If the administration emanated from itself there would be some reason for abridging the rights of the people for its own security," he wrote, "but as the government is the will of the people, for their own happiness and comfort, it is treason against their will to impose restrictions upon them which they did not authorise." By August Bache was fearing Federalist violence and the overthrow of the Constitution. The *Aurora* advised Republicans to arm themselves "for the *tenets* preached up by the wretches who follow in the train of our administration are calculated

to convert the people of these free states into only two classes—
Janisaries and *Mutes!*"⁴⁰

In September citizens began fleeing Philadelphia, but not out of
fears about civil disorder. An epidemic of yellow fever was spreading through the city. Bache refused to leave his newspaper and fell
ill with the disease. He put his affairs in order and died calmly on
September 10. He was eulogized in Republican newspapers in other
states and in the *Aurora* which was continued by his wife, Margaret,
and his employee, William Duane. The widow printed a notice addressed to the "friends of civil liberty and patrons of the *Aurora*"
which described her husband as "a man inflexible in virtue, unap-
palled by power or persecution." Federalist newspapers insisted that
the editor had been merely a product of his philosopher grandfather
and a tool of the Republicans. Benjamin Russell, the Federalist editor of Boston's *Columbian Centinel,* remarked that his correspondents thought Bache's "memory ought to be held up to the execra-
tion of the whole earth, as a monster, who clutched a dagger prepared
to stab the vitals of his country." The editor of the *Aurora,* Russell
said, had labored in the cause of "anarchy, sedition, and French
robbery."⁴¹

Bache died before he could be brought to trial. In the two years
before the "Revolution of 1800," most of the other prominent Republican journalists in the country were either driven from their jobs
or convicted of seditious libel and imprisoned. The First Amendment had not prevented vindictive Federalists from writing and enforcing a law to punish criticism of government. To a large extent,
parties had begun to finance and direct newspaper publishers as they
would for most of the nineteenth century.⁴² The last decade of the
eighteenth century thus represented an inauspicious beginning for a
constitutionally protected press in America, but Jefferson, Madison,
and other Republicans worked to advance the idea that the newly
formed American political system could and should accommodate
critical, aggressive journalism. Libertarians had long believed that a
free press was a natural and necessary adjunct to a free government,
but after the ratification of the Bill of Rights, they could argue as
Bache did that this relationship was recognized by the Constitution
of the United States.

Conclusion

The Constitution of the United States outlines a republican system of politics designed to protect a government from people and a people from government. Early American journalists and libertarian theorists distrusted state power and continually argued that the press should serve as a check on its use. The same writers and thinkers were also faced with the question of how free the press should be to perform this task. Their answers varied to some extent, but their experience and their reasoning pointed toward a free press and produced the press clause of the First Amendment.

The press clause was written and ratified in a country which had witnessed an extraordinary increase in the impact and status of journalism. Not until 1719 was there more than one newspaper in the colonies. By the 1720s and 1730s, however, publications such as the *New-England Courant, American Weekly Mercury, Pennsylvania Gazette, South-Carolina Gazette,* and *New-York Weekly Journal* were using and defending liberty of the press. Whether for reasons of personal ambition, republican principles, Enlightenment ideals, journalistic impartiality, or party allegiance, editors began publishing writings which challenged religious and political authority. Later the issues of the Revolution and the Constitution were debated extensively in the press. By the end of the century, presidents were reeling from press criticism, and authors were writing lengthy treatises on freedom of expression. Witty and worldly in its early years with printers like James and Benjamin Franklin, American journalism had a tenacious sense of professional pride and mission by the time of Benjamin Franklin Bache. The Hydra-headed press, always difficult to control, had become the eyes, ears, and voice of the electorate and its parties.

Along with this increasing importance came a widespread ideology of a free press as an essential means of communication in a democratic republic, as a "bulwark of liberty" and "scourge of tyrants." It was to some a mechanism of equal or seemingly greater importance than the political institutions themselves. "The basis for our governments being the opinion of the people, the very first object should be to keep that right," Thomas Jefferson wrote in 1787, "and were it left to me to decide whether we should have a government without newspapers or newspapers without government, I should not hesitate a moment to prefer the latter."[1] A free, aggressive press could, of course, be highly irritating to those who were criticized. Jefferson himself was outraged by the conduct of journalists during his presidency and for a time regarded the press as useless at best.

Reacting to the assertion that free expression endangered the wellbeing of the state, libertarians such as Jefferson produced sophisticated thought on liberty of the press. Highly regarded essayists as different as Cato and Hume agreed that the press actually protected government from civil unrest by pointing out problems in time for reform. Writers also reasoned that while actions might be properly punished, mere words discussing political issues should not be criminal. James Madison, among others, clearly saw that seditious libel, the crime of criticizing government introduced into the common law by the Star Chamber, was not consistent with the United States Constitution which made the people the highest authority. British precedents and policies, which had led to confrontations between the oligarchy and the populace, were not necessarily relevant in a country where popular sovereignty had been achieved. While English law assumed that the people were to be ruled by their superiors, the new American government was expressly created to invest citizens with the ultimate control and to enable them to keep their leaders in check.

Denying the charge in 1788 that the proposed Constitution would create an oligarchy, Madison observed in the *Federalist* papers that there were "numerous and various" ways to prevent the "degeneracy" of elected officials. "The aim of every political Constitution is or ought to be first to obtain for rulers, men who possess most wisdom to discern, and most virtue to pursue the common good of the society," he wrote, "and in the next place, to take the most effectual precautions for keeping them virtuous, whilst they continue to hold the public trust." In another newspaper essay published three years later, Madison explained the role the First Amendment would play in the political system. Public opinion was the "real sovereign" in every free country, he wrote, and the press—which was to be protected in the Bill of Rights—would keep the public informed. Officials needed to heed the will of the people where it was fixed, he thought, but could influence it where it was not. The result, Madison's essay suggested, was a system where the people and their leaders communicated with each other through the press as part of the governing process.[2]

Yet, though American political thought supported a free press, politicians occasionally did not. When it suited their ends, some—such as the Federalists who passed the Sedition Act of 1798—reverted to the oligarchical notion of Sir William Blackstone that the term freedom of the press meant freedom only from the prior restraints of licensing and censorship and not freedom from later penalty for unprotected forms of expression such as criticism of government. Indeed, court decisions of the nineteenth and twentieth centuries have improperly relied on the idea that the press clause was primarily intended to preclude prior restraint, but not subsequent punishment. Modern courts have even allowed less protection than the Blackstonian formula by creating exceptions to the rule against prior restraint.[3]

Such interpretations contrast sharply with what is known about the history of the press clause. When the right of expression was challenged in early America, journalists and their defenders were defiant and found their responses in libertarian theory—with its view of the press as an agent of enlightenment and a gauge of liberty. What libertarian theory could mean in practice was illustrated by printers like Benjamin Franklin who tried to pursue the republican ideal of political impartiality and make their newspapers marketplaces of opinions, but often chose to reject false and defamatory statements affecting an individual's reputation. Although Franklin and his libertarian contemporaries recognized the importance of unfettered expression in a free society, they could not always offer consistent and precise legal formulations of what constituted the protected "liberty" of the press and its unprotected "licentiousness." Libertarian rallying cries may have helped to gain public support for printers and to sway juries, but libel prosecutions raised complex legal issues.

Libel cases were rarely if ever brought because a journalist had merely discussed the form of government or a choice of policies. Prosecutions were initiated because public persons had been criticized as individuals and wanted to strike back. It was thus often unclear whether the case was one of seditious libel or personal libel. Libertarians saw a need for free discussion of public affairs, but usually believed that anyone—including a person in public office—had at least some right to preserve their reputation. The result was seemingly endless confusion in defamation law. Was truth to be a complete or qualified defense? Would juries be allowed to deliver general verdicts? How would statements of fact be distinguished from statements of opinion? How could comments on conduct in public life be separated from comments on personal character? Could libel be prosecuted as a crime? Varying answers were given then as now on the standards to be used.

Whatever may be the reasoning employed on particular cases historically, positions on libel have been strongly influenced by politics and personal attitudes. Even strong advocates of liberty of the press—such as Jefferson and Franklin—supported some legal limits on expression when they found themselves or their cohorts under journalistic attack. "THE LIBERTY OF THE PRESS, has, for some Ages, been allowed by all Parties in every free Nation, to be one of the most essential Preservatives of the Rights and Freedom of the People," Eleazer Oswald stated in his *Independent Gazetteer*. "But tho' all Parties admitted this, they have all, or at least some of all, in Turn, attempted to restrain it, by censuring and endeavouring to punish as Licentiousness, that Freedom, against themselves, which they claimed a Right to exercise against their Opponents."[4]

Thus, Hamilton could argue in the *Federalist* papers that a constitutional guarantee for the press would amount to nothing since "its security, whatever fine declarations may be inserted in any constitution respecting it, must altogether depend on public opinion, and on the general spirit of the people and of the government." Others were less pessimistic about the prospects for a press protection. In their correspondence of 1788 and 1789, Jefferson expressed fears about government suppression, while Madison insisted the greatest threat to unpopular opinion was the power of a majority of the people. Both agreed, however, that a bill of rights would have some useful effects in discouraging assaults on freedom. Jefferson admitted that it would not always accomplish its purpose, but pointed to "the legal check which it puts into the hands of the judiciary." Madison doubted that "parchment barriers" would protect liberties from the "decided sense of the public," but said that a bill of rights would be gradually incorporated into the national sentiment and when violated by government would be "a good ground for an appeal to the sense of the community."[5]

The demand for the press clause came despite continual statements from the supporters of the Constitution that the federal government would have no power over the press and that making exceptions to authority not given would suggest that the authority existed. "For why declare that things shall not be done which there is no power to do?" Hamilton asked in the *Federalist* papers. "Why for instance, should it be said, that the liberty of the press shall not be restrainted, when no power is given by which restrictions may be imposed?" Similarly, James Wilson told a public meeting in Philadelphia that the "sacred palladium of national freedom" would not be touched by the federal government. "In truth, then, the proposed system possesses no influence whatever upon the press," he said, "and it would have been merely nugatory to have introduced a formal declaration on the subject—nay, that very declaration might have been construed to imply that some degree of power was given, since we undertook to define its extent."[6]

Suspicions nevertheless remained. "All parties apparently agree, that the freedom of the press is a fundamental right, and ought not to be restrained by any taxes, duties, or in any manner whatever," wrote Richard Henry Lee, arguing that some pretexts might be found in the Constitution to suppress publications. "Why should not the people, in adopting a federal constitution, declare this, even if there are only doubts about it?" When Madison introduced his proposed bill of rights to Congress in 1789, he noted the public alarm over the lack of protection for civil liberties in the Constitution and the objections that had been made to listing freedoms to be guaranteed. The purpose of a bill of rights, he said, would be to point out where "the Government ought not to act, or to act only in a particular mode." He referred to liberty of the press as one of the "choicest privileges of the people" and proposed language for the bill of rights saying that it would be "inviolable" as "one of the great bulwarks of liberty."[7]

Before the great clamor arose for a bill of rights, Madison had expressed doubts about stating absolute guarantees that might be cast aside "where emergencies may overrule them." Jefferson, however, had argued that it was better to establish freedom of the press "in all cases . . . than not to do it in any." When the Federalists passed the Sedition Act of 1798, Madison insisted that individuals could use state courts to sue for damage to their reputations, but that there was no authority in the Constitution for federal actions against the press. "This security of the freedom of the press requires that it should be exempt not only from previous restraint by the Executive, as in Great Britain," he wrote, "but from legislative restraint also, and this exemption, to be effectual, must be an exemption not only from the previous inspection of licensers, but from the subsequent penalty of laws." He was able to conclude that "it would seem scarcely possible to doubt that no power whatever over the press was supposed to be delegated by the Constitution, as it originally stood, and that the amendment was intended as a positive and absolute reservation of it."[8]

The essence of conventional libertarian press theory was that individuals could successfully sue a publisher for libel under some circumstances, but that government could not place any restrictions on the press. Although early Americans believed that false aspersions could be a form of personal injury, they understood that a self-governing people required information and that any authority for government suppression was a greater threat to freedom than even the most irresponsible journalism. Courts have often ignored this willingness to trust the marketplace of ideas, and some historians have asserted that such tolerance hardly existed, but the revolutionary generation knew from its experience that the press could serve as an effective check on the abuse of power. Realizing that freedom of expression would always be endangered, those who demanded and ratified the First Amendment used the strongest possible terms in attempting to preserve a fundamental right for themselves and for future generations.

A Note on Sources

The historiography of press freedom in early America is curiously fragmented and frequently unreliable. Several reasons can be suggested. First, the existence of hundreds of eighteenth-century newspapers can be a formidable obstacle to any scholar who would attempt to trace the developments which preceded and immediately followed the adoption of the First Amendment. Fortunately, historians have been well-served by bibliographers of the sometimes fleeting products of clumsy, creaking wooden presses. An essential guide is Clarence S. Brigham, *History and Bibliography of American Newspapers, 1690–1820* (Worcester, Mass., 1947). Also helpful are Isaiah Thomas, *The History of Printing in America* (New York, 1970) and Edward C. Lathem, *Chronological Tables of American Newspapers, 1690–1820* (Barre, Mass., 1972).

Most early American newspapers are available—occasionally in disappointingly incomplete fashion—on microfilm or in microprint. *Newspapers on Microfilm,* published by the Library of Congress with continuous updates, is an indispensable finding aid. The forty thousand non-serial items listed in Charles Evans' *American Bibliography: A Chronological Dictionary of All Books, Pamphlets, and Periodical Publications Printed in the United States of America, 1639–1800* (14 vols., 1903–1959) and ten thousand imprints located since have been reproduced in microprint as a project of the Readex Corporation and the American Antiquarian Society. A convenient list of these publications is Clifford K. Shipton and James E. Mooney, *Na-*

tional Index of American Imprints Through 1800, The Short-Title Evans (Worcester, Mass., 1969).

A second reason for shortcomings in past studies of eighteenth-century press freedom has been the difficulty of recovering sufficiently the political culture in which newspapers operated. The sixty years of American journalism before the Stamp Act crisis has not been examined closely enough. If Daniel Boorstin, Arthur Schlesinger, Sr., Stephen Botein, and other historians noted in the introduction are correct, then the prerevolutionary press was sleepy and suppressed. A more tenable position is that of Gary B. Nash that newspapers had a part in the evolution of a radical mode of politics before the end of the French and Indian War. In this light, the revolutionary press and the early party press can be seen as outgrowths of an older heritage. The journalists Benjamin Franklin knew—from his older brother James through his grandson Benjamin Franklin Bache—challenged power in the radical Whig tradition and were well-versed in libertarian ideology.

Only in the 1960s and 1970s did historians such as Bernard Bailyn, Gordon Wood, Lance Banning, and Henry F. May begin to trace adequately the impact of republican ideas and Enlightenment ideals on popular thought. Although much of what colonial newspaper journalists and their defenders understood about freedom of expression came from Enlightenment philosophies and from English libertarian theory and practice, scholars have been slow to consider the implications of these connections for their understanding of the early American press and the First Amendment. An exception is Irving Brant, whose *The Bill of Rights, Its Origin and Meaning* (Indianapolis, 1965) is devoted largely to the background of the press clause and its interpretation at the time of the Sedition Act. Brant provides a spirited account of libertarian indignation at seditious libel and analyzes the development of the suppressive legal tactics used by British authorities. Aside from John Brewer's *Party Ideology and Popular Politics at the Accession of George III* (Cambridge, 1976) and, to some extent, Robert R. Rea's *The English Press in Politics, 1760–1774* (Lincoln, Nebr., 1963), studies of the press in England have largely ignored the distinctive ideological perceptions of eighteenth-century radical thought. There are, however, serviceable accounts of developments in journalistic freedom which include Laurence Hanson, *Government and the Press, 1695–1763* (London, 1936) and Fredrick S. Siebert, *Freedom of the Press in England, 1476–1776* (Urbana, Ill., 1952).

A third challenge to the historian is to see through the fires of controversy stirred up by Leonard W. Levy's *Freedom of Speech and Press in Early American History: Legacy of Suppression* (New York, 1963). Levy asserted that the First Amendment was not intended to supersede the common law of seditious libel, that the Framers were Blackstonians with regard to press freedom, and that the press was all but completely suppressed as a matter of common experience. Although accepted by many these assertions have produced protests from reviewers and articles offering evidence to the contrary. Among the articles are Gerald J. Baldasty, "Toward an Understanding of the First Amendment: Boston Newspapers, 1782–1791," *Journalism History* 3 (Spring 1976): 25–30, 32; MaryAnn Yodelis Smith and Gerald J. Baldasty, "Criticism of Public Officials and Government in the New Nation," *Journal of Communication Inquiry* 4 (Winter 1979): 53–74; David A. Anderson, "The Origins of the Press Clause," *U.C.L.A. Law Review* 30 (February 1983): 455–541; Jeffery A. Smith, "A Reappraisal of Legislative Privilege and American Colonial Journalism," *Journalism Quarterly* 61 (Spring 1984): 97–103, 141.

Levy revised his book for publication in 1985 as *Emergence of a Free Press*. The new version did not insist that the press was not free in practice, but still maintained that the law and theory were narrow. For critiques of *Emergence of a Free Press,* see David A. Rabban, "The Ahistorical Historian: Leonard Levy on Freedom of Expression in Early American History," *Stanford Law Review* 37 (February 1985): 795–856; David A. Anderson, "Levy Vs. Levy," *Michigan Law Review* 84 (February–April 1986): 777–86.

Having paid particular attention to Jefferson and Franklin, I should express my appreciation to those responsible for the current editorial projects devoted to their letters and other writings. *The Papers of Thomas Jefferson,* ed. Julian P. Boyd et al. (Princeton, 1950–), is an ambitious undertaking and one for which historians of early America are greatly indebted. *The Papers of Benjamin Franklin,* ed. Leonard W. Labaree, William B. Willcox, et al. (New Haven, 1959–), is the fourth major collection of volumes for Franklin and by far the most complete and authoritative. The Labaree et al. edition of Franklin's *Autobiography* (New Haven, 1964) provides helpful notes but lacks the author's cancellations, revisions, and additions available in *The Autobiography of Benjamin Franklin, A Genetic Text,* ed. J. A. Leo Lemay and P. M. Zall (Knoxville, Tenn., 1981).

In addition to Franklin's own *Pennsylvania Gazette,* newspapers to be consulted in any study of Philadelphia journalism include the

American Weekly Mercury, the *Pennsylvania Journal,* and the *Pennsylvania Chronicle.* Franklin's known contributions to London periodicals while he was a colonial agent are collected in *Benjamin Franklin's Letters to the Press, 1758–1775,* ed. Verner W. Crane (Chapel Hill, N.C., 1950). C. William Miller's *Benjamin Franklin's Philadelphia Printing, 1728–1766, A Descriptive Bibliography* (Philadelphia, 1974) is a detailed and well-illustrated examination of the publications turned out by Franklin's presses.

The most useful biography is still Carl Van Doren, *Benjamin Franklin* (New York, 1938). A general introduction to Franklin's business operations is Norma Summers, "Benjamin Franklin—Printing Entrepreneur" (Ph.D. dissertation, University of Alabama, 1979). Arthur B. Tourtellot, *Benjamin Franklin, The Shaping of Genius, The Boston Years* (Garden City, N.Y., 1977) is an exhaustive study of Franklin's youth and his first journalistic efforts. Among the few works to focus entirely on Franklin's writings are James A. Sappenfield, *A Sweet Instruction, Franklin's Journalism as a Literary Apprenticeship* (Carbondale, Ill., 1973) and Bruce I. Granger, *Benjamin Franklin, An American Man of Letters* (Ithaca, 1964). Franklin's most important competitor is the subject of Anna Janney DeArmond, *Andrew Bradford, Colonial Journalist* (Newark, Del., 1949).

Of the many books dealing with a single aspect of Franklin's life, the most valuable include: Alfred O. Aldridge, *Franklin and His French Contemporaries* (New York, 1957); Alfred O. Aldridge, *Benjamin Franklin and Nature's God* (Durham, N.C., 1967); Gerald Stourzh, *Benjamin Franklin and American Foreign Policy,* 2nd ed. (Chicago, 1969); James H. Hutson, *Pennsylvania Politics, 1764–1770, The Movement for Royal Government and Its Consequences* (Princeton, 1972); Benjamin H. Newcomb, *Franklin and Galloway: A Political Partnership* (New Haven, 1972); and Claude-Anne Lopez and Eugenia Herbert, *The Private Franklin, The Man and His Family* (New York, 1975).

Articles of particular relevance to Franklin's press theory and practice are Merton A. Christensen, "Franklin on the Hemphill Trial: Deism Versus Presbyterian Orthodoxy," *William and Mary Quarterly,* 3rd ser., 10 (July 1953): 422–40; Verner W. Crane, "Benjamin Franklin and the Stamp Act," Colonial Society of Massachusetts *Transactions* 32 (February 1934): 56–77; J. Philip Gleason, "A Scurrilous Colonial Election and Franklin's Reputation," *William and Mary Quarterly,* 3rd ser., 18 (January 1961): 68–84; Ralph L. Ketcham, "Benjamin Franklin and William Smith:

New Light on an Old Philadelphia Quarrel," *Pennsylvania Magazine of History and Biography* 88 (April 1964): 142–63; J. A. Leo Lemay, "Franklin's Suppressed 'Busy-Body'," *American Literature* 37 (November 1965): 307–11. On Franklin's closest associates in the printing business, see Robert H. Kany, "David Hall: Printing Partner of Benjamin Franklin" (Ph.D. dissertation, Pennsylvania State University, 1963); James D. Tagg, "Benjamin Franklin Bache and the Philadelphia *Aurora*" (Ph.D. dissertation, Wayne State University, 1973); Alan F. Dyer, "James Parker, Colonial Printer, 1715–1770" (Ph.D. dissertation, University of Michigan, 1977); and Jeffery A. Smith, "Impartiality and Revolutionary Ideology: Editorial Policies of the *South-Carolina Gazette*, 1732–1775," *Journal of Southern History* 49 (November 1983): 511–26.

List of Abbreviations

AHR	*American Historical Review*
APS	American Philosophical Society
Autobiography	*The Autobiography of Benjamin Franklin, A Genetic Text*, ed. J. A. Leo Lemay and P. M. Zall (Knoxville: University of Tennessee Press, 1981).
BF	Benjamin Franklin
BFB	Benjamin Franklin Bache
Cato's Letters	[John Trenchard and Thomas Gordon], *Cato's Letters*, 4 vols. (London: Printed for W. Wilkins, T. Woodward, J. Walthoe, and J. Peele, 1724).
DH	David Hall
HSP	Historical Society of Pennsylvania
JAH	*Journal of American History*
Jefferson, *Works*	*The Works of Thomas Jefferson*, ed. Paul L. Ford, 12 vols. (New York: G. P. Putnam's Sons, 1904–1905).
Jefferson, *Writings*	*The Writings of Thomas Jefferson*, ed. Andrew A. Lipscomb and Albert E. Bergh, 20 vols. (Washington, D.C.: Thomas Jefferson Memorial Association, 1904–1905).
JM	James Madison
JP	James Parker
PBF	*The Papers of Benjamin Franklin*, ed. Leonard W. Labaree, William B. Wilcox, et al. (New Haven: Yale University Press, 1959–).

173

PMHB	*Pennsylvania Magazine of History and Biography*
PT	Peter Timothy
PTJ	*The Papers of Thomas Jefferson,* ed. Julian P. Boyd et al. (Princeton: Princeton University Press, 1950–).
TJ	Thomas Jefferson
WBF	*The Writings of Benjamin Franklin,* ed. Albert H. Smyth, 10 vols. (New York: Macmillan Co. 1905–1907).
WJM	*The Writings of James Madison,* ed. Gaillard Hunt, 9 vols. (New York: G. P. Putnam's Sons, 1900–1910).
WMQ	*William and Mary Quarterly*

Newspapers

AU	[Philadelphia] *Aurora*
ADA	[Baltimore] *American and Daily Advertiser*
AWM	[Philadelphia] *American Weekly Mercury*
BCR	[Hudson, New York] *Balance and Columbian Repository*
BEP	*Boston Evening-Post*
BG	*Boston Gazette*
BJ	[London] *British Journal*
BNL	*Boston News-Letter*
CC	[Hartford] *Connecticut Courant*
CG	[New Haven] *Connecticut Gazette*
CGWR	*Carlisle Gazette, and Western Repository of Knowledge* [Pennsylvania]
CH	*Concord Herald* [New Hampshire]
CoC	[Boston] *Columbian Centinel*
EG	[Salem, Massachusetts] *Essex Gazette*
FG	[Philadelphia] *Federal Gazette*
FJ	[Philadelphia] *Freeman's Journal*
GA	[Philadelphia] *General Advertiser*
GSSC	[Charleston] *Gazette of the State of South Carolina*
HF	[Boston] *Herald of Freedom*
IC	[Boston] *Independent Chronicle*
IG	[Philadelphia] *Independent Gazetteer*
LJ	*London Journal*
MC	[Boston] *Massachusetts Centinel*
MG	[Middletown, Connecticut] *Middlesex Gazette*
NEC	[Boston] *New-England Courant*
NG	[Philadelphia] *National Gazette*
NHG	[Portsmouth] *New-Hampshire Gazette*
NJG	[Burlington] *New-Jersey Gazette*
NM	*Newport Mercury*

NYJ	*New-York Journal*
NYM	*New-York Mercury*
NYPB	*New-York Weekly Post-Boy*
NYWJ	*New-York Weekly Journal*
PC	[Philadelphia] *Pennsylvania Chronicle*
PG	[Philadelphia] *Pennsylvania Gazette*
PJ	[Philadelphia] *Pennsylvania Journal*
P'sG	[Philadelphia] *Porcupine's Gazette*
RG	[New York] *Royal Gazette*
RIG	[Newport] *Rhode-Island Gazette*
RNYG	*Rivington's New-York Gazetteer*
SCG	[Charleston] *South-Carolina Gazette*
UI	[Philadelphia] *Universal Instructor*
VG	[Williamsburg] *Virginia Gazette*
WR	[Boston] *Weekly Rehearsal*

Notes

Preface

1. For a discussion of the legal and historical implications of regarding the press as an institution functioning as a part of the American political system, see David A. Anderson, "The Origins of the Press Clause," *U.C.L.A. Law Review* 30 (February 1983): 456–62.

2. *Poor Richard Improved*, 1757, in *PBF* 7: 86–87. On the interrelationship of rights, principles, practices, and institutions, see Thomas I. Emerson, *The System of Freedom of Expression* (New York: Random House, 1970), p. 4. For review and analysis of the historical studies which have identified and discussed radical Whig thought in early America, see Robert E. Shalhope, "Toward a Republican Synthesis: The Emergence of an Understanding of Republicanism in American Historiography," *WMQ*, 3rd ser., 29 (January 1972): 49–80; Robert E. Shalhope, "Republicanism and Early American Historiography," *WMQ*, 3rd ser., 39 (April 1982): 334–56. See also Joyce Appleby, "Introduction: Republicanism and Ideology," and Linda K. Kerber, "The Republican Ideology of the Revolutionary Generation," *American Quarterly* 37 (Fall 1985): 461–73, and 474–95, respectively.

3. *Report on the Resolutions*, in *WJM*, 6: 387–89, 398.

4. Leonard W. Levy, "Liberty and the First Amendment: 1790–1800," *AHR* 68 (October 1962): 22n; Anderson, "The Origins of the Press Clause," pp. 536–37.

Introduction

1. Arthur S. Miller, "An Inquiry into the Relevance of the Intentions of the Founding Fathers, With Special Emphasis Upon the Doctrine of

Separation of Powers," *Arkansas Law Review* 27 (Winter 1973): 596, 598; Leonard W. Levy, *Judgments: Essays on American Constitutional History* (Chicago: Quadrangle Books, 1972), p. 71. On Constitutional rationales, see Philip Bobbitt, *Constitutional Fate, Theory of the Constitution* (New York: Oxford University Press, 1982). On the Supreme Court's attempts to use history, see Alfred H. Kelly, "Clio and the Court: An Illicit Love Affair," *Supreme Court Review* 1965 (1965): 119–58; Charles A. Miller, *The Supreme Court and the Uses of History* (Cambridge: Harvard University Press, 1969); Wilcomb E. Washburn, "The Supreme Court's Use and Abuse of History," *Organization of American Historians Newsletter* 11 (August 1983): 7–9. Portions of this introduction are taken, with permission, from Jeffery A. Smith, "Legal Historians and the Press Clause," *Communications and the Law* 8 (August 1986): 69–80.

2. Thomas I. Emerson, "Colonial Intentions and Current Realities of the First Amendment," *University of Pennsylvania Law Review* 125 (1977): 737–60; Vincent Blasi, "The Checking Value in First Amendment Theory," *American Bar Foundation Research Journal* 1977 (Summer 1977): 523–28. See also Stephen W. Gard, "The Absoluteness of the First Amendment," *Nebraska Law Review* 58 (1979): 1053–86.

3. Philip B. Kurland, "The Irrelevance of the Constitution: The First Amendment's Freedom of Speech and Freedom of Press Clauses," *Drake Law Review* 29 (1979–1980): 4, 5; Leonard W. Levy, *Emergence of a Free Press* (New York: Oxford University Press, 1985), p. 348.

4. TJ to Judge Johnson, June 12, 1823, in *The Writings of Thomas Jefferson,* ed. H. A. Washington, 9 vols. (Washington, D.C.: Taylor and Maury, 1853–54), 7: 296; JM to John G. Jackson, December 27, 1821, in *WJM,* 9: 74; JM to Spencer Roane, May 6, 1821, ibid., p. 59; JM to M. L. Hurlbert, May 1830, ibid., p. 372. On the importance of the original intention, see Raoul Berger, *Government by Judiciary* (Cambridge: Harvard University Press, 1977), pp. 363–72.

5. Leonard W. Levy, *Freedom of Speech and Press in Early American History, Legacy of Suppression* (New York: Harper & Row, 1963), pp. xxi, 309; Merrill Jensen, review of *Legacy of Suppression, Harvard Law Review* 75 (1961): 457. For reactions similar to Jensen's review, see James Morton Smith, review of *Legacy of Suppression, WMQ,* 3rd ser., 20 (January 1963): 156–59; Lawrence H. Leder, "The Role of Newspapers in Early America 'In Defense of Their Own Liberty'," *Huntington Library Quarterly* 30 (November 1966): 1–16. For examples of research that has challenged Levy's thesis, see Dwight L. Teeter, "A Legacy of Expression: Philadelphia Newspapers and Congress During the War for Independence, 1775–1783" (Ph.D. dissertation, University of Wisconsin, 1966); MaryAnn Patricia Yodelis, "Boston's Second Major Paper War: Economics, Politics, and the Theory and Practice of Political Expression in the Press, 1763–1775" (Ph.D. dissertation, University of

Wisconsin, 1971); Gerald J. Baldasty, "Toward an Understanding of the First Amendment: Boston Newspapers, 1782–1791," *Journalism History* 3 (Spring 1976): 25–30, 32; MaryAnn Yodelis Smith and Gerald J. Baldasty, "Criticism of Public Officials and Government in the New Nation," *Journal of Communication Inquiry* 4 (Winter 1979): 53–74. See also Jeffery A. Smith, "Research Raises New Challenge to Levy View of First Amendment," *Media Law Notes,* Newsletter for the Law Division of the Association for Education in Journalism and Mass Communication and the Mass Communications Law Section of the Association of American Law Schools, 11 (April 1984): 1–2.

6. Levy, *Emergence of a Free Press,* pp. vii, x, xii, xiii–xiv.

7. Anderson, "The Origins of the Press Clause," pp. 533, 534.

8. Ibid., p. 534.

9. Levy, *Emergence of a Free Press,* pp. xvii, 12. On the evolution of American law at this time, see Morton J. Horwitz, "The Emergence of an Instrumental Conception of American Law, 1780–1820," *Perspectives in American History* 5 (1971): 287–326.

10. Stewart Macaulay, "Law and the Behavioral Sciences: Is There Any There There?" *Law & Policy* 6 (April 1984): 149–87; Richard L. Abel, "Law Books and Books about Law," *Stanford Law Review* 26 (November 1973): 175–228.

11. Bernard Bailyn, *The Ideological Origins of the American Revolution* (Cambridge: The Belknap Press of Harvard University Press, 1967); Gordon S. Wood, *The Creation of the American Republic, 1776–1787* (Chapel Hill: University of North Carolina Press for the Institute of Early American History and Culture, 1969); Lance Banning, *The Jeffersonian Persuasion, Evolution of a Party Ideology* (Ithaca: Cornell University Press, 1978). For studies of the pressures faced and not always resisted by early American printers, see, e.g., Alfred L. Lorenz, *Hugh Gaine, A Colonial Printer-Editor's Odyssey to Loyalism* (Carbondale: Southern Illinois University Press, 1972); Dwight L. Teeter, "Benjamin Towne: The Precarious Career of a Persistent Printer," *PMHB* 89 (July 1965): 316–30. On public support, see Jeffery A. Smith, "Public Opinion and the Press Clause," *Journalism History,* forthcoming. I have proposed a theory statement which says: "Extra-legal efforts by individuals to restrain or free the press increase as unresolved tensions in political, economic, or social systems increase." Jeffery A. Smith, "Further Steps Toward a Theory of Press Control," *Journalism History* 8 (Autumn-Winter 1981–1982): 95.

12. *BG,* May 26, 1755. For the view that the colonial press was stunted but sprang to life at the Revolution, see Levy, *Emergence of a Free Press,* pp. x, 15, 16; Daniel J. Boorstin, *The Americans, The Colonial Experience* (New York: Random House, 1958), p. 335; Arthur M. Schlesinger, *Prelude to Independence, The Newspaper War on Britain, 1764–1776* (New York: Alfred A. Knopf, 1958), pp. vii–viii, 61–66,

296–97; Clinton Rossiter, *Seedtime of the Republic, The Origin of the American Tradition of Political Liberty* (New York: Harcourt, Brace and Co., 1953), pp. 28–31. See also Thomas C. Leonard, "News for a Revolution: The Exposé in America, 1768–1773," *Journal of American History* 67 (June 1980): 27. For an alternative view, see Gary B. Nash, "The Transformation of Urban Politics, 1700–1765," *Journal of American History* 60 (December 1973): 606, 616–20.

13. Harold L. Nelson, "Seditious Libel in Colonial America," *American Journal of Legal History* 3 (April 1959): 160–72; Levy, *Emergence of a Free Press*, pp. xii, 17, 83.

14. Levy, *Emergence of a Free Press*, p. 14; Jeffery A. Smith, "A Reappraisal of Legislative Privilege and American Colonial Journalism," *Journalism Quarterly* 61 (Spring 1984): 97–98.

15. Levy, *Emergence of a Free Press*, p. 84; Smith, "A Reappraisal of Legislative Privilege and American Colonial Journalism," pp. 98–103.

16. Levy, *Emergence of a Free Press*, p. 84; *NEC*, July 9, 1722; *CG*, April 10, 1756; *NYPB*, March 15, November 8, 1756; Smith, "A Reappraisal of Legislative Privilege and American Colonial Journalism," pp. 98–99, 101.

17. Levy, *Emergence of a Free Press*, pp. 84, 182–83, 185; Dwight L. Teeter, "Press Freedom and the Public Printing: Pennsylvania, 1775–83," *Journalism Quarterly* 45 (Autumn 1968): 445–51.

18. Worthington C. Ford, et al., eds. *Journals of the Continental Congress, 1774–1789*, 34 vols. (Washington, D.C.: U.S. Government Printing Office, 1904–1937), 4: 18–20; Levy, *Emergence of a Free Press*, p. 177; [William Goddard], *The Prowess of the Whig Club* (Baltimore, [1777]); Ward L. Miner, *William Goddard, Newspaperman* (Durham, N.C.: Duke University Press, 1962), pp. 150–62, 168–73.

19. Levy, *Emergence of a Free Press*, p. xii; James Alexander, *A Brief Narrative of the Case and Trial of John Peter Zenger, Printer of the New York Weekly Journal*, ed. Stanley N. Katz, 2nd ed. (Cambridge: Belknap Press of Harvard University Press, 1972), p. 84.

20. Levy, *Emergence of a Free Press*, pp. 48–51, 127; *Minutes of the Provincial Council of Pennsylvania*, 16 vols. (Philadelphia and Harrisburg: Severns, Fenn, 1851–53), 3: 143, 145, 369–70; Alexander, *A Brief Narrative of the Case and Trial of John Peter Zenger*, p. 84.

21. *FG*, September 12, 1789; Bernard Schwartz, ed., *The Bill of Rights: A Documentary History*, 2 vols. (New York: Chelsea House, 1971), 1: 235, 266, 278, 284, 287, 300, 335, 342, 378; "The Virginia Constitution," in *PTJ*, 1: 344–45, 353, 363; Levy, *Emergence of a Free Press*, pp. 192, 250.

22. Frank L. Mott, *Jefferson and the Press* (Baton Rouge: Louisiana State University Press, 1943); Leonard W. Levy, *Jefferson & Civil Liberties, The Darker Side* (New York: Quadrangle, 1973), pp. 42–69; Jan

C. Robbins, "Jefferson and the Press, the Resolution of an Antinomy," *Journalism Quarterly* 48 (Autumn 1971): 421–30, 465.

23. *Autobiography*, p. 17. Franklin describes the *Courant* as the second newspaper to appear in the colonies, but it was founded after the *Boston News-letter* (1704), *Boston Gazette* (1719), and *American Weekly Mercury* (1719). James Franklin was the first printer of the *Gazette*, which was the second continuously published newspaper in America. Massachusetts authorities suppressed Benjamin Harris' *Publick Occurrences* after one issue in 1690. Edward C. Lathem, comp., *Chronological Tables of American Newspapers, 1690–1820* (Barre, Mass.: American Antiquarian Society and Barre Publishers, 1972), p. 2.

24. Levy, *Emergence of a Free Press*, pp. 119–21, 192–93; Leonard W. Levy, ed., *Freedom of the Press from Zenger to Jefferson* (Indianapolis: Bobbs-Merrill Co., 1966), pp. 3–4; Clinton Rossiter, "The Political Theory of Benjamin Franklin," *PMHB* 76 (July 1952): 274; James A. Sappenfield, *A Sweet Instruction, Franklin's Journalism as a Literary Apprenticeship* (Carbondale: Southern Illinois University Press, 1973), p. 108; Stephen Botein, " 'Meer Mechanics' and an Open Press: The Business and Political Strategies of Colonial Printers," *Perspectives in American History* 9 (1975): 127–225; Stephen Botein, "Printers and the American Revolution," in Bernard Bailyn and John B. Hench, eds., *The Press & the American Revolution* (Worcester, Mass.: American Antiquarian Society, 1980), pp. 11–57.

25. On Franklin's range of intellectual traits and place in Enlightenment thought, see Adrienne Koch, "Pragmatic Wisdom and the American Enlightenment," *WMQ*, 3rd ser., 18 (July 1961): 313–22, 329; Michael Kammen, *People of Paradox, An Inquiry Concerning the Origins of American Civilization* (New York: Alfred A. Knopf, 1972), pp. 194–96; Henry F. May, *The Enlightenment in America* (New York: Oxford University Press, 1976), pp. 126–32.

26. *AWM*, February 12, 1740. The subject of the letter was Franklin's "low Craft" in neglecting to include Governor George Thomas' reasons for not approving a revenue measure in the printed *Votes* of the Pennsylvania Assembly.

Chapter I. The English Experience

1. BF to William Strahan, October 27, 1753, in *PBF*, 5: 82–83.

2. *Autobiography*, pp. 68, 95–96, 108, 119; BF to Thomas Darling and Nathan Whiting, November 25, 1754, in *PBF*, 5: 440–41; Carl Bridenbaugh, *Cities in Revolt, Urban Life in America, 1743–1776* (New York: Oxford University Press, 1971), p. 185. The networks within the colonial printing trade, including Franklin's various connections, are the subject of Charles W. Wetherell, "Brokers of the Word: An Essay in

the Social History of the Early American Press, 1639–1783" (Ph.D. dissertation, University of New Hampshire, 1980).

3. Winnifred R. Reid, "Beginnings of Printing in New Haven," in *Papers in Honor of Andrew Keogh* (New Haven: Privately Printed, 1938), pp. 67–88; JP to BF, June 11, 1766, in *PBF*, 13: 301–302. On Thomas Clap and the New Light/Old Light controversy, see Richard L. Bushman, *From Puritan to Yankee, Character and the Social Order in Connecticut, 1690–1765* (Cambridge: Harvard University Press, 1967): 235–66; Louis L. Tucker, *Puritan Protagonist: President Thomas Clap of Yale College* (Chapel Hill: University of North Carolina Press for the Institute of Early American History and Culture, 1962).

4. *CG, February* 7, 1756.

5. *CG,* April 12, 1755.

6. *HF,* September 15, 1788.

7. *FJ,* April 25, 1781.

8. TJ to Spencer Roane, September 6, 1819, in Jefferson, *Works,* 12: 136.

9. On the obstacles to the acceptance of orthodox religion in England, see Keith Thomas, *Religion and the Decline of Magic, Studies in Popular Beliefs in Sixteenth and Sevententh Century England* (London: Weidenfeld and Nicolson, 1971), pp. 151–73.

10. The most satisfactory account of press freedom in sixteenth-century England is Fredrick S. Siebert, *Freedom of the Press in England, 1476–1776, The Rise and Decline of Government Control* (Urbana: University of Illinois Press, 1952), pp. 21–104.

11. Siebert, *Freedom of the Press in England,* pp. 107–78; Joseph Frank, *The Beginnings of the English Newspaper, 1620–1660* (Cambridge: Harvard University Press, 1961); *BG,* June 2, 1755. On the Prynne case, see Brian Manning, *The English People and the English Revolution, 1640–1649* (London: Heinemann, 1976), pp. 2–3; Edward, Earl of Clarendon, *The History of the Rebellion and Civil Wars in England Begun in the Year 1641,* 6 vols. (Oxford: Clarendon Press, 1888), 1: 265–70; Proceedings Against John Bastwick, Henry Burton, and William Prynn, 3 Howell's State Trials 711 (1637).

12. Siebert, *Freedom of the Press in England,* pp. 179–302; Bernard Capp, *English Almanacs, 1500–1800, Astrology and the Popular Press* (Ithaca: Cornell University Press, 1979). On Lilly, see Capp, *English Almanacs,* pp. 44, 48–49, 57–58, 73–86; Derek Parker, *Familiar to All, William Lilly and Astrology in the Seventeenth Century* (London: Jonathan Cape, 1975); William Lilly, *Mr. William Lilly's History of his Life and Times, from the Year 1602, to 1681,* 2nd ed. (London: Printed for J. Roberts, 1715).

13. *Journals of the House of Commons,* 11: 305–6. For the argument that this action remedied a defect in the Bill of Rights, see, e.g., *"The Liberty of the PRESS,"* in *Gentleman's Magazine* 8 (January 1738): 35.

The Walpole administration was, however, successful in imposing theater censorship. Vincent J. Liesenfeld, *The Licensing Act of 1737* (Madison: University of Wisconsin Press, 1984).

14. Siebert, *Freedom of the Press in England,* pp. 305–45; J. A. Downie, *Robert Harley and the Press, Propaganda and Public Opinion in the Age of Swift and Defoe* (Cambridge: Cambridge University Press, 1979); Edward Hughes, "The English Stamp Duties, 1664–1764," *English Historical Review* 56 (April 1941); 234–64; John L. Bullion, *A Great and Necessary Measure, George Grenville and the Genesis of the Stamp Act, 1763–1765* (Columbia: University of Missouri Press, 1982); Edmund S. and Helen M. Morgan, *The Stamp Act Crisis, Prologue to Revolution,* rev. ed. (New York: Collier Books, 1963); *The Craftsman,* 14 vols. (London: Printed for R. Francklin, 1731–37), 8: 73–74; Laurence Hanson, *Government and the Press, 1695–1763* (London: Oxford University Press, 1936), p. 119. The *Craftsman* observed that some journalists were "appearing at first on the *popular Side,* with no other view than being *bought off,* and *setting Themselves to Market." Craftsman,* 8: 247.

15. Arthur Aspinall, "Statistical Accounts of the London Newspapers in the Eighteenth Century," *English Historical Review* 63 (April 1948): 201–32; Samuel Johnson, *The Idler and the Adventurer,* ed. W. J. Bate, John M. Bullitt, and L. F. Powell (New Haven: Yale University Press, 1963), p. 94. On the politics and press of this period, see John Brewer, *Party Ideology and Popular Politics at the Accession of George III* (Cambridge: Cambridge University Press, 1976); Robert R. Rea, *The English Press in Politics, 1760–1774* (Lincoln: University of Nebraska Press, 1963); Thomas W. Perry, *Public Opinion, Propaganda, and Politics in Eightenth-Century England, A Study of the Jew Bill of 1753* (Cambridge: Harvard University Press, 1962).

16. Siebert, *Freedom of the Press in England,* pp. 346–63; Benjamin B. Hoover, *Samuel Johnson's Parliamentary Reporting, Debates in the Senate of Lilliput* (Berkeley: University of California Press, 1953); *Gentleman's Magazine* 8 (January 1738): 28. For examples of publishers being reprimanded, see *Journal of the House of Lords,* 19: 253; 27: 107–9.

17. Brewer, *Party Ideology and Popular Politics at the Accession of George III,* pp. 163–200; Pauline Maier, "John Wilkes and American Disillusionment with Britain," *WMQ,* 3rd ser., 20 (July 1963): 373–95; Richard J. Hooker, "The American Revolution Seen Through a Wine Glass," *WMQ,* 3rd ser., 11 (January 1954): 52–57; BF to William Franklin, April 16, 1768, in *PBF* 15: 98–99.

18. Rea, *The English Press in Politics,* pp. 59–69, 174–87, 201–11; Siebert, *Freedom of the Press in England,* pp. 378–80, 385–88; Peter D. G. Thomas, "The Beginning of Parliamentary Reporting in Newspapers, 1768–1774," *English Historical Review* 74 (October 1959): 623–36;

Peter D. G. Thomas, "John Wilkes and Freedom of the Press (1771),"
Bulletin of the Institute of Historical Research 33 (1960): 86–98.

19. William Strahan to DH, November 9, 1771; November 4, 1772,
in "Correspondence Between William Strahan and David Hall, 1763–
1777," *PMHB* 12 (1888): 121, 245–46; Tobias Smollett, *The Expedition
of Humphry Clinker* (London: Oxford University Press, 1966), pp.
102–3.

20. *BJ*, September 22, 1722. On the problems with party labels, see
Sir Lewis Namier, *England in the Age of the American Revolution*, 2nd
ed. (New York: St. Martin's Press, 1966), pp. 180–81. For statements
on the inevitability and importance of parties and political journalism in
free nations, see J. A. W. Gunn, ed., *Factions No More, Attitudes to
Party in Government and Opposition in Eighteenth-Century England,
Extracts from Contemporary Sources* (London: Frank Cass, 1972), pp.
113, 115, 168, 194, 197, 229, 234. For a general discussion of English
writings on freedom of the press and the view that libertarian ideas on
the subject were not the product of any one political group, see G. Stuart
Adam, "The Press and Its Liberty: Myth and Ideology in Eighteenth-
Century Politics," (Ph.D. dissertation, Queens University, 1978).

21. Caroline Robbins, *The Eighteenth-Century Commonwealthman,
Studies in the Transition, Development and Circumstance of English
Liberal Thought from the Restoration of Charles II until the War With
the Thirteen Colonies* (Cambridge: Harvard University Press, 1959),
pp. 115–25; David L. Jacobson, ed., *The English Libertarian Heritage,
From the Writings of John Trenchard and Thomas Gordon in The Independent Whig and Cato's Letters* (Indianapolis: Bobbs-Merrill Co.,
1965), pp. xvii–lx.

22. *Cato's Letters*, 1: 99, 102, 256; 3: 242, 243, 248. For an example
of these arguments being paraphrased and used against the Sedition Act
of 1798, see *AU*, July 10, 1798. Cato's essays on freedom of expression
originally appeared in the *LJ*, February 4, June 10, 1721; *BJ*, October
20, 27, 1722.

23. Isaac Kramnick, *Bolingbroke and His Circle: The Politics of Nos-
talgia in the Age of Walpole* (Cambridge: Harvard University Press,
1968); Simon Varey, ed., *Lord Bolingbroke, Contributions to the Craftsman* (Oxford: Clarendon Press, 1982), pp. xiii–xxviii; Bailyn, *The
Origins of American Politics*, pp. 45–48; Banning, *The Jeffersonian
Persuasion*, pp. 57–60; Robert M. Weir, "The Role of the Newspaper
Press in the Southern Colonies on the Eve of the Revolution: An Interpretation," in Bailyn and Hench, eds., *The Press & the American Revolution*, pp. 119–22; May, *The Enlightenment in America*, pp. 74, 90,
293; Charles B. Sandford, *Thomas Jefferson and His Library, A Study
of His Literary Interests and of the Religious Attitudes Revealed by
Relevant Titles in His Library* (Hamden, Conn.: Archon Books, 1977),

pp. 84, 121–22, 142, 149; TJ to Francis Eppes, January 19, 1821, in Jefferson, *Works*, 12: 194–95.

24. Trial of Richard Francklin, 17 Howell's State Trials 625; Abel Boyer, ed., *The Political State of Great-Britain*, 60 vols. (London: Printed for T. Cooper, 1710–1740), 42: 88; Hanson, *Government and the Press*, pp. 23, 67–68; *Craftsman*, 7: 246, 8: 93–94.

25. *Craftsman*, 8: 24, 285–97; [William Arnall], *The Case of Opposition Stated, Between the Craftsman and the People* (London: Printed for J. Roberts, 1731), pp. 38, 43–58. See also *The Doctrine of Innuendo's Discuss'd; Or the Liberty of the Press Maintain'd* (London: Printed for the Author, 1731) and *The Craftsman's Doctrine and Practice of the Liberty of the Press, Explained to the Meanest Capacity* (London: Printed for J. Roberts, 1732). On Bollingbroke's activities against the press, which apparently did not include the idea for the Stamp Act of 1712, see Downie, *Robert Harley and the Press*, pp. 151–54. Bolingbroke may have been more interested in the appearance of suppression than the reality. He released a number of prisoners who apologized. Daniel Defoe and Jonathan Swift were among those who felt that the ministry did far too little to control the press. Hanson, *Government and the Press*, pp. 62–63; *The Prose Works of Jonathan Swift*, ed. Herbert Davis, 14 vols. (Oxford: Basil Blackwell, 1939–1968), 7: 103–6.

26. Hanson, *Government and the Press*, pp. 69–70, 140; *Gentleman's Magazine* 7 (September 1737): 551, and 8 (January 1738): 28–30, 32–34, 35–37; William Cobbett, ed., *The Parliamentary History of England*, 36 vols. (London: Printed for T. C. Hansard, 1806–1820), 8: 1269; E. Raymond Turner, "The Excise Scheme of 1733," *The English Historical Review* 42 (1927): 34–57; J. H. Plumb, *Sir Robert Walpole, The King's Minister* (London: Cresset Press, 1960), pp. 140–43, 250–71. From jail, Henry Haines described his plight in *Treachery, Baseness, and Cruelty Display'd to the Full. . . .* (London: Printed for Henry Haines, 1740).

27. *Autobiography*, pp. 37–40; Robert W. Kenny, "James Ralph: An Eighteenth-Century Philadelphian in Grub Street," *PMHB* 64 (April 1940): 218–42; Hanson, *Government and the Press*, pp. 2, 52, 68, 71–72, 118–21; *The Champion*, 2 vols. (London: Printed for J. Huggonson, 1741), 2: 88–95.

28. [James Ralph], *The Case of Authors By Profession or Trade. . . .* (London: Printed for R. Griffiths, 1758), pp. 20, 22, 37–38.

29. *SCG*, March 23, 1765. On the use of Cato and other radical Whig writers in the colonial press, see Gary Huxford, "The English Libertarian Tradition in the Colonial Newspaper," *Journalism Quarterly* 45 (Winter 1968): 677–86. For a discussion of the reasonableness of American fears, see Gordon S. Wood, "Conspiracy and the Paranoid Style: Causal-

ity and Deceit in the Eighteenth Century," *WMQ*, 3rd ser., 39 (July 1982): 401–41.

30. Paul S. Boyer, "Borrowed Rhetoric: The Massachusetts Excise Controversy of 1754," *WMQ*, 3rd ser., 21 (July 1964): 328–51; *NYJ*, February 15, March 22, 1770; Smith, "A Reappraisal of Legislative Privilege and American Colonial Journalism," p. 102. For a loyalist's view of the McDougall episode, see Thomas Jones, *History of New York During the Revolutionary War*, ed. Edward Floyd De Lancey, 2 vols. (New York: New York Historical Society, 1879), 1: 24–33.

31. Cobbett, ed., *Parliamentary History*, 16: 1153, 1154, 1155, 1166. For examples of the press being referred to as the palladium or bulwark of English liberties, see pp. 1133, 1164, 1260, 1262, 1282, 1290.

32. Cobbett, ed. *Parliamentary History*, 16: 1166, 1282, 1290.

Chapter II. The Marketplace of Ideas Concept

1. Robert Ashton, *The English Civil War, Conservatism and Revolution, 1603–1649* (London: Weidenfeld and Nicolson, 1978), pp. 249–50; J. H. Hexter, "Power Struggle, Parliament, and Liberty in Early Stuart England," *Journal of Modern History* 50 (March 1978): 47–48; George Rudé, *Wilkes and Liberty, A Social Study of 1763 to 1774* (Oxford: Clarendon Press, 1962); Brewer, *Party Ideology and Popular Politics at the Accession of George III*, p. 24; Banning, *The Jeffersonian Persuasion*, pp. 130–34. Bolingbroke and his cohorts were among those who ridiculed the idea that corruption preserved the Constitution. *Craftsman*, 8: 66.

2. *IG*, April 13, 1782; *The Essays of Michel de Montaigne*, trans. and ed. Jacob Zeitlin, 3 vols. (New York: Alfred A. Knopf, Inc., 1934–1936), 3: 129–31, 134, 135, 137, 229. On the significance of the competition of scientific explanations, see Thomas S. Kuhn, *The Structure of Scientific Revolutions*, 2nd ed. (Chicago: University of Chicago Press, 1970). For examples of the marketplace of ideas concept being espoused in legislatures, see *Journals of the House of Burgesses of Virginia, 1727–1734, 1736–1740*, ed. H. R. McIlwaine (Richmond, Virginia, 1910), p. 176; *Journals of the General Assembly and House of Representatives, 1776–1780*, ed. William E. Hemphill, Wylma A. Wates, and R. Nicholas Olsberg (Columbia: University of South Carolina Press, 1970), p. 53.

3. Sir Simonds D'Ewes, *A Compleat Journal of the Votes, Speeches and Debates, Both of the House of Lords and House of Commons Throughout the Whole Reign of Queen Elizabeth, Of Glorious Memory* (London, Paul Bowes, 1693; reprint ed., Wilmington, Delaware: Scholarly Resources, Inc., n.d.), pp. 237, 239. On Wentworth, see J. E. Neale, "Peter Wentworth," *The English Historical Review* 39 (January, April 1924): 36–54, 175–205; J. B. Black, *The Reign of Elizabeth, 1558–1603* (Oxford: Clarendon Press, 1959), pp. 215–26. On the development

of free debate in Parliament, see J. E. Neale, "The Commons' Privilege of Free Speech in Parliament," in R. W. Seton-Watson, ed., *Tudor Studies* (London: Longmans, Green & Co., 1924), pp. 257–86. This paragraph and some of those which follow in this chapter are adapted with permission of the publisher from Jeffery A. Smith, "Freedom of Expression and the Marketplace of Ideas Concept from Milton to Jefferson," *Journal of Communication Inquiry* 7 (Summer 1981): 47–63.

4. Christopher Hill, *The World Turned Upside Down: Radical Ideas During the English Revolution* (New York: The Viking Press, 1972), pp. 82–85; Christopher Hill, *Milton and the English Revolution* (New York: The Viking Press, 1978), pp. 150–57; "Robinson's Farewell Address to the Pilgrims Upon Their Departure From Holland, 1620," in *Words of John Robinson, Old South Leaflets No. 142*, pp. 1–2; Jeremy Taylor, *A Dicourse on the Liberty of Prophesying* (London: Printed for R. Royston, 1647), p. 6.

5. William Haller, ed., *Tracts on Liberty in the Puritan Revolution, 1638–1647*, 3 vols. (New York: Columbia University Press, 1934), 3: 39, 69, 91, 94, 135, 164–66, 172.

6. *Areopagitica* in *Complete Prose Works of John Milton*, ed. Don M. Wolfe, 7 vols. (New Haven: Yale University Press, 1953–1975), 2: 504, 551, 553, 554, 561. On the circumstances of the composition of *Areopagitica*, see Don M. Wolfe, *Milton in the Puritan Revolution* (New York: Thomas Nelson and Sons, 1941), pp. 120–38; Hill, *Milton and the English Revolution*, pp. 4–5, 93–116, 149–62.

7. Richard Baxter, *Aphorismes of Justification* (1649), "To the Reader," quoted in William Haller, *Liberty and Reformation in the Puritan Revolution* (New York: Columbia University Press, 1955), pp. 171–72. For Leveller views, see Wolfe, *Milton in the Puritan Revolution*, pp. 128–38; Don M. Wolfe, ed., *Leveller Manifestoes of the Puritan Revolution* (New York: Thomas Nelson and Sons, 1944), pp. 128, 327–28; William Haller and Godfrey Davies, eds., *The Leveller Tracts, 1647–1653* (New York: Columbia University Press in cooperation with Henry E. Huntington Library and Art Gallery, 1944), pp. 166–67.

8. Milton, *Areopagitica*, p. 565; H. Sylvia Anthony, "*Mercurius Politicus* Under Milton," *Journal of the History of Ideas* 27 (October-December 1966): 593–609; Mark Fackler and Clifford G. Christians, "John Milton's Place in Journalism History: Champion or Turncoat?" *Journalism Quarterly* 57 (Winter 1980): 569. On Nedham, see Joseph Frank, *Cromwell's Press Agent: A Critical Biography of Marchmont Nedham, 1620–1678* (Lanham, Md.: University Press of America, 1980).

9. Ernest Sirluck, "*Areopagitica* and a Forgotten Licensing Controversy," *Review of English Studies*, n.s. 11 (1960): 260–74. The pamphlets by Tindal, Gregory, and Defoe are reprinted in Stephen Parks, ed., *Freedom of the Press: Six Tracts, 1698–1709* (New York: Garland Publishing, Inc., 1974). For the debate on Milton's contemporary influ-

ence, see William R. Parker, *Milton's Contemporary Reputation* (Columbus: Ohio State University Press, 1940), pp. 1–65; Haller, *Liberty and Reformation in the Puritan Revolution,* p. 187; Hill, *Milton and the English Revolution,* pp. 220–30; Blair Worden, "Milton Among the Radicals," *Times Literary Supplement,* December 2, 1977, pp. 1394–95.

10. [Anthony Ashley Cooper, 3rd earl of Shaftesbury], *Characteristics of Men, Manners, Opinions, Times,* 3 vols. (London, 1711), 1: 61, 64, 69, 74–75; *Cato's Letters,* 3: 245, 248–49.

11. *PG,* June 10, 1731; July 24, 1740; *NYWJ,* November 12, 19, 1733. On Milton's importance, see George F. Sensabaugh, *Milton in Early America* (Princeton: Princeton University Press, 1964).

12. *NYPB,* May 2, 1752; *CG,* February 7, 1756. Franklin's almanac said, *"Craft* must be at charge for clothes, but *Truth* can go naked." *Poor Richard,* 1747, in *PBF,* 3: 104.

13. William Bollan, *The Freedom of Speech and Writing Upon Public Affairs, Considered* (London: Printed by S. Baker, 1766), p. 3; *NYJ,* January 5, 1775; *NYM,* January 9, 1775.

14. Lathem, comp., *Chronological Tables of American Newspapers,* pp. 5–6, 9–13; *NYJ,* March 22, 1770; August 18, 1774; *RNYG,* August 11, 1774. On Holt's financial problems, see Beverly McAnear, "James Parker versus John Holt," New Jersey Historical Society *Proceedings* 59 (April, July 1941): 77–95, 198–212.

15. Lathem, comp., *Chronological Tables of American Newspapers,* pp. 14–22.

16. *IG,* April 13, 1782. On the conduct of Oswald and rival editor Francis Bailey, whose *Freeman's Journal* was aligned with the "Constitutionalists," see Teeter, "Legacy of Expression," pp. 205–33.

17. Lathem, comp., *Chronological Tables of American Newspapers,* pp. 44–75; *ADA,* May 16, 1799. See William David Sloan, "The Early Party Press: The Newspaper Role in American Politics, 1788–1812," *Journalism History* 9 (Spring 1982): 18–24.

18. *AU,* March 1, 1797.

19. [Benjamin Franklin Bache], *Truth Will Out!* ([Philadelphia, 1798]), p. iii.

20. *The Complete Writings of Thomas Paine,* ed. Philip S. Foner, 2 vols. (New York: The Citadel Press, 1945), 1: 320, 352. On Paine as a radical writer, see Eric Foner, *Tom Paine and Revolutionary America* (New York: Oxford University Press, 1976).

21. *Speeches of Lord Erskine,* ed. James L. High, 4 vols. (Chicago: Callaghan & Co., 1876), 1: 495, 519, 527–33, 565.

22. High, ed., *Speeches of Lord Erskine,* 1: 579–80.

23. "A Bill for Establishing Religious Freedom," in *PTJ,* 2: 546; TJ to George Washington, September 9, 1792, in Jefferson, *Works,* 7: 146–47; "Inaugural Address," March 4, 1801, ibid., 9: 195–96. See also, TJ to John Tyler, June 28, 1804, in Jefferson, *Writings,* 11: 33–34. When

John Jay expressed concerns about being attacked in the press in 1785, Jefferson assured him that he had the support of public esteem and that public servants had to accept the inevitability of assaults on their reputations. Jay replied that truth would ultimately prevail. John Jay to TJ, December 9, 1785; May 5, 1786, in *PTJ*, 9: 87, 450; TJ to John Jay, January 25, 1786, in ibid., 9: 215. For a denial of the marketplace of ideas concept by defenders of the Sedition Act in Jefferson's state, see *The Address of the Minority in the Virginia Legislature to the People of that State* ([Richmond, 1799]), p. 11.

24. TJ to John Norvell, June 14, 1807, in Jefferson, *Works*, 10: 417, 418; JM to N.P. Trist, April 23, 1828, in *Letters and Writings of James Madison*, 4 vols. (Philadelphia: J. B. Lippincott & Co., 1865), 3: 630. On the Norvell letter, see Mott, *Jefferson and the Press*, pp. 54–59.

25. TJ to Walter Jones, January 2, 1814, in Jefferson, *Works*, 11: 373; TJ to John Adams, February 25, 1823, in Jefferson, *Writings*, 15: 416; TJ to Adamantios Coray, October 31, 1823, ibid., p. 489.

Chapter III. The Ideals of the Enlightenment

1. Lester G. Crocker, "The Problem of Truth and Falsehood in the Age of Enlightenment," *Journal of the History of Ideas* 14 (October 1953): 575–603.

2. [Samuel Hartlib], *A Description of the Famous Kingdom of Macaria . . . An Example to other Nations. In a Dialogue between a Scholar and a Traveller* (London: Printed for Francis Constable, 1641), pp. 6–7, 13–14; [Thomas Hayter], *An Essay on the Liberty, of the Press, Chiefly as It Respects Personal Slander* (London: Printed for J. Raymond, [1755]), p. 5.

3. William Berkeley to the Lords of the Committee of Colonies, June 20, 1671, in George Chalmers, ed., *Political Annals of the Present United Colonies, From Their Settlement to the Peace of 1763* (London: Printed for the Author by J. Bowen, 1780), p. 328.

4. Leonard W. Labaree, ed., *Royal Instructions to British Colonial Governors, 1670–1776*, 2 vols. (New York: D. Appleton-Century Co., 1935), 2: 495–96; Josiah Quincy, *Reports of Cases Argued and Adjudged in the Superior Court of Judicature of the Province of Massachusetts Bay, Between 1761 and 1772* (Boston: Little, Brown, and Co., 1865), p. 309.

5. On the importance of the press in spreading the ideas of the Enlightenment and American Revolution, see Stow Persons, "The Cyclical Theory of History in Eighteenth Century America," *American Quarterly* 6 (Summer 1954): 161; Bernard Bailyn, "Political Experience and Enlightenment Ideas in Eighteenth-Century America," *AHR* 67 (January 1962): 343–44; Gordon S. Wood, "Rhetoric and Reality in the American Revolution," *WMQ*, 3rd ser., 23 (January 1966): 3–32. For background

on the development of the printing trade and its relationship to Western thought, see Elizabeth L. Eisenstein, *The Printing Press as an Agent of Change, Communications and Cultural Transformations in Early-Modern Europe*, 2 vols. (Cambridge: Cambridge University Press, 1979).

6. Eugene F. Miller, "On the American Founders' Defense of Liberal Education in a Republic," *Review of Politics* 46 (January 1984): 65–90; H. Trevor Colbourn, *The Lamp of Experience, Whig History and the Intellectual Origins of the American Revolution* (Chapel Hill: University of North Carolina Press for the Institute of Early American History and Culture, 1965), pp. 127–133, 158–84; *Autobiography*, p. 72; George Simpson Eddy, "Dr. Benjamin Franklin's Library," *Proceedings of the American Antiquarian Society* 34 (October 1924): 206–26; Margaret B. Korty, "Benjamin Franklin and Eighteenth-Century American Libraries," *Transactions of the American Philosophical Society*, n.s., 55 (1965): 1–72; Sanford, *Thomas Jefferson and His Library*, pp. 17–114.

7. "Proposals Relating to the Education of Youth in Pennsylvania," in *PBF*, 3: 405–6; Ralph L. Ketcham, "Benjamin Franklin and William Smith: New Light on an Old Philadelphia Quarrel," *PMHB* 88 (April 1964): 142–63; Joshua L. Chamberlain, ed., *University of Pennsylvania*, 2 vols. (Boston: R. Herndon Co., 1902), 1: 69; "To the Trustees of the College of Philadelphia," in Horace W. Smith, *Life and Correspondence of the Rev. William Smith, D.D.*, 2 vols. (Philadelphia: Ferguson Bros. & Co., 1880), 1: 125–27; BF to Ebenezer Kinnersley, July 28, 1759, in *PBF*, 8: 415–16; *Autobiography*, p. 119.

8. "Bill for the More General Diffusion of Knowledge," in *PTJ*, 2: 526–27; TJ to Horatio G. Spafford, March 17, 1814, in Jefferson, *Writings*, 14: 120; TJ to JM, February 17, 1826, in Jefferson, *Works*, 12: 456.

9. JM to W. T. Barry, August 4, 1822, in *WJM*, 9: 103–5; *NG*, December 19, 1791.

10. "To the Inhabitants of the Province of Quebec," October 26, 1774, in Ford, ed., *Journals of the Continental Congress, 1774–1789*, 1: 108; *Cato's Letters*, 3: 246–47.

11. *Autobiography*, p. 164. On Voltaire and Hume and freedom of thought and expression, see May, *The Enlightenment in America*, pp. 105–21; Peter Gay, *The Enlightenment, An Interpretation*, 2 vols. (New York: Alfred A. Knopf, 1969), 2: 24–26, 72–83, 398–401, 448–55.

12. Robert Darnton, *The Literary Underground of the Old Regime* (Cambridge: Harvard University Press, 1982); "Liberty of the Press," in *Works of Voltaire*, trans. William F. Fleming, 42 vols. (New York: St. Hubert Guild, 1901), 11: 130–34.

13. Ernest C. Mossner, *The Life of David Hume*, 2nd ed. (Oxford: Oxford University Press, 1980), pp. 319–35; Desmond Flower, ed. *Voltaire's England* (London: The Folio Society, 1950), pp. 43, 50; *David Hume's Political Essays*, ed. Charles W. Hendel (Indianapolis: Bobbs-Merrill Co., 1953), pp. 5, 7, 123, 124.

14. Hayter, *An Essay on the Liberty, of the Press,* p. 5; Charles Louis de Secondat, Baron de la Brède et de Montesquieu, *The Spirit of Laws,* ed. David W. Carrithers (Berkeley: University of California Press, 1977), pp. 92, 93.

15. *BG,* March 14, 1768. On Adams as a politician and propagandist, see Nash, *Urban Crucible,* pp. 278–79, 352–54; Pauline Maier, "Coming to Terms with Samuel Adams," *AHR* 81 (February 1976): 12–37; Leonard, "News for a Revolution," pp. 29–32.

16. *MG,* November 8, 1785; *NHG,* October 7, 1756; Paul M. Spurlin, *Rousseau in America, 1760–1809* (University, Alabama: University of Alabama Press, 1969).

17. *CC,* October 29, December 3, 17, 1764; January 8, 21, 1765; *MG,* November 8, 29, December 6, 1785; January 10, 1786.

18. Ralph, *The Case of Authors,* p. [73]; *The Spectator,* ed. Donovan F. Bond, 5 vols. (Oxford: Clarendon Press, 1965), 1: xl–xli, lxxxv–lxxxvii, 44; *NYJ,* April 19, 1770. For examples of American newspapers stating their intention to be "useful and entertaining," see *WR,* September 27, 1731; *NHG,* October 7, 1756; *RNYG,* April 22, 1773; *NJG,* December 5, 1777; *CGWR,* August 17, 1785; *FG,* October 18, 1788. Explaining why he rejected personal libel, Franklin stated in his memoirs that he had contracted with his subscribers "to furnish them with what might be either useful or entertaining" and therefore "could not fill their Papers with private Altercation in which they had no Concern without doing them manifest Injustice." *Autobiography,* p. 95. The metaphor of the newspaper as a spring or fountain of knowledge was used from time to time in the press. See, e.g., *HF,* September 15, 1788; *CH,* January 6, 1790.

19. J. A. Passmore, "The Malleability of Man in Eighteenth-Century Thought," in Earl R. Wasserman, ed., *Aspects of the Eighteenth Century* (Baltimore: The Johns Hopkins Press, 1965), pp. 21–46; Carl L. Becker, *The Heavenly City of the Eighteenth-Century Philosophers* (New Haven: Yale University Press, 1932), pp. 64–65; Gay, *The Enlightenment,* 2: 511–16; Montesquieu, *The Spirit of Laws,* p. 93; *NYM,* January 27, 1755; *NM,* March 1, 1790.

20. Milton, *Areopagitica,* pp. 492, 553, 559.

21. [Matthew Tindal], *A Letter to a Member of Parliament, Shewing, that a Restraint Press Is Inconsistent with the Protestant Religion, and Dangerous to the Liberties of the Nation* (London: Printed by J. Darby, 1698), pp. 9, 11, 22, 24–26, 30–31.

22. *SCG,* February 17, 1733; *CG,* May 10, 1755; *The Letters of Junius,* ed. John Cannon (Oxford: Clarendon Press, 1978), p. 14; *Address of the General Assembly to the People of the Commonwealth of Virginia,* in *WJM,* 6: 337.

23. *AWM,* April 6, 1732. James Parker apparently knew this essay. In 1759 he began a pamphlet objecting to New York's provincial stamp tax

by remarking that "in all Countries where Liberty truly reigns, every one hath a Privilege of declaring his Sentiments upon all Topicks with the utmost Freedom, provided he does it with proper Decency and a just Regard to the laws." Levy interprets Parker's remark as "a neat way to say that all sentiments short of seditious libel were free, an epitome of the American view of the matter." Levy thus seems to suggest that Parker accepted the law of seditious libel, but he notes elsewhere that Parker published a number of pieces saying that it was no longer good law and should be abolished. Similarly, Levy assumed that Bishop Hayter "probably meant seditious libel" when he listed "Treason" along with blasphemy and perjury as the types of expression which fell under the cognizance of government. Hayter's idea of treason or sedition, however, appears to have been Jacobite views which would deny constitutional principles and undermine the liberties of the people. It was essential, Hayter argued, that the press be able to ring the "Alarm-Bell" to put the royal family and the public on guard against their enemies. Hayter, a zealous Whig, had earlier resigned a position in the royal household due to the increasing influence of Lord Bute's "cabal." James Parker, *A Letter to a Gentleman in the City of New-York* (New York: James Parker, 1759), p. 1; Levy, *Freedom of Speech and Press in Early American History*, pp. 80–81, 142–45; Hayter, *An Essay on the Liberty of the Press*, pp. 8–9, 12–14, 16–32, 39, 44–47; *Memoirs of John Almon* (London, 1790), pp. 146–47.

24. *AWM*, April 6, 1732.

Chapter IV. Sovereignty and Seditious Libel

1. Samuel Miller, *A Brief Retrospect of the Eighteenth Century*, 2 vols. (New York: Printed by T. and J. Swords, 1803), 2: 249, 251, 253, 254, 255.

2. Miller, *A Brief Retrospect of the Eighteenth Century*, 2: 254, 255. On the journalistic treatment of Jefferson as a candidate, see Charles O. Lerche, Jr., "Jefferson and the Election of 1800: A Case Study in the Political Smear," *WMQ*, 3rd ser., 5 (October 1948): 467–91.

3. James Morton Smith, *Freedom's Fetters, The Alien and Sedition Laws and American Civil Liberties* (Ithaca: Cornell University Press, Cornell Paperbacks ed., 1966). See also, John C. Miller, *Crisis in Freedom, The Alien and Sedition Acts* (Boston: Little, Brown and Co., 1951).

4. "Resolutions of 1798," in *WJM*, 6: 328–29. On the reaction against the Sedition Act, see, e.g., James Morton Smith, "The Grass Roots Origins of the Kentucky Resolutions," *WMQ*, 3rd ser., 27 (April 1970): 221–45; Adrienne Koch and Harry Ammon, "The Virginia and Kentucky Resolutions: An Episode in Jefferson's and Madison's Defense of Civil Liberties," *WMQ*, 3rd ser., 5 (April 1948): 145–76.

5. *Annals of Congress*, 5 Cong. 3 sess., pp. 2884–2906, 2988–90.

6. TJ to JM, February 26, 1799, in Jefferson, *Works*, 9: 61; *Annals of Congress*, 5 Cong. 3 sess., pp. 3009, 3012, 3014, 3016–17.

7. *Annals of Congress*, 5 Cong. 3 sess., pp. 2989, 3011. For an analysis of the party-line votes on the Sedition Act, see John D. Stevens, "Congressional History of the 1798 Sedition Law," *Journalism Quarterly* 43 (Summer 1966): 247–56.

8. Irving Brant, *The Bill of Rights, Its Origin and Meaning* (Indianapolis: Bobbs-Merrill Co., 1965), pp. 91–92; Van Vechten Veeder, "The History of the Law of Defamation," in *Select Essays in Anglo-American Legal History*, 3 vols. (Boston: Little, Brown, and Co., 1907–1909), 3: 446–73; Statutes of Westminster, The First, 3 Edw. 1, c. 34.

9. Case De Libellis Famosis, 5 Coke Reports 125a (1606); Brant, *The Bill of Rights*, pp. 113–130, 154–73. On the procedures used by the Star Chamber, which included torture and compulsory self-incrimination, see pp. 87–88; Siebert, *Freedom of the Press in England*, pp. 120–26.

10. Rex v. Tutchin, 14 Howell's State Trials 1095 at 1128 (1704).

11. On this period, see J. P. Kenyon, *Revolution Principles, The Politics of Party, 1689–1720* (Cambridge: Cambridge University Press, 1977); J. H. Plumb, *The Origins of Political Stability, England, 1675–1725* (Boston: Houghton Mifflin, 1967); B. W. Hill, *The Growth of Parliamentary Parties, 1689–1742* (London: George Allen & Unwin Ltd., 1976).

12. Sir William Blackstone, *Commentaries on the Laws of England*, 4 vols. (Philadelphia: Printed by Robert Bell, 1771–1772), 4: 151, 152, 153.

13. Daniel J. Boorstin, *The Mysterious Science of the Law, An Essay on Blackstone's Commentaries* (Cambridge: Harvard University Press, 1941); *Annals of Congress*, 5 Cong. 3 sess., p. 3009; Blackstone, *Commentaries on the Laws of England*, 4: 150, 152, 152n.

14. Bolingbroke to the Earl of Strafford, July 23, 1712, in *Letters and Correspondence, Public and Private, of the Right Honourable Henry St. John, Lord Viscount Bolingbroke, During the Time He was Secretary of State to Queen Anne*, ed. Gilbert Parke, 2 vols. (London: Printed for G. G. and J. Robinson, 1798), 1: 600; Cobbett, ed. *Parliamentary History*, 16: 1164–65; Quincy, *Reports of Cases*, pp. 244, 246, 263.

15. Proceedings against the Dean of St. Asaph, 21 Howell's State Trials 847 at 1040 (1784). On Mansfield's reputation in America, see, e.g., Bailyn, *Ideological Origins of the American Revolution*, p. 123. On Hutchinson, see Bernard Bailyn, *The Ordeal of Thomas Hutchinson* (Cambridge: Belknap Press of Harvard University Press, 1974); John Phillip Reid, "The Ordeal by Law of Thomas Hutchinson," in Hendrik Hartog, ed., *Law in the American Revolution and the Revolution in the Law* (New York: New York University Press, 1981), pp. 20–45. Among the editors who rejected the Blackstonian formulation was William Cobbett, also known as "Peter Porcupine." Reacting to a statement by Judge

Thomas McKean that liberty of the press meant freedom from censorship but not from subsequent penalty, Cobbett expressed scorn. "What precious *advantage* do we have then?" he asked. "A man may *publish his sentiments* in Prussia, in Russia, in Turkey, or even in that den of slaves, France. They can't know that he has done it, 'till it is done; and when they do know it, they can do no more than *punish him for it." P'sG,* December 4, 1797.

16. See, e.g., "The Freedom of Investigation Considered as a Preventative of Revolution," in Tunis Wortman, *A Treatise, Concerning Political Enquiry, And the Liberty of the Press* (New York: Printed by George Forman, 1800), pp. 183–92. On the nature and extent of mob activity, see, especially, Brian Manning, *The English People and the English Revolution, 1640–1649* (London: Heinemann, 1976); George Rudé, "The London 'Mob' of the Eighteenth Century," *The Historical Journal* 2 (1959): 1–18; Pauline Maier, "Popular Uprisings and Civil Authority in Eighteenth-Century America," *WMQ*, 3rd ser., 27 (January 1970): 3–35; Pauline Maier, *From Resistance to Revolution, Colonial Radicals and the Development of American Opposition to Britain, 1765–1776* (New York: Alfred A. Knopf, 1972).

17. *Cato's Letters,* 3: 243–44.

18. [Robert Molesworth, Viscount], *An Account of Denmark, As It was in the Year 1692,* 3rd ed. (London: Printed for Timothy Goodwin, 1694); *AWM*, March 28, April 25, 1734.

19. *The Works of Tacitus,* trans. Thomas Gordon, 2 vols. (London: Printed for Thomas Woodward and John Peele, 1728, 1731), 1: 105–6; Hendel, ed., *David Hume's Political Essays,* p. 6; Hayter, *An Essay on the Liberty, of the Press,* p. 39; Cannon, ed., *Letters of Junius,* p. 23; *Cato's Letters,* 1: 99, 100; *NYM*, January 27, 1755; *CG,* April 12, 1755. The author of the *Mercury* piece, number 10 in the "Watch-Tower" series arranged by the "New York Triumvirate," may have been Noah Welles (1718–1776), an associate of William Livingston. See *The Independent Reflector,* ed. Milton Klein (Cambridge: The Belknap Press of Harvard University Press, 1963), p. 150n.

20. *CG,* February 7, 1756; Montesquieu, *The Spirit of Laws,* pp. 254, 255, 441, 445.

21. Hendel, ed., *David Hume's Political Essays,* pp. 3–7. On the influence of Hume and Montesquieu on the founding fathers, see Garry Wills, *Explaining America: The Federalist* (Garden City, New York: Doubleday and Co., 1981). On Hume, see Douglass G. Adair, "That Politics May Be Reduced to a Science: David Hume, James Madison, and the Tenth *Federalist,"* in Jack P. Greene, ed., *The Reinterpretation of the American Revolution, 1763–1789* (New York: Harper & Row, 1968), pp. 487–503. On Montesquieu, see Paul M. Spurlin, *Montesquieu in America, 1760–1801* (Baton Rouge: Louisiana State University Press, 1940).

22. Cannon, ed., *Letters of Junius,* pp. 14–15, 34–35, 39.

23. For reaction in Parliament, see, e.g., Cobbett, ed., *Parliamentary History,* 16: 1240–41; *Journals of the House of Lords,* 30: 429. On the matter of sovereignty, see John V. Jezierski, "Parliament or People: James Wilson and Blackstone on the Nature and Location of Sovereignty," *Journal of the History of Ideas* 32 (January-March, 1971): 95–106; H. T. Dickinson, "The Eighteenth-Century Debate on the Sovereignty of Parliament," *Transactions of the Royal Historical Society,* 5th ser., 26 (1976): 189–210; Beverly Z. Rowsome, "How Blackstone Lost the Colonies: English Law, Colonial Lawyers, and the American Revolution" (Ph.D. dissertation, Indiana University, 1971). Although the *Commentaries* did not appear until the Revolutionary period, Leonard Levy claims that Blackstone, a reactionary English jurist, was "the oracle of the common law in the minds of the Framers." Levy, *Freedom of Speech and Press in Early American History,* p. 13.

24. *BG,* April 21, May 12, 19, 26, June 2, 23, 1755. On the political developments which took place in America before the Revolution, see Bailyn, "Political Experience and Enlightenment Ideas in Eighteenth-Century America," pp. 345–51. On the critical issue of sovereignty, see Bailyn, *Ideological Origins of the American Revolution,* pp. 198–229.

25. *Cato's Letters,* 1: 98–99.

26. *FJ,* April 25, 1781; *HF,* September 15, 1788.

27. Schwartz, ed., *The Bill of Rights: A Documentary History,* 1: 235, 266, 278, 284, 287, 300, 335, 342, 378; William Cushing to John Adams, February 18, 1789, in "Hitherto Unpublished Correspondence Between Chief Justice Cushing and John Adams in 1789," *Massachusetts Law Quarterly* 27 (October 1942): 14–15.

28. John P. Kaminski and Gaspare J. Saladino, eds., *Commentaries on the Constitution* (Madison: State Historical Society of Wisconsin, 1981–), 1: 198; Anderson, "The Origins of the Press Clause," pp. 466–75; *IG,* October 29, 1787; Richard Leffler, "Freedom of the Press and the Debate over Ratification of the Constitution," paper presented at the Midwest Mass Communication History Conference, School of Journalism and Mass Communication, University of Wisconsin–Madison, April 23, 1982; John P. Kaminski, "Newspaper Suppression during the Debate over the Ratification of the Constitution, 1787–1788," paper presented at the Midwest Mass Communication History Conference, School of Journalism and Mass Communication, University of Wisconsin–Madison, April 23, 1982. For additional journalistic statements on the need for a press protection in the Constitution, see, e.g., *NYJ,* November 8, 1787; *FJ,* October 24, 1787. For background, see Brant, *The Bill of Rights,* pp. 223–32; Robert A. Rutland, *The Ordeal of the Constitution, The Antifederalists and the Ratification Struggle of 1787–1788* (Norman: University of Oklahoma Press, 1966); Bernard Schwartz, *The Great Rights*

of Mankind: A History of the American Bill of Rights (New York: Oxford University Press, 1977).

29. Merrill Jensen, ed., *The Documentary History of the Ratification of the Constitution* (Madison: State Historical Society of Wisconsin, 1976–), 2: 453–55. For Wilson's criticisms of Blackstone, see *The Works of James Wilson*, ed. Robert Green McCloskey, 2 vols. (Cambridge: Harvard University Press, 1967), 1: 39, 77–80; Jezierski, "Parliament or People," pp. 98–106.

30. "Federalist No. 84," in Jacob E. Cooke, ed., *The Federalist* (Middletown, Conn.: Wesleyan University Press, 1961), pp. 578–80; TJ to JM, July 31, 1788, in Jefferson, *Works,* 5: 426–27.

31. Schwartz, ed., *The Bill of Rights,* 2: 825; JM to TJ, October 17, 1788, in *WJM,* 5: 271; "Amendments to the Constitution," ibid., pp. 380, 381–85; Adrienne Koch, *Jefferson and Madison, The Great Collaboration* (New York: Alfred A. Knopf, 1950), pp. 43–61.

32. "Amendments to the Constitution," in *WJM,* 5: 377, 378.

33. *Journal of the Senate,* 1 Cong. 1 sess., pp. 70, 72; *Annals of Congress,* 1 Cong. 1 sess., p. 751.

34. JM to TJ, October 17, 1788, in *WJM,* 5: 272–73; Neal Reimer, "James Madison's Theory of the Self-Destructive Features of Republican Government," *Ethics* 65 (October 1954): 34–43; Kenneth A. Lockridge, *Settlement and Unsettlement in Early America, The Crisis of Political Legitimacy Before the Revolution* (Cambridge: Cambridge University Press, 1981), pp. 112–21; "The Federalist No. 10," in Cooke, ed., *The Federalist,* p. 65; "Amendments to the Constitution," in *WJM,* 5: 380, 382, 385.

35. *NG,* December 19, 1791. On the *National Gazette,* see "Editorial Note," in *PTJ,* 20: 718–53.

36. *Address of the General Assembly,* in *WJM,* 6: 332, 333, 339.

37. Smith, *Freedom's Fetters,* pp. 112–55; U.S. v. Worrall, in Francis Wharton, ed., *State Trials of the United States During the Administrations of Washington and Adams* (Philadelphia: Casey and Hart, 1849), pp. 189–99; *Address of the General Assembly,* in *WJM,* 6: 333–35.

38. "Amendments to the Constitution," in *WJM,* 5: 380; "Resolutions of 1798," in *WJM,* 6: 327; *Report on the Resolutions,* ibid., pp. 386–88; 389, 394, 397. On the Virginia response to the Sedition Act, see Koch, *Jefferson and Madison,* pp. 174–211; Brant, *The Bill of Rights,* pp. 283–304. On the importance of popular sovereignty in questions of freedom of expression, see Smith, *Freedom's Fetters,* pp. ix–xv, 418–33.

Chapter V. Demands, Defenses, and Distinctions

1. *Address of the General Assembly,* in *WJM,* 6: 335–36; *Cato's Letters,* 1: 260–61; 3: 246. See also *Craftsman,* 8: 222; *Report on the Resolutions,* in *WJM,* 6: 387–89.

2. *Craftsman,* 8: 62, 65–66, 217.

3. Alexander, *A Brief Narrative,* pp. 65–66, 70, 72, 73, 74, 79, 84, 90, 91, 98; "Hamilton's 15 Propositions on the Law of Libel," in Julius Goebel, Jr., et al., eds., *The Law Practice of Alexander Hamilton,* 5 vols. (New York: Columbia University Press, 1964–1981), 1: 841; *BG,* February 29, March 7, 1768. Citing their role as "Guardians of the People's Rights" and therefore of "Liberty of the Press," a majority of the House of Representatives voted to take no notice of the *Boston Gazette. BG,* March 7, 1768.

4. *Cato's Letters,* 1: 98, 3: 249; *NYWJ,* February 18, 1734; Cobbett, ed., *Parliamentary History,* 16: 1288–89. Denying that Walpole had practiced "unprecedented Forbearance" with respect to the press, the *Champion* observed that "some Pieces were published in the Reign of King *William,* without incurring the Resentment of the Government; which would be exceeding *dangerous* to *reprint* now." *Champion,* 2: 95. For a comparable remark, see *BG,* June 2, 1755. On the case of the Seven Bishops, see The Trial of the Seven Bishops, 12 Howell's State Trials 183 (1688); Maurice Ashley, *The Glorious Revolution of 1688* (London: Hodder and Stoughton, 1966), pp. 195, 199–202; John Miller, *James II, A Study in Kingship* (Hove, East Sussex: Wayland Publishers, 1977), pp. 182–87.

5. *NG,* December 19, 1791. Newspaper essayists also affirmed the importance of the overt acts test. See, e.g., *BG,* May 26, 1755. For a disparaging review of theoretical writings distinguishing words from actions, see Levy, *Freedom of Speech and Press in Early American History,* pp. 90–91, 93, 154–57; 164–71, 188–89, 251–52, 255–56.

6. Montesquieu, *Spirit of the Laws,* p. 222.

7. Father of Candor [pseud.], *A Letter Concerning Libels, Warrants, the Seisure of Papers, and Sureties for the Peace of Behaviour,* 7th ed. (London: Printed for John Almon, 1771), pp. 20, 23, 34, 39, 46, 161. John Almon was charged with contempt of the Court of the King's Bench for publishing the Father of Candor pamphlet, but the case was eventually dropped. Rea, *The English Press in Politics,* pp. 110–19. Father of Candor's view that words could not be equated with an actual breach of the peace had been stated in a dissent of seventeen members of the House of Lords during the debate over the Wilkes case in 1763. *Journals of the House of Lords,* 30: 427.

8. Bond, ed., *The Spectator,* 1: 97, 99, 422, 423; *Cato's Letters,* 1: 258; Quincy, *Reports of Cases,* p. 267; Smollett, *Humphry Clinker,* p. 104; Cannon, ed., *Letters of Junius,* p. 14. The *Craftsman* also suggested that personal abuse was "a just Tax upon *high Stations." Craftsman,* 8: x.

9. *Cato's Letters,* 1: 252, 253, 254–56, 257, 258, 259, 261, 3: 253.

10. *Craftsman,* 8: viii–x, 39–48, 84; *Champion,* 2: 95; Cannon, ed., *Letters of Junius,* p. 14.

11. *IC,* June 4, 1778; *CH,* January 6, 1790; *MC,* September 24, 1785. For evidence of the public-private distinction being made dozens of times in the press of one American city in the decade preceding the First Amendment, see Baldasty, "Toward an Understanding of the First Amendment: Boston Newspapers, 1782–1791," pp. 26–29. For additional examples of discussion of the responsibility of the press with regard to public and private reputations, see *AWM,* April 25, 1734, November 6, 1740; *EG,* August 2, 1768; *SCG,* May 7, 1772; *RNYG,* September 2, 1774; *IG,* April 13, 1782; *FG,* October 1, 1788.

12. Alexander, *A Brief Narrative,* pp. 79, 81.

13. The Case of Henry S. Woodfall, 20 Howell's State Trials 895 at 899, 903 (1770); Siebert, *Freedom of the Press in England,* pp. 387–88. For examples of other cases where the public-private distinction was made, see the account of the trial of Abijah Adams in *IC,* April 15, 18, 1799; *A Report of an Action for a Libel, Brought by Dr. Benjamin Rush, Against William Cobbett. . . .* (Philadelphia: Printed by W. W. Woodward, 1800), pp. 1–2.

14. *PG,* November 17, December 8, 1737.

15. Hayter, *An Essay on the Liberty, of the Press,* pp. 10, 26; Father of Candor, *A Letter Concerning Libels,* p. 48. Most of the wording of Father of Candor's remark was an echo of a statement made by Andrew Hamilton at Zenger's trial. Alexander, *A Brief Narrative,* p. 99.

16. *BG,* June 2, 1755; A Friend to Harmony [pseud.], *Candid Considerations on Libels* (Boston: Printed by E. Freeman and L. Andrews, 1789). For another example of the argument that punishing private defamation imperilled press freedom, see the essay by "Brutus" in *GSSC,* August 27, 1783. Jefferson observed at one point that press freedom could not be limited without being lost and that published attacks on a public servant's reputation were part of the price to be paid for liberty. TJ to John Jay, January 25, 1786, in *PTJ,* 9: 215; TJ to James Currie, January 28, 1786, ibid., p. 239.

17. [Arnall], *The Case of Opposition Stated,* p. 39.

18. Quincy, *Reports of Cases,* pp. 266, 267–68; Trial of John Almon, 20 Howell's State Trials 803 at 837 (1770). At Zenger's trial, Andrew Hamilton rejected the notion that legal action could simply be initiated against guilty officials, noting the difficulties involved in taking a governor to court and the influence one branch of government could have on another. Alexander, *A Brief Narrative,* pp. 80–81. See also William Cushing to John Adams, February 18, 1789, in "Hitherto Unpublished Correspondence," p. 15.

19. Case De Libellis Famosis, 5 Coke Reports 125a (1606); Blackstone, *Commentaries on the Laws of England,* 4: 150. For examples of Star Chamber doctrine being used in the eighteenth century, see Trial of John Tutchin, 14 Howell's State Trials 1095 at 1119 (1704), Trial of Richard Francklin, 17 Howell's State Trials 625 at 658–59 (1731); Trial

of John Almon, 20 Howell's State Trials 803 at 837 (1770). On the development of the truth defense, see Clifton O. Lawhorne, *Defamation and Public Officials, The Evolving Law of Libel* (Carbondale: Southern Illinois University Press, 1971), pp. 1–37.

20. *Cato's Letters*, 1: 253, 258, 259, 260, 261; 3: 249, 254–55; Cobbett, ed., *Parliamentary History*, 16: 1273–74. See also Father of Candor, *A Letter Concerning Libels*, p. 47.

21. Trial of William Owen, 18 Howell's State Trials 1203 at 1222, 1227–29 (1752); Cobbett, ed., *Parliamentary History*, 16: 1321–22; Cannon, ed., *Letters of Junius*, pp. 9, 206–17.

22. Proceedings against the Dean of St. Asaph, 21 Howell's State Trials 847 at 1008, 1040 (1784); H. M. Lubasz, "Public Opinion Comes of Age: Reform of the Libel Law in the Eighteenth Century," *History Today* 8 (July 1958): 453–61; James Fitzjames Stephen, *A History of the Criminal Law in England*, 3 vols. (London: Macmillan and Co., 1883), 2: 343–45, 383.

23. For a discussion of slander cases in one colony, see Raphael Semmes, *Crime and Punishment in Early Maryland* (Baltimore: The Johns Hopkins Press, 1938), pp. 207–31. Two famous and fiercely contested personal libel suits involving public officials were In Re Knowles v. Douglass (1748–1749), Court Files of Suffolk County, Boston, Massachusetts, 209, group nos. 24871, 24961; 399, no. 64145; 401, no. 64529; 403, no. 64940; 407, no. 65550; Hopkins v. Ward (1757), Worcester County Court of Common Pleas, Worcester, Massachusetts, 5: 76–92. On Knowles v. Douglass, see John Noble, "Notes on the Libel Suit of Knowles v. Douglass in the Superior Court of Judicature," *Publications of the Colonial Society of Massachusetts, Transactions* 3 (1895–1897): 213–39; John Lax and William Pencak, "The Knowles Riot and the Crisis of the 1740's in Massachusetts," *Perspectives in American History* 10 (1976): 201–4. On Hopkins v. Ward, see David S. Lovejoy, *Rhode Island Politics and the American Revolution, 1760–1776* (Providence: Brown University Press, 1958), pp. 11–12; Warner Papers Rhode Island Historical Society, Providence, Rhode Island, 3, nos. 715, 722, 723, 725, 743, 744. One of the most highly publicized cases was the libel trial of journalist William Cobbett in 1799. See Winthrop and Frances Neilson, *Verdict for the Doctor, The Case of Benjamin Rush* (New York: Hastings House, 1958).

24. Smith, "A Reappraisal of Legislative Privilege and American Colonial Journalism," pp. 97–103, 141.

25. On the relationship between the British and American sedition laws, see Manning J. Dauer, *The Adams Federalists* (Baltimore: The Johns Hopkins Press, 1953), pp. 157–59. One of the libertarian responses to the British legislation was written by one of the country's great men of letters, Samuel T. Coleridge, *The Plot Discovered; or An Address to the People, Against Ministerial Treason* (Bristol, 1795). On Hamilton's

view of the Sedition Act of 1798 and on the ineffectiveness of its libertarian provisions, see Smith, *Freedom's Fetters,* pp. 106–11, 128–30,
153–55, 421–24.

26. *Annals of Congress,* 5 Cong. 2 sess., pp. 2151–54, 2163–64; 3
sess., p. 3014. For the questionable interpretation that there was a "sudden, radical, and transforming" breakthrough in libertarian thought on
freedom of expression in 1798, see Levy, "Liberty and the First Amendment, 1790–1800," p. 22.

27. *Address of the General Assembly,* in *WJM,* 6: 334–35, 337; *Report on the Resolutions,* ibid., pp. 393, 397.

28. Wortman, *A Treatise Concerning Political Enquiry,* pp. 152–53,
157–60, 170–71; 259, 260.

29. Hortensius [George Hay], *An Essay on the Liberty of the Press;
Respectfully Inscribed to the Republican Printers Throughout the United
States* (Philadelphia: Printed at the *Aurora* Office, 1799), pp. 37–38, 40,
43; George Hay, *An Essay on the Liberty of the Press, Shewing, That
the Requisition of Security for Good Behaviour from Libellers, Is Perfectly Compatible with the Constitution and Laws of Virginia* (Richmond: Printed by Samuel Pleasants, Jr., 1803), pp. 26, 28–29, 37.

30. Wortman, *A Treatise Concerning Political Enquiry,* pp. 252–56;
Hay, *An Essay on the Liberty of the Press,* pp. 28–29, 37; *Annals of
Congress,* 5 Cong. 2 sess., p. 2162; *Address of the General Assembly,* in
WJM, 6: 337; *Report on the Resolutions,* ibid., p. 396.

31. Trial of James Thompson Callender, in Wharton, ed., *State Trials
of the United States,* pp. 688–89, 692–93; Smith, *Freedom's Fetters,* pp.
334–58; [Hay], *An Essay on the Liberty of the Press,* pp. 43–44, 46.

32. *Cato's Letters,* 1: 258; Rex v. Tutchin, 14 Howell's State Trials
1095 at 119, 1120, 1124 (1704). Although he recognizes that individuals
as well as the state could prosecute for personal libels, Leonard Levy
maintains that the Americans who wrote and ratified the First Amendment to the U.S. Constitution did not intend to eliminate seditious libel
prosecutions for criticism of government. He fails to see that libertarians
before 1798 might have approved of a right to make any statements
against a politician's policies, but might also have accepted the idea of
legal action being taken in some cases against those who attacked his personal character. After citing an instance of Franklin taking this position
in 1789, for example, Levy improperly concludes that he never went on
record opposing seditious libel or abandoning the concept that a state
could be criminally assailed by mere words. In this way, Levy continually misses the significance of libertarian arguments that political observations could be made freely, but not necessarily all personal attacks on
public persons. Levy, *Freedom of Speech and Press in Early American
History,* pp. x, xxiv, 2–3, 10, 186–88, 213–14. For the view that the
Jeffersonians opposed the Sedition Act because the limits on free expression were imposed by the national government rather than the states, see

Walter Berns, *The First Amendment and the Future of American Democracy* (New York: Basic Books, 1976), pp. 80–146.

33. Father of Candor, *A Letter Concerning Libels,* p. 48.

34. Alexander, *A Brief Narrative,* pp. 84, 87; Father of Candor, *A Letter Concerning Libels,* pp. 10–15, 23, 45–46, 48.

35. *CGWR,* August 10, 1785; William Cushing to John Adams, February 18, 1789, and John Adams to William Cushing, March 7, 1789, in "Hitherto Unpublished Correspondence," pp. 14–16.

36. St. George Tucker, "Of the Right of Conscience, and of the Freedom of Speech and of the Press," in Levy, ed., *Freedom of the Press From Zenger to Jefferson,* pp. 318–26. On Tucker's legal thought, see Charles T. Cullen, "St. George Tucker and Law in Virginia, 1772–1804" (Ph.D. dissertation, University of Virginia, 1971).

37. Julian S. Waterman, "Thomas Jefferson and Blackstone's *Commentaries,*" *Illinois Law Review* 27 (1933): 629–59; TJ to JM, February 26, 1826, in Jefferson, *Writings,* 16: 156; "The Virginia Constitution," in *PTJ,* 1: 344–45, 353, 363; TJ to A. Coray, October 31, 1823, in Jefferson, *Writings,* 15: 489.

38. "Draft of a Constitution for Virginia," 1783, in *PTJ,* 6: 304; TJ to JM, July 31, 1788, in *PTJ,* 13: 442; TJ to JM, August 28, 1789, in *PTJ,* 15: 367; "Draft of a Charter of Rights," June 3, 1789, ibid., p. 168; "Notes for a Constitution," [1794?], in Jefferson, *Works,* 8: 161–62. For examples of TJ's disgust at newspaper falsehoods during this time, see "Observations on Démeunier's Manuscript," 1786, in *PTJ,* 10: 55; TJ to Maria Cosway, October 12, 1786, ibid., pp. 447, 448; TJ to C. W. F. Dumas, December 25, 1786, ibid., p. 631.

39. "Kentucky Resolutions," 1798, in Jefferson, *Works,* 8: 463–65; TJ to Levi Lincoln, March 24, 1802, in Jefferson, *Works,* 9: 358.

40. TJ to Thomas McKean, February 19, 1803, in Jefferson, *Works,* 9: 451–52; TJ to Abigail Adams, September 11, 1804, in Jefferson, *Writings,* 11: 51–52; "Second Inaugural Address," March 4, 1805, in Jefferson, *Writings,* 3: 380–82; TJ to Thomas Seymour, February 11, 1807, in Jefferson, *Works,* 10: 367–69; TJ to Wilson Cary Nicholas, June 13, 1809, in Jefferson, *Works,* 11: 108–11; TJ to Gideon Granger, March 9, 1814, in Jefferson, *Writings,* 14: 115–17. The possibly sinister implications of Jefferson's conduct with regard to the Connecticut cases is explored in Levy, *Jefferson & Civil Liberties,* pp. 60–66. The prosecutions were in a federal court but state law—which allowed the truth defense—would have been applied. Jefferson apparently did not realize at first that the charge was *seditious* libel of the president. Ibid., pp. 62–63.

41. *BCR,* August 23 and 30, 1803.

42. People v. Croswell, 3 Johnson's Cases 337 (New York, 1804); *The Speeches . . . in the Great Cause of the People, Against Harry Croswell. . . .* (New York: Printed by G. and R. White, 1804), pp. 63, 64, 72–73, 76, 78. On Hamilton's support of legal actions to suppress the

opinions of political opponents, see James M. Smith, "Alexander Hamilton, the Alien Law, and Seditious Libels," *Review of Politics* 16 (July 1954): 305–33.

43. On the Croswell case and the developments which followed, see Donald Roper, "James Kent and the Emergence of New York's Libel Law," *American Journal of Legal History* 17 (July 1973): 223–31; Margaret A. Blanchard, "Filling in the Void: Speech and Press in State Courts prior to *Gitlow*," in Bill F. Chamberlin and Charlene J. Brown, eds., *The First Amendment Reconsidered, New Perspectives on the Meaning of Freedom of Speech and Press* (New York: Longman, 1982), pp. 20–43; Goebel et al., eds., *The Law Practice of Alexander Hamilton,* 1: 775–848.

44. Lawhorne, *Defamation and Public Officials,* pp. 57–276; New York Times v. Sullivan, 376 U.S. 254 at 279–80 (1964).

45. Garrison v. Louisiana, 379 U.S. 64 (1964). On the development of libel law after *New York Times v. Sullivan,* see Clifton O. Lawhorne, *The Supreme Court and Libel* (Carbondale: Southern Illinois University Press, 1981), pp. 35–107.

Chapter VI. The Colonial Journalist:
Good Humour'd Unless Provok'd

1. TJ to Samuel Smith, August 22, 1798, in Jefferson, *Works,* 8: 443.

2. TJ to JM, February 5, 1799, in Jefferson, *Works,* 9: 34; *Autobiography,* p. 12. Jefferson admired the easy prose of Franklin as well as that of Thomas Paine. TJ to Francis Eppes, January 19, 1821, in Jefferson, *Works,* 12: 195. On Franklin's view of the problems and potential of communication, see Philip D. Beidler, "The 'Author' of Franklin's *Autobiography*," *Early American Literature* 16 (Autumn 1981–1982): 257–69.

3. Peter Folger, *A Looking Glass for the Times, or the Former Spirit of New England Revived in This Generation* (n.p., 1725), pp. 14, 15; *Autobiography,* p. 6. Folger's *Looking Glass* may have been circulated only in manuscript before 1725 since no printed copy before this date can be found. On Folger and other critics of prevailing practices and opinions in Massachusetts, see Leo P. Bradley, Jr., "The Press and the Declension of Boston Orthodoxy, 1674–1724" (M.A. thesis, University of Washington, 1977).

4. *Autobiography,* pp. 8, 10, 11, 12, 14; Albert Furtwangler, "Franklin's Apprenticeship and the *Spectator,*" *New England Quarterly* 52 (September 1979): 377–96. In his almanac, Franklin paid tribute to Joseph Addison, one of the authors of the *Spectator,* as the man whose "writings have contributed more to the improvement of the minds of the British nation, and polishing their manners, than those of any other English pen whatever." *Poor Richard, Improved,* 1748, in *PBF,* 3: 254.

5. *NEC,* August 14, 1721; January 22, 1722. On James Franklin, see Jeffery A. Smith, "James Franklin and Freedom of the Press in Massachusetts and Rhode Island, 1717–1735," paper presented at the annual convention of the Association for Education in Journalism, East Lansing, Michigan, August 11, 1981; Jeffery A. Smith, "James Franklin," in Perry J. Ashley, ed., *American Newspaper Journalists: 1690–1872* (Detroit: Gale Research Co., 1985), pp. 212–18. On the *Courant* and its contributors, see Worthington C. Ford, "Franklin's *New-England Courant,*" Massachusetts Historical Society *Proceedings* 57 (April 1924): 336–53; Arthur B. Tourtellot, *Benjamin Franklin, The Shaping of Genius, The Boston Years* (Garden City, N.Y.: Doubleday & Co., 1977), pp. 233–310.

6. *BNL,* August 28, 1721; *BG,* January 15, 29, 1722. On the activities of the Hell-Fire Club in England, see *NEC,* February 12, 1722.

7. General Court Records, Massachusetts Archives, Boston, Massachusetts, 11, p. 113; *BNL,* April 3, 1721. On the conflicts in Massachusetts politics at this time, see Thomas Hutchinson, *The History of the Colony and Province of Massachsetts-Bay,* ed. Lawrence Shaw Mayo, 3 vols. (Cambridge: Harvard University Press, 1936), 2: 174–208; G. B. Warden, *Boston, 1689–1776* (Boston: Little, Brown & Co., 1970), pp. 80–99; William Pencak, *War, Politics, & Revolution in Provincial Massachusetts* (Boston: Northeastern University Press, 1981), pp. 61–80.

8. Bradley, "The Press and the Declension of Boston Orthodoxy," pp. 111–16; Clyde A. Duniway, *The Development of Freedom of the Press in Massachusetts* (New York: Longmans, Green, & Co., 1906), pp. 93–96; [Daniel Defoe], *News from the Moon, A Review of the State of the British Nation* ([Boston: James Franklin, 1721]); *BNL,* March 6, 1721; *BG,* March 6, 13, 1721.

9. *NEC,* September 11, December 4, 1721. For other essays by James Franklin, see, e.g., *NEC,* September 4, 1721; January 22, February 5, 12, 1722. For other essays by Cato, see, e.g., *NEC,* October 9, 16, 23, 30, 1721. On the *Courant* as a dispenser of radical Whig ideology, see T. H. Breen, *The Character of the Good Ruler, A Study of Puritan Political Ideas in New-England, 1630–1730* (New Haven: Yale University Press, 1970), pp. 261–69.

10. *NEC,* November 20, December 4, 1721.

11. John B. Blake, "The Inoculation Controversy in Boston: 1721–1722," *New England Quarterly* 25 (December 1952): 489–506; C. Edward Wilson, "The Boston Inoculation Controversy: A Revisionist Interpretation," *Journalism History* 7 (Spring 1980): 16–19, 40; *NEC,* December 4, 1721; January 22, February 5, 1722.

12. *NEC,* August 21, September 4, December 4, 1721; Kenneth Silverman, *The Life and Times of Cotton Mather* (New York: Harper & Row, 1984), pp. 336–63. James Franklin's commitment to Puritan beliefs is open to question, but he may have attended either the theologically moderate Old South Church or the more liberal Brattle Street Church. Cotton

and Increase Mather were copastors of the conservative Second Church. For *Courant* attacks on the Mathers, see, in particular, *NEC,* August 7, November 6, December 4, 1721; January 22, February 5, 12, May 21, 1722. See also, *A Friendly Debate; Or, a Dialogue between Rusticus and Academicus About the Late Performance of Academicus* (Boston: Printed by J. Franklin, 1722). For an example of a Mather reply, see *A Vindication of the Ministers of Boston, From the Abuses & Scandals, Lately Cast Upon Them, in Diverse Printed Papers* (Boston: Printed by B. Green, 1722).

13. *Autobiography,* pp. 17–18; *NEC,* April 16, 1722; Bruce Granger, *American Essay Serials From Franklin to Irving* (Knoxville: University of Tennessee Press, 1978), pp. 15–24.

14. *NEC,* March 26, April 9, 30, May 7, 14, 28, June 11, 1722; *English Advice to the Freeholders, & c. of the Province of Massachusetts-Bay* (Boston: Printed by James Franklin, 1722); General Court Records, 11, pp. 319–20; 370; *Autobiography,* p. 19. The title of the election pamphlet appears to have been taken from a spirited British polemic comparing Whigs and Tories, [Francis Atterbury], *English Advice, to the Freeholders of England* (n.p., 1714).

15. *Autobiography,* p. 19; *NEC,* June 18, 1722. This unsigned essay is ignored in the Franklin *Papers,* but it clearly seems to be the product of his pen and to foreshadow the Silence Dogood essay of September 24, 1722, on *"Night-Walkers."* Janus reappears in a BF essay published in the *Courant* of February 11, 1723. On Janus, the Roman god with two faces, see *NEC,* August 19, 1723. When Janus was introduced the second time, the *Courant*—perhaps in a reference to James and Benjamin Franklin—describes its editor as having two faces and as being able to "look two ways at once." *NEC,* February 11, 1723.

16. *NEC,* June 18, July 2, 9, 23, 1722; *Autobiography,* pp. 19, 31.

17. *NEC,* July 16, 30, August 27, September 17, 1722.

18. *NEC,* January 14, 21, 1723; General Court Records, 11, pp. 491, 493.

19. Council Records, Massachusetts Archives, Boston, Massachusetts, 7, pp. 452–53; Suffolk County Court Files, Boston, Massachusetts, 146, No. 16480; *NEC* January 28, February 4, 1723; *AWM,* February 26, 1723. On Boston politics, see G. B. Warden, "The Caucus and Democracy in Colonial Boston," *New England Quarterly* 43 (March 1970): 19–33; Gary B. Nash, *The Urban Crucible,* pp. 80–88, 139–40.

20. *Autobiography,* p. 19; *NEC* February 11, 1723. Thomas Fleet, a Boston printer who was a member of the Hell-Fire Club and later a dauntless though impartial newspaper publisher, was one of two persons who put up £50 for Franklin's bond. Records of the General Session of the Peace, Suffolk County, Boston, Massachusetts, 1719–1725, p. 186.

21. *NEC,* May 6, 1723.

22. *NEC,* May 13, 1723. Records of the Superior Court of Judicature,

Boston, Massachusetts, 1721–1725, p. 119. Documents related to both of James Franklin's cases are reprinted in Duniway, *The Development of Freedom of the Press in Massachusetts,* pp. 163–66.

23. *Autobiography,* pp. 14–16.

24. *Autobiography,* pp. 18, 19, 20–27; *NEC* September 30, 1723.

25. *NEC,* March 16, November 9, 1724. For the *Courant*'s coverage of the Massachusetts prosecution of John Checkley for libel, see *NEC,* June 8, 15, July 20, December 7, 1724. For an extract from a British paper criticizing the flexibility of seditious libel law, see *NEC,* July 20, 1724. For an example of a complaint about personal scurrility in the *Courant,* see *NEC,* September 2, 1723.

26. [James Franklin], *The Life and Death of Old Father Janus. . . .* (Boston: Printed by James Franklin, 1726), pp. 2–5, 7. On the economic conditions in Boston, see Warden, *Boston,* p. 81. For a description of Newport at this time, see Edwin S. Gaustad, *George Berkeley in America* (New Haven: Yale University Press, 1979), pp. 1–13. Franklin did die without a large estate. Appraisers set the total at £163. Samuel Wickham and Josias Lyndon, "Inventory of the Estate of James Franklin," May 5, 1735, Town Council Book, Newport Historical Society, Newport, Rhode Island, 7, pp. 236–38.

27. Carl Bridenbaugh, *Fat Mutton and Liberty of Conscience: Society in Rhode Island, 1636–1690* (Providence: Brown University Press, 1974); Lawrence L. Lowther, "Rhode Island Colonial Government, 1732" (Ph.D. dissertation, University of Washington, 1964); [James Franklin], *Mr. Samuel Gorton's Ghost: Or, The Spirit of Persecution Represented in the Similitude of a Dream* (Newport, R.I.: Printed by James Franklin, 1728); "Samuell Gorton, New England Firebrand," *New England Quarterly* 7 (September 1934): 405–44; Philip F. Gura, "The Radical Ideology of Samuel Gorton: New Light on the Relation of English to American Puritanism," *WMQ,* 3rd ser., 36 (January 1979): 78–100; Philip F. Gura, "Samuel Gorton and Religious Radicalism in England, 1644–1648," *WMQ,* 3rd ser., 40 (January 1983): 121–24; John E. Alden, *Rhode Island Imprints, 1727–1800* (New York: R. R. Bowker Co. for the Bibliographical Society of America, 1949), pp. 1–13; Clarence S. Brigham, "James Franklin and the Beginnings of Printing in Rhode Island," Massachusetts Historical Society *Proceedings* 65 (March 1936): 538–44; [James Franklin], *The Rhode-Island Almanack for 1734* (Newport, R.I.: Printed by James Franklin, 1734). "Poor Robin" had been the pen name of William Winstanley, a highly successful seventeenth-century almanac maker whose work was suppressed when it first appeared in 1662. See Thomas, *Religion and the Decline of Magic,* pp. 335–36; Capp, *English Almanacs,* pp. 39–40, 123–27, 385. Poor Robin's poem was taken from verse which appeared in the *SCG,* January 8, 1732, and *PG,* November 16, 1733.

28. *RIG,* October 18, 25, November 8, 16, 1732.

29. *RIG,* November 23, 1732.

30. *RIG,* January 11, 1733, *Autobiography,* pp. 98–99; Isaiah Thomas, *The History of Printing in America,* ed. Marcus A. McCorison (New York: Weathervane Books, 1970), pp. 176–78, 315–17; 325–26; BF to Jane Mecom, January 13, 1772, in *PBF,* 19: 28. Hall, who apparently never settled his debt to BF, left Newport in 1768 to start the *Essex Gazette* in Salem, Massachusetts. For an example of a defense of press freedom in his paper, one in which a correspondent quoted Cato and complained about officials turning legitimate criticisms into "arguments against you as *disturbers of the peace,* and *movers of sedition in the state,*" see *EG,* May 7, 1771.

Chapter VII. The Enlightened Printer: Virtue and Vituperation

1. *Autobiography,* pp. 114–16.

2. *Autobiography,* pp. 11, 14, 15, 43, 58, 59, 76; *A Dissertation. . . .* in *PBF,* 1: 57–71; BF to Benjamin Vaughn, November 9, 1779, in *WBF,* 7: 412. Franklin stated more than once that he believed in a God who governed by providence and who should be worshipped. Men, he thought, had immortal souls and faced judgment for conduct in life. For his religious creed, see *Autobiography,* pp. 58–59, 76–78, 92; BF to Josiah and Abiah Franklin, April 13, 1738, in *PBF,* 2: 202–4; BF to Joseph Huey, June 6, 1753, in ibid., 4: 504–6; BF to Ezra Stiles, March 9, 1790, in *WBF,* 10: 83–85. On Franklin and moral conduct, see David M. Larson, "Franklin on the Nature of Man and the Possibility of Virtue," *Early American Literature* 10 (Fall 1975): 111–20; Norman J. Fiering, "Benjamin Franklin and the Way to Virtue," *American Quarterly* 30 (Summer 1978): 199–223.

3. *NEC,* April 16, 1722; "Plan of Conduct," in *PBF,* 1: 99, 100; "Articles of Belief and Acts of Religion," November 20, 1728, in *PBF,* 1: 107, 108; *Autobiography,* pp. 78–83, 86–91.

4. *Autobiography,* pp. 87, 93, 94.

5. *PG, August* 2, 1733.

6. *Autobiography,* pp. 16, 107, 154–55. Franklin himself printed Whitefield's sermons and journals. Ibid., p. 105.

7. *Autobiography,* p. 35.

8. *Autobiography,* pp. 24, 31, 53–59. On BF's self-control and relationship with his father, see Hugh J. Dawson, "Fathers and Sons: Franklin's 'Memoirs' as Myth and Metaphor," *Early American Literature* 14 (Winter 1979–1980): 269–92. On Franklin's success as a businessman, see Norma S. Summers, "Benjamin Franklin—Printing Entrepreneur" (Ph.D. dissertation, University of Alabama, 1979).

9. *Autobiography,* pp. 63–64; [Samuel Keimer], *Advertisement* ([Philadelphia], 1728); *UI,* January 21, 1729; *AWM,* January 28, 1729.

10. *AWM,* February 18, 25, March 4, 1729; *UI,* February 25, March

13, 1729. For reactions to BF's style of writing, see *UI*, March 20, April 10, June 5, 1729. In 1750, BF's *Poor Richard* observed, "He that can bear a Reproof, and mend by it, if he is not wise, is in a fair way of being so." In that year, the almanac also said, "Clean your Finger, before you point at my Spots." *Poor Richard Improved*, 1750, in *PBF*, 3: 446, 447.

11. *AWM*, March 27, April 3, 10, 1729. On the printing of two editions of the March 27 issue of the *Mercury*, see J. A. Leo Lemay, "Franklin's Suppressed 'Busy-Body'," *American Literature* 37 (November 1965): 307–11.

12. *AWM*, September 18, 25, 1729; *Minutes of the Provincial Council of Pennsylvania*, 3: 369–70; Anna Janney DeArmond, *Andrew Bradford, Colonial Journalist* (Newark, Del.: University of Delaware Press, 1949), pp. 16–19; *UI*, September 18, 25, 1729; *Autobiography*, p. 64; *PG*, October 2, 9, 1729.

13. *Autobiography*, pp. 27, 64, 67, 69; *A Modest Enquiry into the Nature and Necessity of a Paper-Currency*, in *PBF*, 1: 141–57.

14. *Autobiography*, pp. 69, 101; Alexander Spotswood to BF, October 12, 1739, in *PBF*, 2: 235–36; *AWM*, November 20, 27, December 4, 18, 1740; *PG*, November 13, December 11, 1740; Sappenfield, *A Sweet Instruction*, pp. 92–100; Wallace B. Eberhard, "Press and Post Office in Eighteenth-Century America: Origins of a Public Policy," in Donovan H. Bond and W. Reynolds McLeod, eds., *Newsletter to Newspapers: Eighteenth-Century Journalism* (Morgantown: School of Journalism, West Virginia University, 1977), pp. 145–149; "Additional Instruction to the Deputy Postmasters of North America," March 10, 1758, in *PBF*, 7: 390–92. For examples of the *Gazette*'s treatment of Bradford and his newspaper, see *PG*, March 19, 1730; November 9, 1732; August 15, 1734. For a discussion of one of Franklin's efforts to ridicule Bradford during their magazine competition, see Alfred O. Aldridge, "A Humorous Poem by Benjamin Franklin," *Proceedings of the American Philosophical Society* 98 (December 1954): 397–99. One reason for Franklin's conduct may have been that about 1730 Bradford put an end to marriage plans Franklin had made by telling the prospective bride's parents that Franklin was unlikely to prosper as a printer. *Autobiography*, pp. 69–70.

15. *Autobiography*, pp. 61, 99–100; "Standing Queries for the Junto," [1732?], in *PBF*, 1: 255–59.

16. *Autobiography*, pp. 71–72, 117, 121–23. No attempt is made here to chronicle Franklin's promotion of civic improvements in the press, but seemingly no matter was too small to escape his attention. See, e.g., his essay on slippery sidewalks. *PG*, January 11, 1733.

17. *Autobiography*, p. 70; *PG*, September 9, 12, 1732; July 12, 1733; March 21, April 11, 1734. On the mystery of William Franklin's mother, see Claude-Anne Lopez and Eugenia W. Herbert, *The Private Franklin*,

The Man and His Family (New York: W. W. Norton & Co., 1975), pp. 22–23. In 1740 John Webbe accused Franklin of "blackening" his private reputation in the magazine controversy of that year. *AWM*, November 20, 1740.

18. *AWM*, January 6, 1736; February 14, 21, 1738; *PG*, February 15, 1738. On the chancery court dispute, see Stanley N. Katz, "The Politics of Law in Colonial America: Controversies over Chancery Courts and Equity Law in the Eighteenth Century" *Perspectives in American History* 5 (1971): 266–71. On the death, see Julius F. Sachse, *Benjamin Franklin as a Free Mason* (Philadelphia, 1906), pp. 49–75.

19. *PG*, March 13, 1730; September 23, 1731.

20. *Autobiography*, p. 93; "The Speech of Miss Polly Baker," in *PBF*, 3: 120–25; Max Hall, *Benjamin Franklin and Polly Baker: The History of a Literary Deception* (Chapel Hill: University of North Carolina Press for the Institute of Early American History and Culture, 1960).

21. *PG*, July 30, October 22, 1730.

22. *PG*, June 10, 1731; May 8, July 24, 1740. On the *Gazette*'s editorial treatment of the Great Awakening and Franklin's surprisingly cordial relationship with Whitefield, see Alfred O. Aldridge, *Benjamin Franklin and Nature's God* (Durham: Duke University Press, 1967), pp. 103–23; Melvin H. Buxbaum, *Benjamin Franklin and the Zealous Presbyterians* (University Park: Pennsylvania University Press, 1975), pp. 125–52.

23. *Autobiography*, pp. 96–97; *PG*, April 10, 1735; "A Defence of the Rev. Mr. Hemphill's Observations," in *PBF*, 2: 113, 125; Merton A. Christensen, "Franklin on the Hemphill Trial: Deism Versus Presbyterian Orthodoxy," *WMQ*, 3rd ser., 10 (July 1953): 422–40. For one example of an acerbic treatment of a pessimistic theological position, see Alfred O. Aldridge, "A Religious Hoax by Benjamin Franklin," *American Literature* 36 (May 1964): 204–9. For a sardonic reaction to religious orthodoxy, see the verses Franklin wrote and sent to his partner, James Parker, on addresses composed by Governor Sir William Gooch and his Council after a fire destroyed the capitol at Williamsburg, Virginia, in 1747. Parker published them as a supplement to his newspaper. *NYPB*, June 1, 1747. On some of the deistic writings Franklin printed in the *Pennsylvania Gazette*, see Alfred O. Aldridge, "Benjamin Franklin and the *Maryland Gazette*," *Maryland Historical Magazine* 44 (September 1949): 177–89. See also, Alfred O. Aldridge, "Franklin's 'Shaftesburian' Dialogues Not Franklin's: A Revision of the Franklin Canon," *American Literature* 21 (May 1949): 151–59.

24. *Poor Richard Improved, 1751*, in *PBF*, 4: 96; *Poor Richard Improved, 1757*, in *PBF*, 7: 82; BF to ———, December 13, 1757, ibid., pp. 294–95.

25. "Parable against Persecution," July 1755, in *PBF*, 6: 114–24; "A New Version of the Lord's Prayer," [1768?], in *PBF*, 15: 299–303; "Franklin's Contributions to an Abridgment of the Book of Common

Prayer," [before August 5, 1773], in *PBF*, 20: 343–52; BF to Sarah Franklin, November 8, 1764, in *PBF*, 11: 449; *Autobiography*, pp. 23, 77, 96.

26. BF to Ezra Stiles, March 9, 1790, in *WBF*, 10: 84–85.

27. "OBSERVATIONS on my Reading History in Library," May 9, 1731, in *PBF*, 1: 192–93; *Autobiography*, p. 95.

28. *PG*, December 22, 1730; Samuel Chew, *The Speech of Samuel Chew, Esq.: Chief Justice . . . Nov. 21, 1741* (Philadelphia: Franklin, 1741); Samuel Chew, *The Speech of Samuel Chew, Esq.: Chief Justice . . . Aug. 20, 1742* (Philadelphia: Franklin, 1742); *NYPB*, May 21, 1744.

29. *Autobiography*, pp. 64–65, 67–68; DeArmond, *Andrew Bradford*, pp. 87–95; *PG*, September 28, October 11, 18, 1733. The reasons for Hamilton's political realignment of 1732–33 remain obscure. A number of early American political figures—including, to some extent, Franklin—seemed to fluctuate between "court" and "country." See Eugene R. Sheridan, *Lewis Morris, 1671–1746, A Study in Early American Politics* (Syracuse: Syracuse University Press, 1981), pp. 204–5.

30. *AWM*, October 18, 1733; *PG*, November 16, 1733.

31. *PG*, November 17, 24, December 1, 8, 1737.

32. *AWM*, April 13, May 25, 1738; August 6, 1741; *PG*, August 6, 1741.

33. "Old Mistresses Apologue," June 25, 1745, in *PBF*, 3: 27–31; *Poor Richard Improved, 1750*, ibid., p. 449. Another example of a potentially damaging piece which was published elsewhere at this time is Franklin's "Verses on the Virginia Capitol Fire," June 1, 1747, ibid., pp. 135–40.

34. *Autobiography*, p. 109; *Plain Truth, 1747*, in *PBF*, 3: 198, 203; Richard Peters to the Proprietaries, November 29, 1747, ibid., pp. 215–17; BF to Cadwallader Colden, November 27, 1747, ibid., p. 213.

35. *Autobiography*, pp. 109–13; Thomas Penn to Richard Peters, June 9, 1748, Penn Letter Book, 2, HSP, p. 232. "The People happen to love me," Franklin later acknowledged. BF to Peter Collinson, November 5, 1756, in *PBF*, 7: 13.

36. *Autobiography*, p. 120. For a brief account of Pennsylvania politics at this time, see Marc Egnal, "The Pattern of Factional Development in Pennsylvania, New York, and Massachusetts, 1682–1776," in Patricia U. Bonomi, ed., *Party and Political Opposition in Revolutionary America* (Tarrytown, N.Y.: Sleepy Hollow Press, 1980), pp. 51–54.

37. On the famous snake cartoon, see BF to Richard Partridge, May 8, 1754, in *PBF*, 5: 272–75. The combination of colonial snakes and strong rhetoric was not new to Franklin. In 1751, he had written a caustic letter to the *Pennsylvania Gazette* about Britain's policy of transporting criminals to populate the colonies. Writing as "AMERICANUS," he suggested that provincial rattlesnakes be sent to England in exchange

and placed in the gardens of the prime ministers, members of Parliament, and Lords of Trade. *PG,* May 9, 1751.

Chapter VIII. The Prerevolutionary Printer: The Ideal of Impartiality

1. On Franklin's business relations with other printers, which began when he entered business for himself in Philadelphia through a brief partnership with Hugh Meredith, see *Autobiography,* pp. 56, 64–66, 108; Carl Van Doren, *Benjamin Franklin* (New York: Viking Press, 1938), pp. 116–23. Franklin's joint ventures with printers for Pennsylvania's German population involved newspapers which were published in 1732, 1749 to 1752, 1752 to 1753, and 1755 to 1757. On Franklin's German papers and his chief competitors in German-language publishing, see Stephen L. Longenecker, *The Christopher Sauers* (Elgin, Ill.: Brethren Press, 1981). When a London friend suggested that German printing houses be suppressed in order to check the growth of German power in Pennsylvania, Franklin replied that such an action would "seem too harsh" and would be unnecessary if other steps were taken. BF to Peter Collinson, [1753?], in *PBF,* 5: 159. For Franklin's relationship with Mecom, see Wilberforce Eames, "The Antigua Press and Benjamin Mecom, 1748–1765," *Proceedings of the American Antiquarian Society,* n.s., 38 (October 1928): 303–48. Franklin's connections with other printers were extensive by mid-century. In 1753, Franklin expressed concern about a report in a Boston newspaper regarding efforts of the Susquehannah Company to buy Indian land within the boundaries of Connecticut. Afraid that it would cause the French or others to take countermeasures, Franklin observed that such schemes should not be announced to the public until they are ripe for execution. "I shall endeavour to prevent the reprinting of that Paragraph in the Papers here and to the Southward," he wrote. BF to Thomas Clap, August 20, 1753, in *PBF,* 5: 21–22.

2. *PG,* November 16, 1733; *SCG,* January 8, October 14, 1732; Jeffery A. Smith, "Impartiality and Revolutionary Ideology: Editorial Policies of the *South-Carolina Gazette,* 1732–1775," *Journal of Southern History* 49 (November 1983): 513–15.

3. *SCG,* February 2, 1734.

4. Smith, "Impartiality and Revolutionary Ideology," pp. 515–24; *SCG,* March 30, 1747.

5. Smith, "Impartiality and Revolutionary Ideology," pp. 518–19, 520–21; *SCG,* January 25, March 28, April 4, July 9, 16, 25, 29, August 1, 8, 1748.

6. *NYPB,* February 24, 1752. On Parker and his business dealings, see Beverly McAnear, "James Parker Versus William Weyman," New Jersey Historical Society *Proceedings* 59 (January 1941): 1–23; Beverly McAnear, "James Parker Versus John Holt," pp. 77–95, 198–212; Alan F.

Dyer, "James Parker, Colonial Printer, 1715–1770" (Ph.D. dissertation, University of Michigan, 1977). Parker repeated his request five months later when he asked that articles concerning church or state be signed. He noted that this policy might be seen as abridging English liberties, but said that he did not have time to offer a full explanation. *NYPB*, July 13, 1752. Several weeks later he presented an essay which repeated the arguments of Franklin's "Apology for Printers." *NYPB*, August 3, 1752, quoted in Dyer, "James Parker," pp. 73–74. William Smith of Philadelphia, who was Franklin's friend at this time and later a writer of stinging, pseudonymous political essays, wrote to Parker to complain that a policy of requiring names made it difficult for writers to oppose vice and tyranny. Albert F. Geggenheimer, *William Smith, Educator and Churchman, 1727–1803* (Philadelphia: University of Pennsylvania Press, 1943), pp. 6–7.

7. *NYPB*, January 27, February 3, April 27, May 4, 11, 1752; Alfred O. Aldridge, "Franklin's Deistical Indians," *American Philosophical Society Proceedings* 94 (August 1950): 398–410; BF to Cadwallader Colden, May 14, 1752, in *PBF*, 4: 310–12; Dyer, "James Parker," pp. 70–72; Julius Goebel, Jr., and T. Raymond Naughton, *Law Enforcement in Colonial New York* (New York: The Commonwealth Fund, 1944), pp. 153–54. The idea that suppression made a work more sought after was a common one. See, e.g., *Cato's Letters*, 1: 104; 3: 256; *NEC*, January 22, 1722; *AWM*, April 10, 1729; *PG*, August 9, 1733. In 1747, Parker successfully resisted an effort by Clinton to suppress a remonstrance of the governor's conduct produced by the Assembly. The legislators ordered Parker to print the protest and accused Clinton of attempting to violate liberty of the press. *NYPB*, October 26, November 2, 1747; *Journal of the Votes and Proceedings of the General Assembly of the Colony of New-York*, 2 vols. (New York: Hugh Gaine, 1766), 2: 191–93, 198, 202, 272; Victor H. Paltsits, "A Rare Factional Pamphlet, Printed at New York by James Parker in 1747," *Literary Collector* 7 (November 1903): 1–5. On Parker and Clinton, see Dyer, "James Parker," pp. 62–70.

8. Milton M. Klein, ed., *The Independent Reflector* (Cambridge: The Belknap Press of Harvard University Press, 1963), pp. 57, 336–42; *The Independent Reflector*, "The Preface," [New York: Henry De Foreest, 1754], p. 8; Dyer, "James Parker," pp. 75–87. Gaine, an Anglican, was later persuaded by Livingston and his associates to publish their side of the college issue for a year in return for £50. The result was their "Watch-Tower" series which began in 1754. Dyer, "James Parker," pp. 94–95; *The Journals of Hugh Gaine, Printer*, ed. Paul L. Ford, 2 vols. (New York: Dodd, Mead, & Co., 1902), 1: 10–19; Lorenz, *Hugh Gaine*, pp. 15–18.

9. *NYPB*, September 3, 1753.

10. "The Preface," pp. 2–3.

11. *NYPB*, January 6, 1755. Five months later Parker wrote that he

wished to avoid placing party controversies and personal invective in his New Haven newspaper, but would print disputes separately. He said that he did not want endless debates crowding out other subjects and making the paper a "meer Vehicle of Controversy." *CG,* June 7, 1755. A year later the paper said it would not "meddle with Characters, either public or private, on the detracting Side, unless when it can be done consistently with that Constitution which punishes no Man, nor permits his Property or Character to be touched till he has justly deserved it, and has had a fair Tryal to make it manifest to the World." Reacting to the prevalent use of pseudonyms, the statement went on to ask why the paper should publish pieces authors were either afraid or ashamed to sign, *CG,* May 22, 1756.

12. Alexander Colden to James Parker, July 28, 1755, in *PBF,* 6: 114; Ford, ed., *Journals of Hugh Gaine,* 2: 3; Dyer, "James Parker," pp. 136-44; *NYPB,* March 15, 1756; *Journal of the Votes and Proceedings of the General Assembly of the Colony of New-York,* 2: 487–89. A week before the letter in question was published, another correspondent had stated that the war effort required unanimity and newspaper writers should be cautious about what they said. *NYPB,* March 8, 1756. Of particular concern were newspaper accounts of troop movements. Fearing that such information would help the enemy, authorities sought and sometimes managed to obtain the power to suppress such items. See, e.g., *Journals of the House of Representatives of Massachusetts, 1755* (Boston: The Massachusetts Historical Society, 1957), p. 155; *Minutes of the Provincial Council of Pennsylvania,* 7: 339, 447.

13. *NYPB,* November 8, 1756. Parker and other colonial printers published critical comments about Anglo-American conduct in the war but also exceedingly patriotic essays. The week before this exchange, for instance, the first page of *Post-Boy* was largely devoted to reprinting a piece which contrasted the glories of British liberties with the tyrannies of France and other nations. This was the eleventh in the "Virginia-Centinel" series. The tenth Virginia Centinel, which Parker did not print, was so scathing in its assessment of Colonel George Washington and his regiment, however, that the future president gave thought to resigning his commission. *NYPB,* November 1, 1756; *VG,* September 3, 1756; Worthington C. Ford, "Washington and 'Centinel X'," *PMHB* 22 (1898): 436–51. Some of the newspaper criticisms of the war effort may be found in Alan Rogers, *Empire and Liberty, American Resistance to British Authority, 1755–1763* (Berkeley: University of California Press, 1974).

14. Mack Thompson, "Massachusetts and New York Stamp Acts," *WMQ,* 3rd ser., 26 (April 1969): 253–58; *NYPB,* October 4, December 20, 27, 1756; April 18, October 17, 1757; Parker, *A Letter to a Gentleman in the City of New York,* p. 4; Beverly McAnear, "James Parker Versus New York Province," *New York History* 22 (July 1941): 321–30. Hugh Gaine approved of the tax as a defense measure. *NYM,* December

20, 1756. In Massachusetts, on the other hand, printer Thomas Fleet, a one-time member of James Franklin's Hell-Fire Club, vigorously objected to the stamp tax. See, e.g., *BEP*, March 17, 1755; April 19, August 9, 1756; January 10, May 2, 1757.

15. Robert H. Kany, "David Hall: Printing Partner of Benjamin Franklin" (Ph.D. dissertation, Pennsylvania State University, 1963), pp. 93–103; Stephen R. Siegert, "War and the Pennsylvania Assembly, 1739–41 and 1754–56: Influence of the Society of Friends as Reflected in the English-Language Press of Pennsylvania" (M.S. thesis, West Virginia University, 1981), p. 54; Robert D. Harlan, "A Colonial Printer as Bookseller in Eighteenth-Century Philadelphia: The Case of David Hall," *Studies in Eighteenth-Century Culture* 5 (1976): 355–69; Robert Hunter Morris to Franklin and Hall, March 19, 1755, in *PBF*, 5: 532; Franklin and Hall to Robert Hunter Morris, March 20, 1755, ibid., pp. 534–35.

16. *Autobiography*, pp. 143–52; BF to Peter Collinson, June 26, 1755, in *PBF*, 6: 86; William Smith to Thomas Penn, [September ? 1755], ibid., pp. 211–12; BF to Peter Collinson, August 27, 1755, ibid., pp. 169, 171; *PG*, December 18, 1755; March 4, 1756. For Franklin's dislike of the altercations he was entering, see BF to Peter Collinson, August 27, 1755, in *PBF*, 6: 171. For examples of BF's unfavorable attitude as Poor Richard toward parties in 1751 and 1753, see *PBF*, 4: 95–96, 405.

17. William Smith, *A Brief State of the Province of Pennsylvania*, 2nd ed. (London: R. Griffiths, 1755); "Reply to the Governor," [September 29, 1755], in *PBF*, 6: 195; Humphrey Scourge [pseud.], *Tit for Tat, or the Score Wip'd Off* [Philadelphia, 1755]; *PG*, January 1, 8, 1756.

18. Ketcham, "Benjamin Franklin and William Smith," pp. 146–53; *PG*, March 4, April 15, 1756; *PJ*, March 25, April 15, 22, May 6, 20, 1756.

19. Gertrude MacKinney and Charles F. Hoban, eds., *Pennsylvania Archives*, 8th ser., 8 vols. (Harrisburg: State Printers, 1931–1935), 5: 4272–74; [William Smith], *The Second Edition, with Additions, of, A Remonstrance, by Obadiah Honesty* ([Philadelphia, 1757]).

20. "Pennsylvania Assembly Committee: Report on Grievances," in *PBF*, 7: 136–42; BF to [Isaac Norris], January 14, 1758, ibid., p. 362; "Petition to the King in Council," February 2, 1759, in *PBF*, 8: 269; BF to Joseph Galloway, April 7, 1759, ibid., p. 313; BF to Joseph Galloway, February 17, 1758, in *PBF*, 7: 374.

21. "Examination of David Hall," January 18, 1758, in Penn Manuscripts, Wyoming Controversy, Smith and Moore vs. Assembly, HSP, 5: 223–25; *PG*, December 1, 1757; MacKinney and Hoban, eds., *Pennsylvania Archives*, 8th ser., 6: 4707.

22. *PJ*, February 23, 1758; *American Magazine* 1 (January, February, April, 1758): 199–200, 210–27, 308. Bradford's paper was not the provost's personal organ. On April 6, 1758, the *Pennsylvania Journal*

published a piece that mocked Smith as a self-professed author of libels, falsehoods, and personal attacks. For an account of Smith's battles with the Assembly, see George Dargo, *Roots of the Republic, A New Perspective on Early American Constitutionalism* (New York: Praeger Publishers, 1974), pp. 118–26. See also, Peter C. Hoffer, "Law and Liberty: In the Matter of Provost William Smith of Philadelphia, 1758," *WMQ*, 3rd ser., 38 (October 1981): 681–701.

23. Ferdinand J. Paris to William Allen, May 13, 1758, Penn Manuscripts, Official Correspondence, HSP, 9: 35; BF to David Hall, June 10, 1758, in *PBF*, 8: 97–98; "Documents on the Hearing of William Smith's Petition," ibid., pp. 29n, 31–41, 49–50.

24. BF to Thomas Leech and Assembly Committee of Correspondence, May 13, 1758, in *PBF*, 8: 62; BF to Isaac Norris, June 9, 1758, ibid., p. 403; Joseph H. Smith, *Appeals to the Privy Council from the American Plantations* (New York: Columbia University Press, 1950), pp. 646–49; Geggenheimer, *William Smith*, pp. 126–49; W. L. Grant and James Munro, eds., *Acts of the Privy Council, Colonial Series*, 6 vols. (London: His Majesty's Stationery Office, 1908–1912), 4: 375–85; BF to Mary Stevenson, March 25, 1763, in *PBF*, 10: 234.

25. BF to Richard Jackson, September 1, 1764, in *PBF*, 11: 239; "Preface to Joseph Galloway's Speech," 1764, ibid., pp. 298–99; *What is Sauce for a Goose is also Sauce for a Gander* (Philadelphia, 1764), pp. 2–7. See, generally, J. Philip Gleason, "A Scurrilous Colonial Election and Franklin's Reputation," *WMQ*, 3rd ser., 18 (January 1961): 68–84; James H. Hutson, "Benjamin Franklin and the Parliamentary Grant for 1758," ibid., 23 (October 1966): 575–95. For background, see William S. Hanna, *Benjamin Franklin and Pennsylvania Politics* (Stanford: Stanford University Press, 1964), pp. 148–68; Benjamin H. Newcomb, *Franklin and Galloway: A Political Partnership* (New Haven: Yale University Press, 1972), pp. 71–104; James H. Hutson, *Pennsylvania Politics, 1764–1770, The Movement for Royal Government and Its Consequences* (Princeton: Princeton University Press, 1972), pp. 84–177.

26. "Protest against the Appointment of Benjamin Franklin as Agent," in *PBF*, 11: 408–12; *Remarks on a Late Protest*, ibid., pp. 430, 438, 441.

27. [William Smith], *An Answer to Mr. Franklin's Remarks* in *PBF*, 11: 490–91; *PG*, December 20, 27, 1764; January 3, 10, 1765; *PJ*, December 20, 27, 1764; January 3, 10, 1765.

28. Verner W. Crane, "Benjamin Franklin and the Stamp Act," Colonial Society of Massachusetts *Transactions* 32 (February 1934): 56–77; Robert D. Harlan, "David Hall and the Stamp Act," *The Papers of the Bibliographical Society of America* 61 (1967): 13–37; Smith, "Impartiality and Revolutionary Ideology," pp. 552–23; Michael D'Innocenzo and John J. Turner, Jr., "The Role of New York Newspapers in the Stamp Act Crisis, 1764–66," *The New York Historical Society Quarterly* 51 (July, October 1967): 215–31, 345–65; Miner, *William Goddard*,

pp. 50–52; *The Constitutional Courant: Containing Matters Interesting to Liberty, and No Wise Repugnant to Loyalty* in Merrill Jensen, ed., *Tracts of the American Revolution* (Indianapolis: Bobbs-Merrill Co., 1967), pp. 80–93.

29. DH to BF, September 6, 1765, in *PBF,* 12: 258; BF to DH, September 14, 1965, ibid., p. 268; DH to William Strahan, September 6, 19, 1765, Hall Papers, APS; *PG,* October 31, 1765; Morgan and Morgan, *The Stamp Act Crisis,* pp. 240–44, 321; Harlan, "David Hall and the Stamp Act," pp. 31–32; Kany, "David Hall," pp. 219–24.

30. Smith, "Impartiality and Revolutionary Ideology," pp. 522–24; *SCG,* August 26, October 19, 31, 1765; June 2, 1766, PT to BF, September 3, 1768, in *PBF,* 15: 200–201.

31. *SCG,* December 14, 1769.

32. JP to BF, October 10, 1765, in *PBF,* 12: 310, JP to BF, June 14, 1765, ibid., pp. 175, 176; JP to BF, September 22, 1765, ibid., p. 277; JP to BF, June 11, 1766, ibid., 13: 300–307; JP to BF, May 6, 1766, ibid., pp. 262–66.

33. JP to BF, October 11, 1766, in *PBF,* 13: 454–57; McAnear, "James Parker Versus John Holt," pp. 200–209; Lorenz, *Hugh Gaine,* pp. 66, 72; Schlesinger, *Prelude to Independence,* pp. 117, 312–13.

34. John Hughes to BF, September 8–17, 1765, in *PBF,* 12: 263–66; BF to David Hall, September 14, 1765, ibid., pp. 267–68; Joseph Galloway to BF, September 20, 1765, ibid., pp. 269–70; Deborah Franklin to BF, September 22, 1765, ibid., pp. 271–72, 274; *PJ,* September 4, 11, 18, 1766.

35. BF to Joseph Galloway, November 8, 1766, in *PBF,* 13: 488; Benjamin H. Newcomb, "Effects of the Stamp Act on Colonial Pennsylvania Politics," *WMQ,* 3rd ser., 23 (April 1966): 257–72. The almanac also said, "Write Injuries in Dust, Benefits in Marble." *Poor Richard,* 1747, in *PBF,* 3: 104.

36. David Hall to William Strahan, June 12, October 9, 1767, Hall Papers, APS.

37. *PC,* February 9, 1767. For examples of Franklin being defended or his writings being reprinted, see *PC,* February 9, 16, 23, March 9, 23, 1767.

38. DH to BF, January 27, 1767, in *PBF,* 14: 17–18; BF to DH, April 14, 1767, ibid., pp. 126–28; William Franklin to BF, November 13, 1766, in *PBF,* 13: 499–501; DH to William Strahan, April 30, May 26, June 12, 1767, Hall Papers, APS.

39. *PC,* March 9, 16, 23, April 6, 13, 1767.

40. William Goddard, *The Partnership. . . .* (Philadelphia, 1770); BF to William Franklin, January 30, 1772, in *PBF,* 19: 51. For Goddard's characterization of himself as a defender of freedom of the press, see *PC,* November 28, 1768. On the *Chronicle,* see Arthur M. Schlesinger, "Politics, Propaganda, and the Philadelphia Press, 1767–1770,"

PMHB 60 (October 1936): 309–22; John J. Zimmerman, "Benjamin Franklin and the *Pennsylvania Chronicle*," *PMHB* 81 (October 1957): 351–64; Miner, *William Goddard*, pp. 65–73.

Chapter IX. The Revolutionary Journalist: The Court of the Press

1. BF to William Franklin, October 6, 1773, in *PBF*, 20: 437; *Poor Richard*, 1745, in *PBF*, 3: 8; "Speech in the Convention, at the Conclusion of its Deliberations," September 17, 1787, in *WBF*, 9: 607–8; *Poor Richard Improved*, 1757, in *PBF*, 7: 87. For the view that the satires represented a cynical, pessimistic side of Franklin, see Linda K. Bates, "Toward the Heart of Darkness: Benjamin Franklin's Satires" (Ph.D. dissertation, University of California, Davis, 1981).

2. *Autobiography*, p. 90; "Speech in the Convention, at the Conclusion of its Deliberations," September 17, 1787, in *WBF*, 9: 607–9. Franklin's remark on qualifying his statements is an echo of Montaigne's essay "Of Cripples." Zeitlin, ed., *The Essays of Michel de Montaigne*, 3: 232. On other examples of Franklin borrowing from Montaigne, including his uncharacteristically misanthropic letter of June 7, 1782, to Joseph Priestley, see Robert Newcomb, "Franklin and Montaigne," *Modern Language Notes* 72 (November 1957): 489–91.

3. *NEC*, February 11, 1723; *PG*, June 10, 1731. When he was forced to make decisions, Franklin could resort to what he referred to as a kind of *"Moral* or *Prudential Algebra"*—lining up reasons for and against a particular action in opposite columns and then choosing what to to. BF to Joseph Priestly, September 19, 1772, in *PBF*, 19: 299–300; BF to Jonathan Williams, April 8, 1779, in *WBF*, 7: 281–82. For an application of personality theory to Franklin's avoiding disputes, see Richard L. Bushman, "On the Uses of Psychology: Conflict and Conciliation in Benjamin Franklin," *History and Theory* 5 (1966): 225–40. On Franklin's relationship with Dashwood, one of the more notorious Englishmen of the eighteenth century, see *Benjamin Franklin at West Wycombe Park* (Philadelphia: American Philosophical Society, 1977). On his friendship with Paine, see Dixon Wecter, "Thomas Paine and the Franklins," *American Literature* 12 (November 1940): 306–17. John Adams attributed "the Elevation to the Government of New Jersey of a base born Brat," William Franklin, to "some kind of Backstairs Intrigues" involving Benjamin Franklin and Bute. *Diary and Autobiography of John Adams*, ed. L. H. Butterfield, 4 vols. (Cambridge: Belknap Press of Harvard University Press, 1961), 4: 151.

4. William Smith, *Historical Memoirs*, ed. William H. W. Sabine (New York, 1956), pp. 71–76; Roger J. Champagne, *Alexander McDougall and the American Revolution in New York* (Schenectady: Union College Press, 1975), pp. 26–28; Dorothy R. Dillon, *The New York Triumvirate* (New York: Columbia University Press, 1949), pp. 91–93.

5. *NYPB,* January 29, February 19, March 19, 26, April 2, 9, 1770; L. F. S. Upton, *The Loyal Whig, William Smith of New York & Quebec* (Toronto: University of Toronto Press, 1969), pp. 69–71.

6. *NYPB,* May 6, 1770; Schlesinger, *Prelude to Independence,* pp. 114–16. For the "Dougliad" series, see *NYM,* April 9 through June 25, 1770. An acrimonious loyalist history claimed that although Parker was "strongly attached to the republican faction," his sudden death was "not without strong suspicions of foul play." Jones, *History of New York During the Revolutionary War,* p. 33.

7. Kany, "David Hall," pp. 246–47; Smith, "Impartiality and Revolutionary Ideology," p. 524; Jack P. Greene, "The Gadsden Election Controversy and the Revolutionary Movement in South Carolina," *Mississippi Valley Historical Review* 46 (December 1959): 469–92; Jack P. Greene, "Bridge to Revolution: The Wilkes Fund Controversy in South Carolina, 1769–1775," *Journal of Southern History* 29 (February 1963): 19–52.

8. *SCG,* March 26, 1772; PT to BF, August 24, 1772, in *PBF,* 19: 283–84; BF to PT, November 3, 1772, ibid., p. 362.

9. *SCG,* May 7, 1772.

10. Smith, "Impartiality and Revolutionary Ideology," pp. 524–25; *SCG,* September 2, 6, 13, 15, 1773. For attacks on Mansfield at this time, see, e.g., *SCG,* April 16, May 9, 14, 1772; September 6, 1773.

11. Smith, "Impartiality and Revolutionary Ideology," pp. 522, 525; PT to BF, June 12, 1777, in Douglas C. McMurtrie, ed., "The Correspondence of Peter Timothy, Printer of Charlestown, with Benjamin Franklin," *South Carolina Historical and Genealogical Magazine* 35 (October 1934): 128.

12. David Hume to BF, May 10, 1762, in *PBF,* 10: 81–82; "A Traveller," May 20, 1765, in *PBF,* 12: 134. On Franklin as a colonial agent, see Jack M. Sosin, *Agents and Merchants, British Colonial Policy and the Origins of the American Revolution, 1763–1775* (Lincoln: University of Nebraska Press, 1965), pp. 142–61; Cecil B. Currey, *Road to Revolution: Benjamin Franklin in England, 1765–1775* (Garden City, New York: Anchor Books, 1968). On Franklin's journalism in London, see *Benjamin Franklin's Letters to the Press, 1758–1775,* ed. Verner W. Crane (Chapel Hill: University of North Carolina Press for the Institute of Early American History and Culture, 1950); Verner W. Crane, "Franklin's Political Journalism in England," in Roy N. Lokken, ed., *Meet Dr. Franklin* (Philadelphia: Franklin Institute, 1981), pp. 125–42. On Franklin's response to the concept of biological degeneration, see Alfred O. Aldridge, "Benjamin Franklin and the Philosophes," *Studies on Voltaire and the Eighteenth Century* 24 (1963): 62–65. According to a story Franklin told Jefferson, when this theory was propounded at a dinner in France, Franklin asked the guests—half American and half French—to rise. The French guests were quite short and the Americans remarkably

tall. *Ben Franklin Laughing,* ed. P. M. Zall (Berkeley: University of California Press, 1980), p. 138.

13. Peter Oliver's *Origin & Progress of the American Rebellion. A Tory View,* ed. Douglass Adair and John A. Schutz (San Marino, California: Huntington Library, 1961), pp. 79–80. Oliver was particularly angered by a hoax which made the rounds of colonial newspapers beginning with the *Pennsylvania Journal* on June 29, 1774. The piece, which had been widely attributed to Franklin, said that Parliament was preparing to consider a substantial tax on American births and marriages. Oliver, *Origin & Progress of the American Rebellion,* pp. 105–6; Schlesinger, *Prelude to Independence,* pp. 199–200.

14. BF to John Whitehurst, June 12, 1763, in *PBF,* 10: 302; BF to William Strahan, June 28, August 8, 1763, ibid., pp. 304, 320; BF to Richard Jackson, February 11, 1764, in *PBF,* 11: 76; BF to William Franklin, April 16, October 5, 1768, in *PBF,* 15: 98–99, 224. In a letter which has been lost, Franklin apparently instructed David Hall not to reprint the *North Briton* No. 45 as other colonial newspaper editors were doing. Hall replied that he had not planned to print it. DH to BF, June 23, 1763, in *PBF,* 10: 293.

15. BF to Joseph Priestly, October 3, 1775, in *PBF,* 22: 218; Verner W. Crane, "The Club of Honest Whigs: Friends of Science and Liberty," *WMQ,* 3rd ser., 23 (April 1966): 210–33; Nicholas Hans, "Franklin, Jefferson, and the English Radicals at the End of the Eighteenth Century," *Proceedings of the American Philosophical Society* 98 (December 1954): 406–21; "Reply to a Defender of Lord Hillsborough," [after September 7, 1772], in *PBF,* 19: 297; BF to James Bowdin, February 25, 1775, in *PBF,* 21: 506; BF to Joseph Galloway, February 25, 1775, ibid., pp. 508–9.

16. "The Final Hearing before the Privy Council Committee for Plantation Affairs on the Petition from the Massachusetts House of Representatives for the Removal of Hutchinson and Oliver," January 29, 1774, in *PBF,* 21: 37–70; "Extract of a Letter from London," February 19, 1774, ibid., pp. 112–15.

17. "Tract Relative to the Affair of Hutchinson's Letters," [1774], in *PBF,* 21: 415–17, 427–28; Max Farrand, ed., *The Records of the Federal Convention of 1787,* 3 vols. (New Haven: Yale University Press, 1911), 2: 348. Franklin's comment that criticism was best ignored was a view held by Samuel Johnson, among others. See George B. Hill, ed., *Boswell's Life of Johnson,* 6 vols. (Oxford: Clarendon Press, 1934–1950), 2: 61.

18. "Revisions of the Pennsylvania Declaration of Rights," [between July 29 and August 15, 1776], in *PBF,* 22: 532.

19. Luther S. Livingston, *Franklin and His Press at Passy* (New York: Grolier Club, 1914); "Supplement to the *Boston Independent Chronicle,"* in *WBF,* 8: 437–47; "Information to Those Who Would Re-

move to America," ibid., pp. 603–14; BF to Richard Price, August 16, 1784, in *WBF*, 9: 256; BF to Jan Ingenhousz, April 29, 1785, ibid., pp. 318–20; "On the Slave Trade," March 23, 1790, in *WBF*, 10: 87–91. One of the printers Franklin helped was Mathew Carey, who had assisted him in France after fleeing prosecution in Ireland for defending Catholics. Franklin did, however, turn down a request from Carey that he sign an endorsement of his *American Museum*. Franklin said such a recommendation was a novel idea, but might seem "impertinent" to the public. BF to Mathew Carey, June 10, 1788, in *WBF*, 9: 660–62. Another was Francis Childs. See, in the Franklin Papers, APS, John Jay to Francis Childs, May 11, 1783; Francis Childs to BF, October 20, 1783; BF to Francis Childs, February 5, 1786; February 22, 1790. Franklin also appears to have been sympathetic to the wage demands of Philadelphia's journeymen printers. See Henry P. Rosemont, "Benjamin Franklin and the Philadelphia Typographical Strikers of 1786," *Labor History* 22 (Summer 1981): 398–429.

20. BF to Richard Price, June 13, 1782, in *WBF*, 8: 457; BF to Sir Edward Newenham, October 2, 1783, in *WBF*, 9: 102.

21. BF to Robert Morris, July 26, 1781, in *WBF*, 8: 288; BF to Francis Hopkinson, December 24, 1782, ibid., pp. 647–48. For examples of a New York loyalist newspaper's treatment of Franklin, see *RG*, February 10, 21, March 21, 1778. For instances of patriot sentiment being directed against Franklin, see Charles Wetherell, ed., " 'For These or Such Like Reasons': John Holt's Attack on Benjamin Franklin," *Proceedings of the American Antiquarian Society* 88 (October 1978): 251–57; John Adams to Thomas McKean, September 20, 1779, McKean papers, 1, p. 31, HSP. Franklin's friends and relatives kept him apprised of his dwindling reputation and political fortunes in the United States. Richard Bache to BF, October 30, 1780, Franklin Papers, APS; Robert Morris to BF, October 25, 1780, September 28, 1782, and May 30, 1783, ibid.; Jane Mecom to BF, December 29, 1780, in *The Letters of Benjamin Franklin & Jane Mecom*, ed. Carl Van Doren (Princeton: Princeton University Press for the American Philosophical Society, 1950), p. 205. On Franklin's relationship with Hopkinson, the patriot satirist, see Dixon Wecter, "Francis Hopkinson and Benjamin Franklin," *American Literature* 12 (May 1940): 200–17. The idea that printers should disassociate themselves from personal libel by printing the material outside of the newspaper was also used by James Parker. See, e.g., *CG*, June 7, 1755.

22. "Centinel I," *IG*, October 5, 1787, in Kaminski and Saladino, eds., *Commentaries on the Constitution, Public and Private*, 1: 326–37; Mathew Carey, *Autobiography* (Brooklyn: Research Classics, 1942), pp. 6, 12–16; Elizabeth Holt Oswald to BF, August 3, 1788, Franklin Papers, APS; BF to Elizabeth Oswald, n.d., ibid. Oswald also challenged Francis Bailey, another Philadelphia printer, to a duel, but Bailey declined the offer. Kaminski and Saladino, eds., *Commentaries on the Constitution,*

Public and Private, 1: xxxiii–xxxvi. For background, see Thomas R. Meehan, "The Pennsylvania Supreme Court in the Law and Politics of the Commonwealth, 1776–1790" (Ph.D. dissertation, University of Wisconsin, 1960), pp. 490–508.

23. *Autobiography,* pp. 94–95; "To the Editors of the *Pennsylvania Gazette,*" 1788, in *WBF,* 9: 639.

24. *FG,* September 12, 1789. Statements from this essay were misquoted and taken out of context by Representative Robert G. Harper to buttress his arguments for the Sedition Act of 1798. See Smith, *Freedom's Fetters,* pp. 137–39; Brant, *The Bill of Rights,* pp. 269–70. As late as 1785, when an old English friend defended him in the press against accusations regarding his conduct at the peace negotiations, Franklin was content to have the defamer "be left to himself" after the vindication was published. "The Writer of the Calumny you have so well refuted, manifests a good deal of Malignancy in his Nature," Franklin wrote to his friend, "and such People are afflicted and punished, when they find those Accusations false, which they wish'd to be true." BF to Caleb Whitefoord, July 27, 1785 (misdated 1787), in *The Whitefoord Papers,* ed. W. A. S. Hewins (Oxford: Clarendon Press, 1898), p. 201.

25. BF to Gaetano Filangieri, January 11, 1783, in *WBF,* 9: 1–2; *FG,* September 12, 1789. Franklin was not alone in seeing advantages in this kind of solution. See Smollett, *Humphry Clinker,* pp. 103–4. The idea had been suggested by a correspondent—perhaps Franklin—a year earlier in the first issue of the *Federal Gazette.* The writer, whose prose resembled Franklin's, advised the editor against printing private scandal and warned that the faults of public officials should be exposed "with decency." *FG,* October 1, 1788. Franklin may have been the author of this piece, but no firm evidence exists at this time according to the former editor of the Franklin *Papers.* William B. Willcox to Jeffery A. Smith, February 23, 1983, personal files of Jeffery A. Smith, Iowa City, Iowa. On Franklin's reaction to criminal laws, see also BF to Benjamin Vaughan, March 14, 1785, in *WBF,* 9: 291–99. Franklin's almanac often complained about the laws and lawyers. See, e.g., *Poor Richard,* 1746, in *PBF,* 3: 67. On the discomfort in the 1780s with laws which did not seem to be based on reason, justice, or morality, see Wood, *The Creation of the American Republic,* pp. 456–57.

26. BF to Charles Vaughan, February 12, 1788, Franklin Papers, APS; *FG,* September 12, 1789. Franklin repeated the comment he made to Vaughan about the people's obedience in BF to Charles Carroll, May 25, 1789, in *WBF,* 10: 7.

27. Francis N. Thorpe, ed., *The Federal and State Constitutions,* 7 vols. (Washington, D.C.: Government Printing Office, 1909), 5: 1275, 3083, 3090, 3100; 7: 569.

28. Thorpe, ed., *The Federal and State Constitutions,* 5: 3100. For the view that the 1790 Constitution adopted Zengerian reforms but left

the common law of seditious libel intact, see Levy, "Liberty and the First Amendment," pp. 24–25. On Pennsylvania politics from 1776 through 1790, see Robert L. Brunhouse, *Counterrevolution in Pennsylvania, 1776–1790* (Harrisburg: Pennsylvania Historical Commission, 1942), pp. 221–27; Wood, *The Creation of the American Republic,* pp. 438–46; Donald S. Lutz, *Popular Consent and Popular Control, Whig Political Theory in the Early State Constitutions* (Baton Rouge: Louisiana State University Press, 1980), pp. 133–42.

29. *IG,* October 15, 1782; January 11, 18, 1783; Dwight L. Teeter, "The Printer and the Chief Justice: Seditious Libel in 1782–83," *Journalism Quarterly* 45 (Summer 1968): 235–42, 260. For the arguments of Oswald's supporters, see, e.g., *IG,* October 19, November 9, December 7, 14, 21, 28, 31, 1782; January 4, 1783.

30. *FJ,* October 30, 1782; January 1, 15, 1783; *PG,* January 8, 15, 22, 1783.

31. *PG,* January 8, 1783.

32. BF to Jane Mecom, January 13, 1772, in *PBF,* 19: 29. On Bache's early childhood, see Lopez and Herbert, *The Private Franklin,* pp. 142, 169–71, 215.

33. A. Owen Aldridge, *Voltaire and the Century of Light* (Princeton: Princeton University Press, 1975), pp. 399–400; James D. Tagg, "Benjamin Franklin Bache and the Philadelphia *Aurora*" (Ph.D. dissertation, Wayne State University, 1973), pp. 35–70; BF to John Quincy Adams, April 21, 1779, in *WBF,* 7: 289; BF to BFB, August 14, 1779, ibid., p. 369; BF to Richard Bache, November 11, 1784, in *WBF,* 9: 279. A diary kept by Bache indicates that he had a reporter's talent for description at a young age. B. F. Bache, Diary, August 1, 1782 to September 14, 1785, B. F. Bache Papers, APS.

34. Tagg, "Benjamin Franklin Bache and the Philadelphia *Aurora*," pp. 71–102; *Constitution of the Franklin Society* ([Philadelphia]: Stewart and Cochran, 1792); *GA,* October 1, 1790. For a statement on postal regulations which made similar observations on the relationship between a free press and self-government, see *GA,* December 1, 1791. Bache said in his first issue that he intended to give more attention than other newspapers to the sciences, literature, and the useful arts—a plan which was "coinciding with the advice which the Publisher had received from his late Grand Father." Ibid., October 1, 1790. This advice suggests that Franklin had begun to appreciate the approach Samuel Keimer had attempted sixty years before with his *Universal Instructor.* During his mission to France, Franklin was among several persons appointed by the Academy of Sciences to look into a project for establishing a European periodical of science and arts. They recommended support, and the *Nouvelles de la République des Lettres et des Arts* was published for ten years. Aldridge, "Benjamin Franklin and the Philosophes," p. 54.

35. *GA,* October 23, 1790; January 1, 1794. Jefferson demonstrated

an interest in Bache's career as early as 1788 when the printer was nineteen. BF to TJ, October 24, 1788, in *Benjamin Franklin's Autobiographical Writings,* ed. Carl Van Doren (New York: Viking Press, 1948), p. 761. Monroe had difficulty collecting the money he had given to Bache. James Monroe to BFB, January 28, 1798, Etting Papers, HSP. Bache originally promised to make the newspaper impartial. B. F. Bache, *Proposals for Publishing . . . The Daily Advertiser* ([Philadelphia, 1790]).

36. James E. Pollard, *The Presidents and the Press* (New York: Macmillan Co., 1947), pp. 14–27; *AU,* December 23, 1796. For examples of libertarian press theory in the Republican newspapers of the 1790s, see Donald H. Stewart, *Opposition Press of the Federalist Period* (Albany: State University Press of New York, 1969), pp. 444–46. On the impact of the Jay Treaty controversy, see Joseph Charles, "The Jay Treaty: The Origins of the American Party System," *WMQ,* 3rd ser., 12 (October 1955): 581–630. On the disclosure of government documents at this time, see Daniel F. Hoffman, "Contempt of the United States: The Political Crime That Wasn't," *American Journal of Legal History* 25 (October 1981): 343–60.

37. *AU,* November 8, 1794.

38. Tagg, "Benjamin Franklin Bache and the Philadelphia *Aurora,*" pp. 556–657, 673–75; John Adams to Abigail Adams, April 24, 1797, in *Letters of John Adams to His Wife,* ed. Charles F. Adams, 2 vols. (Boston: Little and Brown, 1841), 2: 254; Bache, *Truth Will Out!,* pp. ii–iii; TJ to JM, April 26, 1798, in Jefferson, *Works,* 8: 412.

39. *AU,* June 27, 30, 1798; Bache, *Truth Will Out!,* p. iii; Tagg, "Benjamin Franklin Bache and the Philadelphia *Aurora,*" pp. 701–4; James Morton Smith, "The *Aurora* and the Alien and Sedition Laws, Part I: The Editorship of Benjamin Franklin Bache," *PMHB* 77 (January 1953): 18–20; *IC,* July 5, 1798. The U.S. Supreme Court eventually decided that federal courts did not have jurisdiction over common law crimes. U.S. v. Hudson and Goodwin, 7 Cranch 32 (1812). Thomas Adams was indicted under the Sedition Act later in 1798. *IC,* October 25, 1798.

40. *AU,* June 29, July 3, 10, 11, 13, 14, 16, 17, 18, 19, 21, 23, August 3, 6, 30, 1798; Tagg, "Benjamin Franklin Bache and the Philadelphia *Aurora,*" pp. 671–82. For examples of a similar treatment of the Sedition Act, see *IC,* July 5, October 25, 1798.

41. Tagg, "Benjamin Franklin Bache and the Philadelphia *Aurora,*" pp. 706–13; *CoC,* September 19, 1798. Margaret Bache's handbill announcing her husband's death was reprinted in *IC,* September 17, 1798. In the same issue of the *Centinel* which expressed loathing of Bache, a news item reported that the toasts at a gathering honoring President Adams at Quincy included one to the liberty of the press: "May it be *preserved* by a timely *correction* of its licentiousness." In July, Bache had reported on a number of Independence Day celebrations around the

country where Republicans drank toasts to liberty of the press. *AU*, July 7, 12, 16, 19, 20, 26, 1798.
42. On parties and the press, see Sloan, "The Early Party Press," pp. 18–24. On the growth of patronage for the press, see Culver H. Smith, *The Press, Politics, and Patronage, The American Government's Use of Newspapers, 1789–1875* (Athens, Ga.: University of Georgia Press, 1977); Carl E. Prince, "The Federalist Party and Creation of a Court Press, 1789–1801," *Journalism Quarterly* 53 (Summer 1976): 238–41.

Conclusion

1. TJ to Edward Carrington, January 16, 1787, in *PTJ*, 11: 49.
2. "Federalist No. 57," in Cooke ed., *The Federalist*, p. 384; *NG*, December 19, 1791. Madison's "Public Opinion" essay of 1791 was written in the context of the long-standing theoretical problem of how to maintain a democratic republic in a large nation. A similar conclusion about this role of the press was reached two years earlier in France by J. P. Brissot, a French journalist and revolutionary leader who corresponded with Jefferson. See Jeremy D. Popkin, "The Newspaper Press in French Political Thought, 1789–99," *Studies in Eighteenth-Century Culture* 10 (1981): 114–15.
3. See Jeffery A. Smith, "Prior Restraint: Original Intentions and Modern Interpretations," *William & Mary Law Review*, forthcoming.
4. *IG*, April 13, 1782.
5. "Federalist No. 84," in Cooke ed., *The Federalist*, p. 580; TJ to JM, July 31, 1788, in *PTJ*, 13: 442; JM to TJ, October 17, 1788, ibid., 14: 18–20; TJ to JM, March 15, 1789, ibid., 14: 659–60.
6. "Federalist No. 84," in Cooke ed., *The Federalist*, p. 579; *Pennsylvania and the Federal Constitution, 1787–1788*, ed. John Bach McMaster and Frederick D. Stone (Lancaster, Penn., 1888; reprint ed., New York: Da Capo Press, 1970), p. 144.
7. [Richard Henry Lee], *Letters From the Federal Farmer to the Republican*, ed. Walter H. Bennett (University, Ala.: Alabama University Press, 1978), pp. 111–12; "Amendments to the Constitution," June 8, 1789, in *WJM*, 5: 377, 380–85.
8. JM to TJ, October 17, 1788, in *WJM*, 5: 274; TJ to JM, July 31, 1788, in *PTJ*, 13: 442; *Address of the General Assembly to the People of the Commonwealth of Virginia*, in *WJM*, 6: 334; *Report on the Resolutions*, 1799–1800, ibid., pp. 387–88, 391, 393, 397.

Index